Science Discoveries on the Net

Science Discoveries on the Net
An Integrated Approach

Anthony D. Fredericks

A Member of the Greenwood Publishing Group

Westport, Connecticut • London

Libraries Unlimited
A member of Greenwood Publishing Group, Inc.
88 Post Road West,
Westport, CT 06881
www.lu.com

Library of Congress Cataloging-in-Publication Data

Fredericks, Anthony D.
    Science discoveries on the Net : an integrated approach / Anthony D. Fredericks.
        p. cm.
    Includes bibliographical references and index.
    ISBN 1-56308-823-1 (softbound)
    1. Science--Study and teaching--Computer network resources. 2. Internet in education.
I. Title.

Q182.7 .F73 2000
025.06'5--dc21

00-055846

10 9 8 7 6 5 4 3 2   IBT 04 03 02

Contents

Preface

I remember when I first started teaching. In those days, science education meant a couple of textbooks, lots of ditto sheets, and some antiquated science materials such as flasks, eye droppers, a balance scale, and (with luck) a few working thermometers. The science program was sometimes piecemeal and often played "second fiddle" to the reading or math programs.

Science for most students was, I suspect, a less-than-exciting subject. Many students probably thought "Science" was an extension of the reading program simply because they spent so much time reading dull textbooks and memorizing endless tables of information. Undoubtedly, students did not see much relevance between the information they were learning in science and the "real world" outside the classroom. Unfortunately, what resulted may have been a less-than-enthusiastic response to science as a subject and a disdain for anything remotely scientific.

Today, our thoughts about learning science and teaching science are dramatically different. We know that science learning, if it is to be both effective and meaningful, must involve children in numerous interactive experiences. By this, I mean that children must be offered multiple opportunities to ask their own questions, pursue their own answers, and investigate corners of their world simply because they are interested and because they are encouraged to participate. In fact, of all the academic areas, science is the one which offers the most unique opportunities for children to take an active role in their own learning, whether that learning takes place in the classroom or the living room.

Indeed, science is one of the most dynamic subjects youngsters will encounter in their lives; thus, it stands to reason that it must be joyous, exciting, and meaningful to them while they are in school. Helping children achieve a measure of self-initiated direction is a challenge for teachers, not in terms of the vast amount of science information children need to memorize and regurgitate, but rather in terms of assisting children in investigating their own unique questions and reaching their own personal goals.

The Internet has provided classrooms with magical opportunities to enhance and expand the science curriculum in a plethora of ways. No longer do we have to assign dull worksheets: Students can "surf" the Web for up-to-the-minute ideas and information. No longer do we have to require the reading of insipid textbook chapters: Students can chat online with working scientists around the world. No longer do we have to demand the completion of classroom experiments that must be accomplished within a single class period: Students can communicate with youngsters around the country to design and follow through on a host of long-term scientific investigations. Indeed, the Internet has provided us with educational possibilities throughout the entire science program that are unbounded by curriculum guides and unfettered by distance, time, or experience.

In many ways, the Internet connects classrooms with the real world. It taps into the budding scientist in each student and provides "real time" connections with an incredible array of scientific knowledge and scientific adventures. In short, the Internet has not only empowered teachers and their classrooms, it has equally empowered students. It gives students resources unavailable in traditional ways; it is their key, their passageway, their portal, and their supersonic transport through which they can achieve a personal investment in their own learning.

This book is designed to help you integrate the Internet into your science program and enhance the scientific discoveries of your students. It is also designed to take advantage of the natural curiosity of children and the inherent scientist inside each and every youngster. In many ways, this is a book of change—change from tiresome worksheets, change from outdated textbooks, and change from mundane activities and "ho-hum" experiments done year after year. I hope you will consider this book invigorating, exciting, joyful, amazing, magical, and delightful—certainly all the qualities that can, and should be, part of any classroom science program.

—Tony Fredericks

Part I

Science and the Internet

Chapter 1

Introduction

An Adventure of the Mind

Science is fun. Science is an exploration of and an investigation into the unknown. Science is learning more about what we don't know: filling in gaps in our knowledge base, changing old ideas, modifying concepts, and discovering that we don't necessarily have all the answers just because we know a bunch of facts. In some ways, science is a testament to our own innate ignorance, an ignorance born of a desire to know more about ourselves and our world, not one signifying a complete lack of knowledge.

For children, science can and should become a dynamic and interactive discipline. It should allow children to examine new ideas, play around with concepts and precepts, and discover that there is no such thing as a body of finite knowledge. What does this mean for teachers? It means that students must be given a multitude of opportunities to probe, poke, and peek into the mysteries of the universe, whether that universe is their own backyard or a galaxy far away.

Science should also give children a host of opportunities to think, instead of just memorize. Knowing the parts of a frog or the number of planets in the solar system means very little unless youngsters are provided with opportunities to apply that information in some useful way. Asking students to store that information in their minds is not helping them *learn* science, but rather asking them to *parrot* science. Little appreciation of the wonders of the scientific community grows from this procedure, and little application of the facts and figures of science comes about through this "traditional" way of presenting science. Indeed, science is more than numbers, charts, and graphs—it is a venture and an *adventure* of the mind—constantly learning and relearning new data and new ideas. Providing youngsters with opportunities to pose questions about their world, question basic assumptions, or actively seek solutions to various mysteries places a value on the power of the human mind—particularly the minds of children.

Principles of Science Instruction

Students need many opportunities to make sense of their world as well as lay a foundation from which future discoveries can emanate. The following guidelines should be considered as markers from which kids can grow in science:

1. Students need to be provided with a basic body of knowledge that will form the foundation for future discoveries. Being able to identify certain types of leaves may be important in helping students gain an appreciation for conservation measures. Knowing the different types of simple machines provides a basis for students to comprehend the working of more complex machinery. Yet meaningful science programs must move beyond these facts. In short, an accumulation of facts is no more science than a collection of bricks is a house.

2. Children need to use science information in a practical and personal sense. Science instruction should be geared toward offering youngsters many opportunities to put their knowledge into practice, to see science as a daily human activity, and to increase their appreciation of the world around them.

3. Children must take some responsibility for their own learning. They need opportunities to make their own choices or select learning opportunities based on their goals and interests. Kids who are given those choices begin to assume greater control over their personal learning and are more willing to pursue learning for its own sake. In short, science is *learned* more than it is *taught*.

4. Students need to understand the interdependencies and interrelationships that exist among all elements of the world around them. They need to grasp the role of science in promoting those understandings.

5. Children are naturally active. The very nature of science implies an action-oriented and process-oriented approach to learning. By this I mean that children need to "get their hands dirty" in science, to manipulate objects, try out different approaches, spill things, break an occasional dish or test tube, handle substances and animals, look around them, taste various objects, and get involved. Kids do this all the time; it's part of the cycle of learning.

6. Children need to be stimulated in diverse ways. Tasting, hearing, seeing, feeling, and smelling are the avenues by which children learn about their immediate environment as well as environments outside the home. These same senses can be made integral elements of science, too, signifying to children that the skills they have previously relied on can be used to foster a better understanding of new areas of discovery and exploration.

7. Students need to use science information in practical and personal ways. Possessing the skills of science is one thing; being able to use those skills in a meaningful context is quite another. Elementary science instruction should be geared toward offering youngsters a myriad of opportunities to put their knowledge into practice.

8. Children need to be engaged in intellectually stimulating encounters with their world. Science provides children with a host of opportunities to question and think about their world. Students must be provided with critical thinking opportunities and challenging situations that allow them to set their own learning goals and satisfy them through self-discovery.

These principles support the notion that science education, to be productive, requires a partnership between teachers and students, the joy of learning, and youngsters' developing curiosity about their environment. Helping students appreciate their potential for contributing to not only their personal knowledge base but also the world around them can be the basis of a lifelong appreciation of science.

Six Key Ingredients

What distinguishes "good" science instruction from "average" science instruction? Well, through several years of study in "real" classrooms with "real" students, researchers have discovered that the following six key ingredients are essential elements in every science lesson or unit. These "keys" are based on the latest research available about how kids learn and specifically about how kids learn science.

What is most distinctive about these ingredients is that they are all embedded in well-designed science lessons. In short, the mastery of scientific concepts is enhanced when these key ingredients are promoted and emphasized.

- **Hands-on approach**—Children need active opportunities to manipulate science, to handle science, and to "get down and dirty" with science. A hands-on approach to science has long been promoted as one of the most effective instructional strategies for any elementary teacher.

- **Process orientation**—Focusing on the processes of science (e.g., observing, classifying, measuring, inferring, predicting, communicating, and experimenting) helps students appreciate science as a "doing" subject, one that never ends but rather offers multiple opportunities for continual examination and discovery.

- **Integration**—When science is integrated into all aspects of the elementary curriculum, students begin to understand its relevance and relationship to their daily lives outside the classroom. Children begin to comprehend the impact science has on daily activities, both in the present and in the future.

- **Cooperative learning**—When children are provided with opportunities to share ideas, discuss possibilities, and investigate problems together, they can benefit enormously from the background knowledge of their peers as well as the strength that comes from a group approach to learning.

- **Critical thinking**—One of the issues classroom teachers have wrestled with for many years concerns the need to help students become independent thinkers. In other words, effective science instruction is not dependent on helping students memorize lots of scientific information but rather on assisting them in being able to use data in productive and mutually satisfying ways.

- **Authentic assessment**—Weaving together formal and informal assessment procedures naturally and normally throughout all aspects of a lesson (beginning, middle, end) is the crux of good instruction. Students should be provided with active opportunities to take a role in their own assessment; this is both motivating and stimulating.

Science, the Internet, and Your Classroom

The Internet can be a natural and normal part of students' experiences with science. Internet resources provide youngsters with valuable opportunities to extend and expand their knowledge of the world around them as well as discover fascinating information in the life, physical, earth, and space sciences. The Web helps kids develop a rich appreciation for the science concepts, values, and generalizations contained within the science curriculum. The Internet underscores the idea that science is much more than a dry accumulation of facts and figures. Youngsters will learn that Web resources allow them to explore and investigate their immediate and far-flung environment in an arena that has no limits.

By sharing technology with the students with whom you work, you are helping to promote the natural curiosity and inquisitiveness of children and encouraging and stimulating them in the following ways:

1. The Internet provides youngsters with an ever-expanding array of information in a welcome format. Youngsters realize that science is not relegated to the pages of a textbook but can be found in both the near and distant corners of their world.

2. Internet sites extend and expand specific science concepts beyond information typically presented in textbooks. Science Web sites allow students to explore a topic in greater depth and develop a greater appreciation of all its nuances.

3. Well-designed Web sites offer students a variety of information from several angles or points of view. Youngsters learn that science knowledge is never static—it's always growing and changing.

4. Web resources help students understand the many ways in which scientific knowledge can be shared, discussed, and evaluated. A variety of related Web sites help youngsters comprehend science as a dynamic subject.

5. The Internet provides children with new information and knowledge unobtainable in any other format. Topics in which new discoveries are being made at a rapid rate (e.g., space exploration, medical research, tectonic plate theory) can be shared through up-to-the-minute reports on the Web.

6. Science Web sites open up the world and assist students in making their own self-initiated discoveries. In many ways, the Internet encourages kids to ask their own questions and provides them with the impetus to initiate their own investigations. It stimulates their natural inquisitiveness and enhances their appreciation of the known and the unknown.

7. Learning science via the Web is fun. Technology gives students a vehicle with which they can explore, discover, investigate, and examine the world in which they live.

The Internet can be a powerful motivator for the elementary classroom as well as for the natural activities that teachers and children can share. You are encouraged to use this book as a stimulus to youngsters' natural tendencies to seek answers to their innumerable questions. You are further encouraged to use the Web sites cited within this volume as "instigators" for scientific discoveries and investigations throughout the months and years ahead.

Science education, to be fruitful, requires a partnership between the science curriculum, the joy of teaching, and children's inherent curiosity about their environment. The Internet is a vehicle for stimulating science teaching and promoting authentic science learning. Its benefits are many and its possibilities unlimited.

Chapter 2

The Internet and Instruction

The Internet is a powerful, worldwide communications system. Often referred to as a "network of networks," it connects thousands of computer networks all over the world. It does this through data lines that can transmit information at high rates of speed.

It is an equally powerful resource for classroom teachers and their students. In many ways it has reshaped our curriculum and the ways in which knowledge is shared with youngsters. That it has redefined our responsibilities is a given; it has also redefined the ways in which children learn and in which we can facilitate that process.

Researching the Internet

Consider the Internet as a very large library. In a large library the researcher has myriad resources, books, periodicals, microfiche, and the like at her or his fingertips. In a large library there will be excellent research materials as well as materials that are barely appropriate or are far out-of-date. Some of the materials will be easy to find, but it will take an intensive search to locate others. As in most libraries, there will be individuals who can assist in the search process and there will be times when the researcher will be on her or his own in tracking down leads and locating appropriate materials.

Just like a large library, the Internet has its advantages and its disadvantages. Researchers (in this case, students) need to know how to get around in this enormous library, whom to ask for assistance, and the validity of the information they seek. Some of the information they collect will be accurate, up-to-date, and precise; other information will be out-of-date, incomplete, or inappropriate. Just because it's online doesn't necessarily mean that the information is useful any more than a book being in a library means that it is needed or necessary to one's search for information.

7

The information on the Internet is but one tool in a researcher's arsenal. It is as good (or as bad) as any other type of scientific research. In short, just because something is online doesn't make it valid, appropriate, or necessary.

The Internet Research Paradigm

To assist students in the appropriate use of the Internet, I have developed a modification of the six-step research cycle to information problem solving (Eisenberg and Berkowitz, 1990). This paradigm forms the basis for the activities and projects described in Part II of this book. You may wish to describe and discuss the components of this paradigm with your students prior to initiating these units in your classroom.

- **Questions**—Good research emanates from good questions, particularly self-initiated questions. It is always appropriate for students to generate their own questions at the beginning of any research project. This helps them focus on the nature and intent of the project and frame it in terms that are meaningful to them. To assist you in this process, each of the units includes selected research questions you can ask students in groups or individually. These questions should encourage students to ask their own questions and pursue answers to those self-initiated queries.

- **Site investigation**—The research questions provide students with a structure. They must then assemble a list of Internet sites with which to investigate the questions they posed. Checking search engines for appropriate sites and listing and/or eliminating sites are all part of this process. The units in this book provide you and your students with selected Web sites to investigate. As stated elsewhere in this book, other sites may be added to this list as they become available or as others are modified or eliminated.

- **Data gathering**—At this stage in the process students go online to obtain the information they need to answer the questions they have generated. It is here that students should have knowledge about the appropriateness of a site to determine its worthiness as a research tool. Making quick evaluations of sites is an important skill.

- **Data analysis**—After students have accessed the necessary information from selected Web sites, they must analyze it. They must eliminate unnecessary or inappropriate information and keep pertinent and relevant data. This stage may take a substantial amount of time depending upon the amount of preliminary information gathered.

- **Compare and contrast**—Students should have sufficient opportunities to compare and contrast the information collected from the Internet with other information sources. For the units in this book, students can accomplish this comparison process through the use of relevant children's literature. Students will be able to contrast print resources with online resources to determine the depth and breadth of their information and to gauge its validity. Although literature is promoted as a natural mechanism for this evaluation process, students should also be encouraged to utilize other print resources (e.g., monographs, flyers, brochures) for validation purposes.

- **Extend**—Collecting information from one or more Web sites is a valid activity. Students should be offered sufficient opportunities to put that information to work. In this book, each unit contains a variety of "hands-on, minds-on" activities that stimulate intellectual pursuits and offer numerous extensions for comprehending the material collected.

Students can use their newfound knowledge in productive, meaningful, and personal extensions. Students will see the relevance of Internet resources as "promoters" of intellectual curiosity and investigation. The Internet becomes a valid tool in students' lifelong quests for information and the "gainful employment" of the data in personally satisfying quests.

This paradigm is illustrated in figure 2.1. Note that it is a continuous process: After students have engaged in an appropriate number of extending activities, they will undoubtedly generate additional questions about the topic. From those questions the process begins all over again. The Internet becomes but one tool in a student's search for information, purpose, and comprehension. Most important, that quest is student-initiated and directed. Teachers become information facilitators, offering learning opportunities and encouraging students to pursue topics via multiple resources.

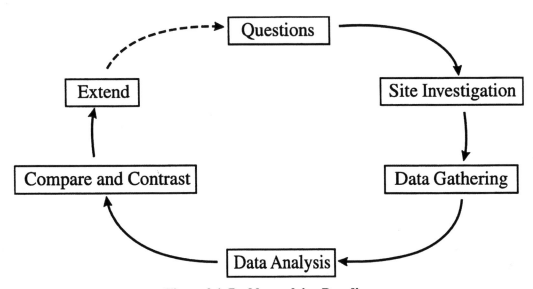

Figure 2.1. Problem-solving Paradigm

A Process of Implementation

This book has been designed for busy teachers. It offers you and your students a plethora of activities, projects, and investigations into every topic and subject in the elementary science curriculum. It is both a resource and a tool. For you and your students to achieve the maximum benefit from this book, follow these procedures:

1. Become familiar with the hardware, software, and systems that you plan to use in your classroom. It is a fact of classroom life that the unexpected should always be expected, particularly in areas of technology, so be prepared.

2. Check each site before assigning it to your students. The Internet is always changing, always evolving. It is quite possible that an address has changed or is no longer current. Pages may have been eliminated and new pages may have been added. As always, knowing what your students will be using will save problems later on.

3. Plan to check any sites for their grade appropriateness. Each unit in this book offers several sites that have been selected for their content and appropriate grade levels.

You need to know if the sites you assign your students are appropriate to their varying reading levels and/or intellectual sophistication.

4. Emphasize to your students that the Internet is only one research tool at their disposal. Make sure students understand the relevance and connection between any Internet projects and the regular curriculum.

5. Set up specific Web sites as "Bookmarks" or "Favorites." This will enable your students to organize their searches more efficiently within a content area. Refer to your browser help screen or manual for directions on how to accomplish this.

6. Have a backup plan available if certain Web sites cannot be accessed. You probably know that it is not always possible to access selected Web sites. Popular sites (such as those maintained by NASA) are frequently busy during regular school hours. Sometimes the system may be off-line, refusing connections, or the receiving modem may be busy. The recommended children's literature and accompanying activities for each unit in this book will provide you with a variety of options to teach a selected concept. Thus, if sites are busy, you will still be able to engage students in meaningful activities.

7. Be sure your students have sufficient opportunities to learn and practice basic computer and Internet skills. Technology is changing so rapidly that not only is it essential that teachers keep up-to-date on the latest innovations, it is equally important that students be provided with necessary instruction and constant practice in computer literacy skills.

8. Check the sites students are accessing and the materials available on those sites frequently. This book, and other similar resources, is designed as an instructional aid. This does not imply that students should be given a task and left to fend for themselves. Student work must be constantly and consistently monitored.

Web Searching

As of the writing of this book there are approximately 900 million pages of text on the Internet, and that number is growing at the rate of about 500 pages every day. To say that there is a lot of information on the Internet would be an obvious understatement. Anyone who has listed a topic on a search engine knows that there can be an unlimited number of pages for any single subject (list "Volcanoes," for example, and you'll get more than 120,000 Web pages).

Search engines are the primary research tool for discovering information on the Internet. A search engine is nothing more than an indexing service of Web sites. These indexes are updated frequently and are organized according to the cataloguing procedures of each search engine. Some Web sites are indexed according to their titles; others are listed according to the full text of the site.

Search engines are accessed by clicking on the Search button on the menu bar of the Web browser or by typing in the URL. When the search program is displayed, a search can be initiated by typing a key word or phrase related to the topic desired. Table 2.1 lists some of the more common search engines.

Table 2.1
Search Engines

AltaVista ....http://www.altavista.com
Deja News ....http://www.deja.com
Dogpile ....http://www.dogpile.com
Excite ....http://www.excite.com
Google ....http://www.google.com
Goto..http://goto.com
HotBot ....http://www.hotbot.com
Infoseek ....http://infoseek.go.com
LookSmart ....http://www.looksmart.com
Lycos...http://www.lycos.com
Magellan ....http://www.magellan.com
Northern Light ....http://www.northernlight.com
Profusion ....http://www.profusion.com
SavvySearch...http://www.savvysearch.com
Snap...http://www.snap.com
Yahoo...http://www.yahoo.com

There are also search engines devoted exclusively to Web sites that are appropriate for children. Each of the Web sites listed on these engines has been prescreened and is considered child-safe for all students. Teachers and parents can rest assured that these search engines prevent access to adult or inappropriate materials. Table 2.2 presents some of the best.

Table 2.2
Child-Appropriate Search Engines

Lycos Kids Guide ....http://www.lycos.com/kids
Magellan ....http://www.magellan.com
Searchopolis ....http://www.searchopolis.com
Yahooligans..http://www.yahooligans.com

For complex topics you can save a lot of time by utilizing a metasearch engine. A metasearch engine submits a request for information to several different search engines at the same time. The results are then arranged on a list from high frequency citations to low frequency citations. Metasearch engines are time-saving and labor-saving ways of obtaining lots of information in a very short amount of time. Table 2.3 lists some of the more popular metasearch engines.

Table 2.3
Metasearch Engines

All in One..http://www.allonesearch.com
Beaucoup Search Engines...http://www.beaucoup.com
C/NET Search...http://search.cnet.com
Internet Search Sites ....http://www.refdesk.com/newsrch.html
Metacrawler http://www.go2net.com/search.html
Webcrawler...http://Webcrawler.com
W3 Search Engines http://osiris.sunderland.ac.uk/rif/W3searches.html

Lesson Plans

You can enhance any lesson in science by accessing a wide variety of lesson plans on the Web. As you might imagine, the quality and content of these lessons vary, but most do offer some unique ways of updating and reinvigorating portions of your science program. Consider the Web sites listed in Table 2.4 as positive adjuncts to your curriculum.

Many of the listed sites also offer course outlines, updated reference and resource materials, curriculum guides, standards-based units, and specific projects and experiments. A careful and judicious review of these materials can add sparkle to "tired" lessons and reinvigorate many areas of the science program.

Table 2.4
Lesson Plan Resources

Address	Description
http://www.cln.org/cln.html	The Community Learning Network is designed to help classroom teachers integrate technology into their classrooms. They have over 250 menu pages with more than 5,400 annotated links to educational World Wide Web (WWW) sites. Truly a magnificent resource!
http://server2.greatlakes.k12.mi.us/	This incredible collection of teacher resources is available for downloading. Included are lesson plans, computer software, Hypercard files, new resources, thematic units, guest speakers, field trips, and student-created material resources.
http://www.learner.org	This Web site was established to help schools and communities improve math and science education. Click on SAMI and discover a searchable database with easy access to curriculum resources, lesson plans and projects, funding sources, computer software resources, and more.
http://www.afredericks.com	This Web site is designed to provide busy classroom teachers with the latest information, the newest activities, the best resources, and the most creative projects in elementary science. It's updated frequently with hundreds of exciting and new ideas.

(continued)

Table 2.4 *Continued*.

Address	Description
http://www.teachers.net/lessons	Take a lesson, leave a lesson at the Teachers Net Lesson Exchange. The lessons cover all subjects and grade levels and include links to the teachers who posted the lessons. This is an excellent Web site that will energize the overall classroom curriculum.
http://www.pacificnet.net/~mandel	This is a wonderful place to share ideas, concerns, and questions with educators from around the world. The material is updated weekly and you'll be able to obtain lesson plans in every curricular area. Also included are teaching tips for both new and experienced teachers.
http://cccnet.com	This site assists teachers in taking advantage of the vast resources of the Internet. It includes teacher discussion and bulletin board areas as well as online projects teachers can do with their classes.
http://www.enc.org	This is the Eisenhower National Clearinghouse for Math and Science Education. It includes detailed descriptions of curriculum materials, articles from professional journals on science teaching, and favorite Internet sites for teachers.
http://www.teachnet.com/lesson/index.html	This site offers classroom teachers an array of lesson plans in every curricular area. This is an easy-to-use resource.
http://www.education-world.com	Education World claims to be the "world's educational resource on the Web." Its database contains more than 120,000 URLs, many of which are annotated. Teachers can search by keyword or by selecting topic areas.
http://www.ceismc.gatech.edu/busyt	The Busy Teachers' Website provides classroom teachers with a host of educational Web sites in a wide variety of curricular areas. Lots to search here.
http://encarta.msn.com/schoolhouse/default.asp	This incredible resource taps into the power of Microsoft. Here you'll find loads of lesson plans and a wide range of updated resources for every aspect of your classroom curriculum.

(continued)

Table 2.4 *Continued*.

Address	Description
http://www.gsn.org	The Global School House offers a diverse collection of Internet sites, videoconferencing opportunities, professional development activities, contests, and discussion lists for teachers and parents.
http://www.scholasticnetwork.com	The Scholastic Network bills itself as "The best Internet research tool for kids." At this all-inclusive site you'll discover an amazing variety of resources for you and your students. There's simply too much to list here, but you won't be disappointed!

Online Experts

Wouldn't it be great if students could have experts visit the classroom to offer their expertise on a subject? Well, they can! Experts are available online to answer questions posed by students and supply them with necessary information.

Students can access the expertise of scientists and others within and throughout any science project. Various Web sites (see below) provide students with opportunities to pose questions to working scientists and receive answers in return. Scientists and experts in fields as diverse as astronomy, zoology, chemistry, paleontology, entomology, and oceanography can be contacted via e-mail to obtain up-to-the-minute answers to personal questions.

Querying working experts in a particular field provides youngsters with relevant data about specific topics. Students should understand, however, that the experts are all working scientists. Every attempt is made to transmit a response back to students in a reasonable amount of time (usually two to three days), but the nature of scientists' daily work obligations or field research may prevent that from happening. The experts utilized on each of the sites below have been carefully selected as responsive to student questions; however, students need to know that they are working scientists first and that the time they have available for answering questions may be limited.

Many of these sites also maintain lists of some of the most frequently asked questions along with their accompanying responses. Invite students to search those lists before posing a question. Often, the question will have been asked (and answered) previously.

Several sites are also appropriate for teacher use. Posing a question to a working scientist can provide you with fresh ideas and new perspectives on a specific topic. It's a wonderful way to stay up-to-date on the latest scientific advancements and discoveries and to reinvigorate tried-and-true lesson plans.

Table 2.5
Online Experts

Address	Description
http://k12science.stevens-tech.edu/curriculum/aska.html	This sites allows you and your students to contact a variety of experts in a variety of subject areas. This site is filled with lots of resources.
http://www.ajkids.com	Ask Jeeves for Kids allows students to pose their own questions (in their own language). This site will then provide youngsters with kid-friendly Web sites through which they can obtain the answer(s) to their questions. This is a great resource for any area of the elementary curriculum.
http://ericir.syr.edu/Qa	AskERIC's question and answer service utilizes the diverse resources and expertise of the national ERIC system. The Ask ERIC staff will respond to your question within two business days with ERIC database citations and publications, Internet resources, and referrals to other sources of information. They state that they respond "to EVERY question with personalized resources."
http://www.xpertsite.com	Wow, what a site! Loads of expert connections in a wide variety of subjects and topics. This is the ideal research tool for teachers.
http://www.askanexpert.com	This site connects students with hundreds of real world experts, ranging from astronauts to zookeepers. These experts have volunteered to answer student questions for free.
http://www.vrd.org/locator/subject.html	The AskA+ Locator is an all-inclusive expert site in a wide variety of topic areas. More than 100 expert sites are listed here (with hyperlinks to each). Ideal for both teachers and students.
http://madsci.wustl.edu	The Mad Scientist Network bills itself as a "collective cranium" of scientists providing answers to questions posed by the general public as well as educators and their students. It also contains archives of thousands of previously asked (and answered) questions. One of my favorites!

Informing Parents

As teachers have long known intuitively and as has been validated with a significant body of research, parents play a major role in the education of any child. It has been proven that the bond established between teachers and parents is also a significant factor in the scholastic achievement of students.

For many parents the "inclusion" of technology in the classroom is both exciting and frightening (just as it is for teachers). It is imperative that parents be informed about Internet use in any classroom—such information helps ensure their participation and support of the overall academic program.

To assist you in that regard, the following "Parental Agreement Form" can be duplicated and sent home to parents at the beginning of the school year. The form informs parents about the utilization of technology in the affairs of the classroom and solicits their support and permission. This ensures that parents are "recruited" as educational partners in your Internet projects.

Parental Agreement Form

Dear Parent/Guardian:

Our class is about to begin some exciting new discoveries and adventures in science. We will be examining Internet Web sites in many different areas. This will be a valuable learning opportunity for your child—one that will expand and enhance the entire science curriculum.

Your child will be assigned several projects and activities related to the Internet. Please be assured that we will carefully monitor and supervise all computer activities. Like you, we do not wish any student to have access to inappropriate materials.

Our guidelines for using the Internet are quite specific and detailed. All students have received the following instructions:

- Students may not list their names or addresses on any outgoing e-mail or subscription services.

- Students may not access inappropriate materials or Web sites not approved by the faculty or staff.

- Students may not use inappropriate language.

- Students have been advised that e-mail is not considered private mail and may be checked as warranted.

Please talk with your child about using the Internet at school and at home. Afterwards, please sign and return the form at the bottom by this date: _____.

My child and I have discussed appropriate uses of the Internet. Although the school will make every attempt to restrict controversial materials, I understand that it may be impossible to filter everything. By my signature below, I give my child permission to engage in appropriate Internet activities at school.

Parent/Guardian: _____ Date: _____

I have discussed appropriate uses of the Internet with my parent/guardian. I fully understand my responsibilities and know that any violation may result in my computer privileges being revoked.

Student: _____ Date: _____

The Internet can be a powerful teaching tool and a powerful learning tool. Its utilization within and throughout your science curriculum can provide your students with a wealth of learning opportunities available in no other format. Equally, it can offer you an enormous variety of teaching opportunities that go far beyond curriculum guides and teacher manuals. In many ways, it is a resource that "breaks down" the four walls of the classroom and opens kids' eyes to the far corners of the world.

References

Eisenberg, M., and R. Berkowitz. 1990. *Information problem-solving: The big six skills approach to library and information skills instruction.* Norwood, NJ: Ablex Publishing.

Chapter 3

How to Use This Book

The units included in Part II of this book emphasize key concepts throughout the science curriculum. In addition, the activities, experiments, and projects included in each unit integrate skills from a variety of areas to ensure a unique, multidisciplinary, and interdisciplinary study of science.

Using a Unit

The units are designed to be complete and thorough guides. However, you are not required to use any single unit in its entirety. You may elect to use selected portions of a unit, combine one section of a unit with other classroom curricular materials, or eliminate some sections of a unit due to lack of materials or time. The true value of these units lies in the fact that they can be easily adapted, modified, or adjusted according to the dictates of your science program, your level of comfort, or students' interests.

The units (which can be used alone, in conjunction with a corresponding thematic unit, or in concert with another unit), offer engaging literature, activities, and Internet projects for a specific scientific concept. Each unit includes activities, questions, Web sites, and related works of literature to provide you with a variety of choices through which to develop targeted content objectives and skills.

Each unit is divided into five separate, yet interrelated, sections, discussed below.

Introduction

Each unit is prefaced with a brief introduction. These introductions are designed to provide you with basic factual information necessary to an understanding of the scientific concepts and ideas promoted in various activities in the unit.

Each introduction is addressed to the teacher using the unit. However, you may choose to share these introductions with your students as a preliminary activity. Students should understand that the introduction provides only a modicum of information and that more in-depth data will need to be accessed via the Web sites and literature. After students have had sufficient opportunities to gather their own data, invite them to prepare and write their own introduction for a selected unit. These introductions, framed in "kid language," may be just the ticket for stimulating other groups or classes of students to pursue a topic later in the year or in succeeding years.

Research Questions

The second section of each unit includes carefully designed research questions. These can be posed to students prior to the start of a unit, while the unit is in process, or at its conclusion. They are not intended to be evaluation questions, but rather as opportunities for students to think about some of the basic concepts behind the designated topic.

Many of the questions for a specific unit can be answered via the Web sites and/or the selected literature. This offers youngsters opportunities to research specific aspects of a topic in some detail. It also offers task-oriented queries through which you can monitor student progress.

The questions listed in this section are suggestions only. You are not obliged to use all of them. You should invite your students to generate their own list of questions and add them to the ones suggested here. Maintain those additional questions in a "question bank" and share them with other groups of students or with students in succeeding years. A collection of student-initiated questions infused into these units can be a powerful stimulant to further exploration and discoveries.

Web Sites

Each unit includes a selection of specific Web sites. These sites are designed to provide you and your students with a broad range of experiences, discoveries, and explorations in various aspects of the topic. Some sites will be general, others more specific.

Please note that the Web site addresses included in any single unit are current and accurate as of the writing of this book. The evolving nature of the Internet is such that some addresses will become defunct, others will change, and new ones will be added to the Internet on a daily basis. You should feel free to add your own favorite sites to the ones suggested here. By the same token, feel free to eliminate those sites that are no longer current or operational.

To assist you in selecting those sites that will be most useful for your students, each site has a brief annotation. These summaries will guide you in selecting those sites that offer you important background information as well as those through which students can gather necessary information. The coding system in table 3.1 is provided to help you select the most appropriate sites for any particular topic.

Table 3.1
Coding System

S: K–3 ....Site is appropriate for students in Grades K–3
S: 4–6..Site is appropriate for students in Grades 4–6
S: All...Site is appropriate for all students
T: K–3 ....Site is appropriate for teachers in Grades K–3
T: 4–6..Site is appropriate for teachers in Grades 4–6
T: All ....Site is appropriate for all teachers

Literature Resources

The literature listed for each unit is designed to offer you and your students multiple opportunities to investigate aspects of the topic in greater detail. Books listed come from a variety of sources and "recommended literature" lists. As you might imagine, some topics have a profusion of related literature sources, whereas for others there is a dearth of relevant books. I have tried, whenever possible, to provide you with the most up-to-date and easily accessible literature available.

The literature reflects a range of reading levels. You should feel free to select and use literature that best meets the needs and abilities of your students in addition to promoting specific scientific concepts. An "energized" science curriculum will include literature selections throughout its length and breadth. You will discover innumerable opportunities for developing, expanding, and teaching scientific principles based on the literature in these units. Remember that the readability or difficulty level of a single book should not determine if or how it will be used; rather, the emphasis should be on whether students are interested and motivated to pursue literature-related activities that promote learning in a supportive and holistic science curriculum.

You are encouraged to substitute and/or include in any unit books that you have found to be particularly noteworthy, those that are old-time favorites or new releases, or recommendations from colleagues or professional resources. The utility of a unit lies in the fact that the literature used can come from a variety of sources and is not relegated to the suggestions made here. Keeping these units "fresh" and updated with new literature resources can be a powerful stimulant for both teacher and student interest.

Activities and Projects

Each unit contains a wide scope of activities designed to promote growth in critical thinking, creative thinking, problem solving, and scientific investigation. This gives students unlimited opportunities to process and interpret information while learning relevant knowledge and concepts. I have suggested a variety of activities. You are encouraged to select the ones most appropriate for your students and your science program objectives.

You are not expected to use all the activities suggested for a unit or all parts of any single activity. Instead, you and your students should decide on those activities that best serve the needs of the science program and of the students themselves. You will discover activities that can be used individually, in small groups, in large groups, or as a whole class. Providing students with opportunities to make some of their own selections can be a powerful and energizing element for the entire science program. When youngsters are given those opportunities, their appreciation of science and their interest in learning important scientific concepts grow tremendously.

As students become involved in the various units, I suggest that you guide them in researching and/or developing other activities based on classroom dynamics and teaching/learning styles. For learning to be meaningful, it must have relevance. I encourage you and your students to adapt the activities included in the units to create a challenging learning environment that will arouse each student's natural curiosity and encourage students to pursue new ideas and formulate their own connections.

I hope you will make these units your own. Add to them, adapt them, and allow students to help you design additional activities, experiments, and projects that will challenge them, arouse their natural curiosity, and create a dynamic learning environment.

Implementing a Unit

Teaching science with these units is not necessarily an "all or nothing" proposition. That is, it is not necessary to use a unit for a full day or a full week. You have several options to consider depending on how you want to present a unit to your class, how much you want it to dominate your daily curriculum, and how involved you and your students want to be. Obviously, your level of comfort with the Internet and the scope and sequence of your classroom or district science curriculum may determine the degree to which you utilize a unit. Following are some options for using the units in your classroom:

1. Teach a unit throughout a school day and for a extended period of several school days.

2. Teach a unit for one-half day for several days in succession.

3. Use a unit for two or more subject areas (e.g., science plus language arts) in combination and the regular curriculum for other subjects.

4. Use a unit as the "curriculum" for science and the regular curriculum for other subjects.

5. Teach a unit for an entire day and follow up with the regular curriculum in succeeding days.

6. Use a unit as a followup to information and data presented in a textbook or curriculum guide.

7. Provide students with a unit as independent work upon completion of lessons in the basal textbook.

8. Teach cooperatively with a colleague to present a unit to both classes at the same time. (This can be done with two classes at the same grade level or two different classes, each at a different grade level.)

9. Use a unit intermittently over the span of several weeks.

How you use a unit may be determined by any number of factors. It is safe to say that there is no ideal way to implement a unit into your classroom plans. This list is only a partial collection of ideas. Your own particular teaching situation, personal experience, and student needs will suggest alternatives to this register of ideas.

Part II
Internet Science Units

Chapter 4

Life Science

Life. It's all around us. From Rover barking in the backyard to the plants in the living room to the tiny speck of mold on the kitchen counter, we are surrounded by life. Understanding how plants and animals grow and develop as well as how they interact with each other is an important part of science. In many ways, life is the area of the scientific world with which students are most familiar and is truly a field ripe for exploration. As students gain an awareness of the life forms around them, they also develop an appreciation for their own place in the gigantic ecosystem that we all participate in each day.

This chapter introduces your students to several of the life sciences. Some of the investigations offer a look into botany: how plants survive, the environments they live in, and how they reproduce. Other investigations provide insights into ecology, the relationship between living things and their environment. Still other investigations explore zoology, from ants to whales.

The study of life in all its forms is one of the basics of science. As students learn about patterns of growth, ecological relationships, and environmental habitats, they gain an appreciation for the majesty of the world around them. This knowledge can then be used in efforts to preserve the living world for successive generations.

Alligators and Crocodiles

 Introduction

Alligators and crocodiles belong to a group of animals known as crocodilians. All crocodilians have short legs and strong tails for swimming. They have remained unchanged for millions of years.

People often confuse these two creatures; however, they are quite easy to distinguish. Crocodiles have thin, pointy snouts, whereas alligators have wide, rounded snouts. Most crocodiles can live in salty water; most alligators live in fresh water. When a crocodile closes its mouth, a tooth sticks up on each side of its lower jaw. In alligators, that tooth is hidden.

 Research Questions

1. What are some basic differences between alligators and crocodiles?

2. Where are most alligators and crocodiles found?

3. How are baby crocodilians born?

4. What kinds of animals prey on the young of alligators and crocodiles?

 Web Sites

http://www.EnchantedLearning.com/subjects/Alligator.shtml
This site is appropriately named All About Alligators. Here students learn about the anatomy, locomotion, habitat, behavior, reproduction, diet, evolution, extinction, classification, and conservation of alligators. (S: 4–6, T: All)

http://www.envirolonk.org/oneworld/tales/crocs/index.html
This site allows students to listen to crocodiles in their many moods and activities. Also included is discussion of myths and tales about crocodiles. (S: K–3)

http://www.flmnh.ufl.edu/natsci/herpetology/brittoncrocs/croccomm.html
At this site kids will be able to listen to the various sounds made by alligators and crocodiles. A super addition to any study of these creatures. (S: All)

http://www.flmnh.ufl.edu/natsci/herpetology/crocs/crocpics.htm#Top
The Crocodilian Photo Gallery offers young viewers a panorama of photos of alligators and crocodiles in all their glory. (S: All)

http://www.fpl.com/html/kid_gator.html

Learning about the life of crocodilians, why some are endangered, and the difference between alligators and crocodiles is the focus of this Web site. (S: 4–6)

Literature Resources

Aruego, Jose & Dewey, Ariane. (1988). *Rockabye Crocodile*. New York: Greenwillow Books.

This simple story presents crocodiles as kind, rather than evil, creatures. Friendship is a key theme for the crocodile in this book.

Curto, Josephine. (1976). *Biography of an Alligator*. New York: Putnam.

This is a nonfiction story of a mother alligator and the way she cares for her young. It discusses how alligators live and the growth of their children.

Mozelle, Shirly. (1994). *Zach's Alligator Goes to School*. New York: HarperCollins.

This book discusses the day that a little boy's alligator goes to school and causes trouble. This is one of a series of books about alligators.

Wallace, Karen. (1996). *Imagine You Are a Crocodile*. New York: Henry Holt.

This book takes the reader through a typical day as a crocodile. What crocodiles see, eat, live in, and do are discussed in this imaginative tale. Students get to use their imaginations and understand the creature in a fun way.

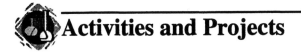

Activities and Projects

1. If possible, obtain both human and crocodilian teeth for use in the classroom. Display both for students to view. Initiate a discussion on losing teeth. Ask students to talk about their personal experiences. In the discussion, allow the students to verbally brainstorm how a crocodilian might lose its teeth. Using the information from the discussion, literature, and Web sites, have students create a story about how the crocodile lost its tooth. Make the stories into shape books of crocodilian teeth to display in the classroom.

2. If possible, arrange a trip to an alligator farm, zoo, or museum that has full-grown crocodilians along with babies and eggs. A tour of the area will give students information about the lifestyle of a crocodilian, a look at how they eat and live, and a look at their life development. Ask students to create a bulletin board display on the life development of a crocodilian from egg to full-grown adult in detail. This information can be obtained from the trip, literature, and Web sites. On the same bulletin board they can display the life development of a human from fetus to adult using similar research. In a corner of the board create a Venn diagram to show the similarities and differences between the two creatures.

3. Teach a lesson on the similarities and differences between alligators and crocodiles. Ask the class to help generate a T-square chart. On one side list characteristics of alligators and on the other side list characteristics of crocodiles. When the chart is completed, call students up to the chart randomly to highlight in yellow the similarities between the two animals. The characteristics that are different should be highlighted in pink. Hang the chart in a place where the color coding can be seen.

4. Obtain a garment or handbag that is made of alligator or crocodile skin. Bring the object to class and teach a lesson about endangered species and hunting animals for material purposes. Invite students to go to the listed Web sites and find addresses for crocodilian conservation organizations. Write, call, or e-mail one of the groups for information on how to help crocodilians.

Ants

Introduction

There are 8,804 known species of ants, and they can be found everywhere. In fact, they are some of the most ubiquitous creatures on the face of the Earth. They are found from tropical regions to Arctic regions. Ant colonies may be as small as several hundred individuals to more than several million creatures.

Ants are true insects. They have a three-part body that includes the head, abdomen, and thorax. They typically live in colonies and are some of the most social creatures in nature. Each ant in a colony has a specific job to perform. There are nurses, ranchers, farmers, and soldiers within a single colony. Usually there is one queen ant, whose sole purpose in life is to produce thousands and thousands of eggs.

Research Questions

1. What do you find amazing about ants?

2. How many different species of ants are there in the world?

3. What is the world's largest ant?

4. What is the world's most deadly ant?

5. What is the most amazing fact about ant life?

6. How are ants different from other insects?

Web Sites

http://monroe2boces.org/shared/esp
    This site has kits to engage students in various activities about ants. Students can learn about building their own ant farm and will be able to answer many of their questions about ants. In addition, there are links to other Web sites on ants in general and specific ants. This site contains resources for both students and teachers. (T & S: K–6)

http://home.apu.edu/~philpi/
    Students learn detailed information about an ant farm on this site. They will discover the home life of an ant and the answers to many research questions. This site is animated with sounds and plenty of visuals. There are also many Web site links that students can access, along with games and activities. (S: 4–6)

http://www.insect–world.earthlife.net/

There are well over one million different known species of insects. Using this Web site, students can discover the world of insects, including ants. Students will be able to answer all their research questions about ants. There are twenty-seven Web site links specifically on ants. (S: 4–6, T: 4–6)

http://www.discovery.com/stories/nature/ants/ants.html

This site is the ultimate guide to ants. Different species of ants, locations, and habits are all highlighted here. (S: 4–6)

http://ant.edb.miyakyo-u.ac.jp/INTRODUCTION/Gakken79E/Page_02.html

This is a wonderful resource for teachers. Tons of information and loads of data highlight this all-inclusive site. (T: All)

 # Literature Resources

Chinery, Michael & Armstrong, Nicholas. (1991). *Ant (Life Story Series)*. New York: Benchmark Books.

This book is an introduction to ants. It shows the physical characteristics, habits, and natural environments of the different types of ants.

Dorros, Arthur. (1987). *Ant Cities (Let's Read and Find Out Science Book)*. New York: Crowell.

This book explains how ants live and work together to build their cities. Each ant has a special job to do and this book describes those jobs. Readers discover the amazing world of ants, in their backyard or around the world.

Fowler, Allan & Rau, Dana Meachen. (1998). *Inside an Ant Colony (Rookie Read–About Science)*. Chicago: Children's Press.

This book takes readers into various ant colonies. Exceptional illustrations capture the attention of young readers.

Julivert, Maria Angels & Socias, Marcel. (1993). *The Fascinating World of . . . Ants*. New York: Barron's Juveniles.

This book describes what an ant is, what it looks like, and its life cycle. It also describes an ant's activities and social habits.

Losi, Carol A. (1997). *The 512 Ants on Sullivan Street*. New York: Scholastic.

At a family picnic, four ants take a barbecue chip, eight take a bacon strip, and the march continues. This book contains math-building skills and activities.

Nickle, John. (1999). *The Ant Bully*. New York: Scholastic.

A young boy learns a lesson about bullying when he is pulled into an ant hole by ants that he has been tormenting.

Parker, Steve. (1999). *It's an Ant's Life*. New York: Reader's Digest Children's Books.

Wonderful illustrations in watercolor and ink highlight this book, with some from an ant's perspective.

Selsam, Millicent E. (1967). *Questions and Answers About Ants*. New York: Four Winds Press.
  This book answers everything youngsters want to know about ants. Filled with simple terms and lots of data for young readers.

Activities and Projects

1. Invite students to visit the Web site http://home.apu.edu/~philpi/ to learn about constructing and maintaining an ant farm. Ask them to build their own ant farm in the classroom. Have them make a list of the materials they think they would need based on the information that they have learned about ants. After you have gathered all the materials, construct an ant farm. Assemble the ant farm with the students and add the ants. Encourage students to keep a journal on what they see. This can be done on a daily basis.

2. Read *It's An Ant's Life* to the students. Encourage them to discuss what it must be like to be an ant. Ask students to imagine themselves as an ant and write a story depicting what a day in their life is like. This story could be fiction or nonfiction. Invite students to share their stories with the rest of the class. Encourage students to display their stories around the classroom.

3. Invite students to investigate the behavior of ants by visiting various Web sites. Encourage them to draw comparisons between the information learned on the site and what they have observed about ants in their yard or neighborhood. Ask students to construct a three-dimensional Venn diagram to portray those differences.

4. Read *Ant (Life Story Series)*, *Inside an Ant Colony*, and *Life of an Ant* to the students. Discuss with them what they have learned from each story. Encourage students to brainstorm different techniques to control ants without using chemicals.

5. Invite students to view an ant hill. Ask them to carefully carve away the opening to the ant nest without tearing up the nest. To carve away the opening, use a butter knife and remove the top of the ant hill at the surface. What do they observe? What did the ants do when the nest was opened? Invite students to carve another ant hill vertically. Have them use the butter knife, to carve another ant hill to the ground surface. What did they observe? Did they see any tunnels? What did the ants do?

6. You and your students can construct an easy classroom ant farm. Look outside for a rotting piece of wood or an area with lots of ants. Scoop up the ants into a large, empty pickle jar with some of the nearby soil. Put the lid on until you return to the classroom. Cover the outside of the jar with black construction paper so that it is completely dark inside. Put some water into a large cake pan, place a small saucer upside down in the middle of the pan, and place the jar on the upturned saucer before removing the lid. (The water prevents the ants from escaping from the jar.) Sprinkle some sugar water over the soil and place two or three bits of fruit inside the jar. The ants will begin to dig their tunnels in the soil. If it is dark enough, they will dig their tunnels next to the sides of the glass. If students remove the black construction paper every week or so, they will see the progress the ants have made in their tunnel building.

Bats

Introduction

Bats are the only mammals that fly. Although they have a bad reputation, most bats are actually beneficial. They live almost exclusively on a diet of insects, although a few species eat fruits and other vegetable matter. Bats live almost anywhere in the world, except in Arctic regions. In the United States, they live mostly in the southwestern states—in trees, caves, houses, under bridges, and in old mines.

Bats have very good hearing and are most active at night. One species, the vampire bat, attacks cattle and sheep in some tropical countries. In fact, its entire diet consists of nothing but blood. It only very rarely attacks humans, although some movies would have us believe otherwise. It is important that kids realize that bats are not scary, but interesting, helpful creatures!

Research Questions

1. Where do most bats live in the United States?

2. What types of places do bats live in?

3. What can bats do that no other mammal can do?

4. How many babies can one bat have in a year?

5. What's the world's largest bat?

Web Sites

http://members.aol.com/bats4kids/

This is a wonderful site with plenty of information about bats, including bat myths, games, a "bat quiz," books, and links to various other bat sites. Questions are answered, such as where bats live, what they eat, and what they look like. (S: All)

http://www.torstar.com/rom/batcave/cave/index.html

This interactive site allows students to explore and read about a real bat cave in St. Clair, Jamaica. Information about and cool pictures of the cave and specific types of bats are the main focus of this interesting site. (S: 4–6)

http://endangered.fws.gov/bats/bats.htm

Lots of information from the U.S. Fish and Wildlife Service provide students with up-to-the-minute data about bats. (S: 4–6) http://www.cccoe.k12.ca.us/bats/default.html

This site offer a world of resources and information for teachers interested in creating a thematic unit on bats. (T: All)

http://www.jaguarpaw.com/Bats.html

This is a great site overflowing with fascinating and unusual information about bats. A well-designed resource. (T: All)

# Literature Resources

Cannon, Janell. (1993). *Stellaluna*. San Diego: Harcourt Brace.

A fabulously illustrated book, *Stellaluna* tells the story of a baby bat separated from its mother and raised by a bird. By reading about the bat having to act like a bird and abandon her bat instincts, children will learn the differences between bats and birds.

Gibbons, Gail. (1999). *Bats*. New York: Holiday House.

This book introduces kids to bats and what they're all about. With its bright, colorful pictures, this book is a good introduction to the world of bats.

Milton, Joyce. (1993). *Bats: Creatures of the Night*. New York: Price Stern Sloan.

In this book, simple sentences packed with lots of information introduce children to bats and their physical characteristics and behaviors.

Perry, Phyllis. (1998). *Bats: The Amazing Upside-Downers*. Danbury, CT: Watts.

Its detailed information about bats, along with conservation organization information, makes this book perfect for older kids. Wonderful photos are a plus.

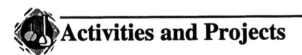# Activities and Projects

1. Ask children to create their own book about the myths about bats. Begin by asking the students what they think they know about bats (facts such as where they live, what they eat, etc.). Create a semantic web on the board and include all the background knowledge of the students. Divide the class into several cooperative groups and invite each group to select a category from the web (habits, habitats, life cycle, diet, etc.) and compile an informational brochure about that topic, a brochure designed to dispel some of the common myths and misperceptions about bats. The completed brochures can be donated to the school library.

2. Read the book *Stellaluna* to the students and illustrate the differences between bats and birds by drawing a Venn diagram on the board. Invite students to consult representative Web sites on bats (see above) and birds and post appropriate factual information in selected parts of the Venn diagram. Students may wish to add additional data throughout their study of bats.

3. Ask students to find out how many insects a bat eats in a certain amount of time (e.g., one hour). This information can be obtained via appropriate Web sites, in encyclopedias, in the school library, and so forth. Encourage the children to each create a chart/graph (bar graph, line graph) depicting a bat's feeding schedule. For example, if a bat eats 1,200 insects in one hour, the chart would show how many insects a bat eats in 10 minutes, half an hour, two hours, or the whole day. Discuss these charts and their accuracy with students. Obviously, bats do not eat every minute of the day, so it is important to help the children realize these charts are not always accurate. Encourage children to create different charts depicting the habits of fruit-eating bats, vampire bats, and meat-eating bats as well.

4. After students have had an opportunity to collect relevant data on bats, invite them to post a map of the United States on one wall of the classroom. Have them use lengths of yarn to note the migratory routes of selected species within the United States. Plan time for students to discuss any similarities or differences between these routes.

Bears

Introduction

Bears evoke our awe and curiosity. Not only do they come in all shapes and sizes; they can be found throughout the world. A favorite creature of zoos and circuses, some species are on the endangered species list.

Most bears are primarily herbivores or insectivores, although some are also carnivores. Throughout their evolutionary process, bears have become the largest terrestrial carnivores in the world, with the largest, the polar bear, reaching a weight of over 1,750 pounds. There are six species of bears: polar bear, sun bear, sloth bear, brown bear, black bear, and panda. Except for the panda, bears are all basically single colored, with some splashes of color on the chest area.

Research Questions

1. What are six different species of bear?
2. Which bear is the largest? The smallest?
3. When do bears hibernate? How long do they hibernate?
4. What kinds of things do bears like to eat?
5. What is the average life span of a bear?
6. How do bears communicate with one another?
7. How do bears care for their young?

Web Sites

http://www.bearden.org/
This site contains easy to understand information on all types of bears. There is a page dedicated to the preservation of bears. Students can submit their questions, comments, and ideas about saving the bears. In addition, there is a section where students can take a quiz to match different types of bears. (S: All, T: All)

http://www.nature-net.com/bears/
The Bear Den is the title of this site. Here students can hear bear sound effects, read stories from zoos around the world, and have a chance to share "bear news" with children around the world. There are lots of great close-up bear pictures, as well as detailed facts to accompany these photos. Also, children can find classification facts for each member of the Ursidae (bear) family. (S: 4–6, T: All)

http://www-nais.ccm.emr.ca/schoolnet/issues/risk/mammals/emammal/polrbear.html

This is a site dedicated to polar bears. Students discover detailed information on what polar bears eat, when they have cubs, and how they can be protected. There are also incredible photos of these creatures on this site. (S: All)

http://www.nationalgeographic.com/bearcam/

The world's largest gathering of bears is at McNeil Falls, Alaska. At this site kids can see live video of these bears as they feed in the McNeil River. The site also has brightly colored maps that show exactly where the bears being shown are located. (S: All)

http://www.gomontana.com/bearman/bears.html

Yellowstone's Bears is a great site for children who wish to learn more about grizzly and black bears. The site provides lots of information, including the average life span, weight, hibernation, and eating habits. In addition, there are ideas on how students can help protect the bears. (S: All)

http://www.nature–net.com/bears/cubden.html

This site, The Cub Den, is for young learners who want to know more about bears. The information provided here is interesting, yet easy to read. The site includes 10 "Amazing Facts About Bears." (S: K–3, T: K–3)

 # Literature Resources

Bailey, Jill. (1992). *Earth's Endangered Creatures: Project Panda*. Austin, TX: Steck-Vaughn.
This book describes the endangered giant panda and the efforts of those in China who are working to save it from extinction.

Bonners, Susan. (1978). *Panda.* New York: Delacorte Press.
This book describes the life of a giant panda from the time that she was born until the birth of her first cub.

Bright, Michael. (1989). *Project Wildlife: Polar Bear*. New York: Gloucester Press.
This book provides students with information on these beautiful polar bears. The pictures, maps, and diagrams make the book fun to read and easy to follow.

Buxton, Jane Heath. (1986). *Baby Bears and How They Grow*. Washington, DC: National Geographic Society.
This wonderful book provides kids with information on a variety of different bears, including polar, grizzly, and black bears, as they grow and change over the years.

Dudley, Karen. (1997). *The Untamed World: Giant Pandas*. Austin, TX: Steck-Vaughn.
The life of a panda bear is examined in great detail, including its social behavior, life cycle, food habits, and habitat.

George, Jean Craighead. (1982). *The Grizzly Bear with the Golden Ears*. New York: Harper & Row.
This fictional story about a bear who bluffs rather than hunts for his food and then learns an important lesson is a great way to introduce students to the eating habits of bears.

Johnston, Ginny & Cutchins, Judy. (1985). *Andy Bear: A Polar Cub Grows up at the Zoo*. New York: Morrow.

This story of a young bear who was raised in Atlanta, Georgia, by a zookeeper is one of excitement, suspense, and triumph. Children can learn a lot about polar bears through learning about Andy Bear.

Olson, Donald. (1997). *Eyes on Nature: Bears*. Chicago: Kidsbooks.

This book is packed with intriguing information on all types of bears: polar bears, black bears, grizzly bears, sun bears, and more! There are also tons of up-close and personal photographs that will bring kids closer to these bears than they have ever been.

Pringle, Laurence. (1989). *Bearman: Exploring the World of Black Bears*. New York: Scribner.

This book tells how Lynn Rogers became a bearman and spent more than 20 years living with and studying black bears.

Stirling, Ian. (1992). *Sierra Club Wildlife Library: Bears*. San Francisco: Sierra Club Books for Children.

This book talks about the origins, evolution, habitats, behavior, and life cycles of bears. It is an excellent introduction to different species of bears.

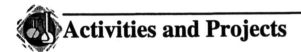

Activities and Projects

1. Invite students to log onto http://www.bearden.org/ and explore the different types of bears that are discussed on this page. Ask each student to choose one or more of these bears that they would like to learn more about. Have students collect facts about their bears and record them in journals. In addition, allow students to print pictures of their bear(s) off the site. Then, provide each student with a large piece of paper in the shape of a bear. Invite each one to write down information, attach printouts, and draw pictures about the bear on this paper. When everyone is finished, put the pages together as a class book. Read it together and then display it in the classroom library for future use.

2. Invite an expert on bears, a trainer or keeper from a local zoo or a park ranger, to talk to the class about bears. Before the visit, ask the students to prepare for their visitor a list of questions about bears. After the visit, ask students to make "Bear Information" posters to show what they learned during the presentation. Display these throughout the school.

3. Ask students to think about the types of sounds that bears make. They may wish to log on to http://www.nature-net.com/bears/ and listen to the bear sound effects. Ask them to think of how they might hear a bear if they were in a forest, in the snow, and so forth. Provide the students with musical instruments and a tape recorder. Allow them to tape their own "Bear Soundtrack" by themselves or in a group. They may wish to use their own voice, instruments, their feet, or other objects in the classroom or brought from home.

4. Ask the students to work together in groups to create a play about bears. They may focus on any kind of bear that they wish and should think about where that bear lives, what it eats, who it lives with, and what it does for fun. Allow the student to create costumes, masks, props, and backgrounds for their skit. Provide the students with time to practice the play. Then have the groups visit different classrooms and perform their bear skits for those students.

5. Ask the students to imagine what it would be like to live in a zoo. After students have finished commenting, read them *Andy Bear: A Polar Cub Grows up at the Zoo.* Have the students record their thoughts about how they would feel if they were a bear living in the zoo. Encourage students to consider how the book changed their views. Then, form small groups and provide the opportunity for students to discuss their thoughts, ideas, and feelings with other students.

6. Divide students into groups of three or four and provide each group with a long sheet of paper. Ask each group to choose one type of habitat that is home for one or more types of bears. Provide the students with selected literature and Web site addresses. Invite each group to draw a mural of the bear or bears that live there and a detailed picture of their habitat. Ask the students to label the different items on their mural. Display these murals in the hallways of the school.

7. Invite the students to explore information on several different species of bears. They may do this via the Internet and the various books provided in the classroom and school libraries. Then have them choose one fact or statistic that they find interesting, such as the average weight of a certain species, the type of food a certain bear eats, or the average life span of each species. Ask students to gather this information for each of the different species of bear. Provide the students with a large piece of posterboard and allow them to make a graph or chart to represent the information. Display these statistics around the classroom.

Bees

Introduction

Bees are often portrayed as angry insects. In reality, bees only sting when they feel their lives, or their hives, are in danger. Two of the most common types of bees are honeybees and bumblebees. Bees live together in colonies and use pollen and nectar from flowers to manufacture honey. Queen bees, worker bees, and drones live together in the hive and help to maintain the cycle of life.

Research Questions

1. Approximately how many eggs does a queen bee lay each day?

2. How many bees may live in one hive?

3. What is another name for the many little rooms inside a hive?

4. What happens to male bees after they mate with queen bees?

5. Describe how the world looks through the eyes of a honeybee.

6. What are some of the symptoms associated with a systemic bee allergy?

7. Why do bees make honey?

8. How many times per minute do the wings of a honeybee vibrate?

Web Sites

http://agnews.tamu.edu/bees/

This site is an excellent resource for students and teachers. A variety of information is presented about Africanized honeybees, otherwise known as "killer bees." This site offers information about the habitat, ways to identify "killer bees," where to find them, and how to protect yourself. A number of educational tools are also available for purchase. (S: 4–6, T: 4–6)

http://www.honey.com/kids/facts.html

Not only does this site provide the viewer with interesting facts about honeybees, it also is dedicated to honey. There are lots of things for students to do, including honey trivia, honey history, a honey glossary, recipes, and games. Teachers are provided with a number of recipes for everything from breakfast to dessert, and links to bee-related books and Web sites. (S: All, T: All)

http://www.lanakids.com/beeware.html

This site provides children with a variety of information that could help to protect against bee stings. If someone gets stung, this site offers tips on how to get the bite taken care of immediately. (S: K–3)

http://www.pa.msu.edu/~sciencet/ask_st/073097.html

At this site viewers can learn all about how bees make honey. Lots of information here makes this a good complement to any unit. (T: 4–6)

http://tqjunior.thinkquest.org/3715/pollin5.html

This site contains lots of colorful information about bees' role in the pollination of flowers. (S: 4–6)

Literature Resources

Cole, Joanna. (1996). *The Magic School Bus Inside a Beehive*. New York: Scholastic.

The children in Miss Frizzle's class experience life from the perspective of worker bees. The children shrink to the size of bees and experience life inside a beehive. They carry pollen grains and nectar into the hive, work at making comb cells, enjoy samples of honey, and help feed the baby bees. Each page includes important facts about the lives of bees.

High, Linda Oatman. (1998). *Beekeepers*. Honesdale, PA: Boyds Mills Press.

In this story set in early spring, the reader is taken through the beginning of an average day for a beekeeping family. A grandfather and his grandchild take care of the hives and watch for honey. Usually it is the grandfather's responsibility to call in the swarms, but on this particular day he passes his swarm-gathering tool to his grandchild, and the bees zoom into the hives.

Parker, Nancy Winslow & Wright, Joan Richards. (1987). *Bugs*. New York: Greenwillow Books.

This book examines a variety of insects found throughout the world. The book includes a picture of each insect discussed, along with a measurement demonstrating the actual size of the insect. The picture glossary in the end of the book includes examples of growth stages, how bugs grow, and a diagram of a typical bug or insect.

Polacco, Patricia. (1993) *The Bee Tree*. New York: Philomel Books.

This book demonstrates a grandfather's attempts to help his granddaughter find reading exciting and adventurous. He successfully accomplishes this by taking her in search of a bee tree. The pair trap several honey bees inside a jar, letting them free one by one, and chasing after each bee until they find the bee tree. Along the way a variety of others join in on the chase.

Activities and Projects

1. If possible, arrange for a local beekeeper to come and speak to your class about raising honeybees. Prior to the visit, assist your students in making a K-W-L chart. Invite the class to compile a list of things they know and would like to know about honeybees. After the beekeeper's presentation the students can complete the last section of the chart. Each student should be able to share one interesting fact about honeybees and/or beekeeping. Display the completed K-W-L chart in the science center.

2. Discuss the various types of bees in a honeybee colony with your students. Encourage them to visit http://honey.com/kids/facts.html, or related sites, for additional information. Divide your class into three groups, with several students in each group. For smaller groups, create two groups for each type of honeybee. Provide each group with one specific type of bee to study. Allow time for each group to research their topic, using books, magazines, newspaper articles, videos, and so forth. Using the information gathered, each group should create a skit to help their classmates become more familiar with that particular type of honeybee.

3. Talk about other animals that have special defense systems. Ask students to come up with a list of five animals that have a special way of protecting themselves. Invite each student to create a drawing of her or his favorite animal from the list. After each child has completed the drawing, have the children share their drawings with the rest of the class. Encourage each child to tell the class something about the animal, including what it does to protect itself.

4. After discussing beehives with your students, create a classroom hive in the science center of your classroom. Explain to your students that beehives are composed of combs, which are made of wax, and are shaped like hexagons (six-sided figures). Teach your students that the bees use the combs to make and store honey. Provide each student with a sheet of paper shaped like a honeycomb. Encourage each student to create a comb to display in the class hive. Allow each child to choose the color for the comb, and encourage your students to fill their individual combs with interesting facts about bees. They may choose to include species, habitats, habits, life cycles, or diet. When each child has completed a honeycomb, encourage the students to share what they have written on the combs with the rest of the class. Display the completed honeycombs in the "beehive" section of the classroom.

5. Arrange for the school nurse, or an emergency room technician, to come into the classroom to discuss first aid for bee stings. Encourage your speaker to touch on the subject of allergies and bee stings. The speaker should be sure to inform your class of the dangers of an untreated bee sting for a person with bee allergies. At the conclusion of the presentation, ask your students to work in small groups to compile a list of things they now know about bee stings. Have each group share what they have learned with the class.

6. Students can construct their own homemade beehives as follows. Gather together about 25 drinking straws. Plug up one end of each straw with modeling clay. Mix up the straws so that some plugged ends face one way and some the other. Tape the bundle together tightly with masking tape. With string or tape, fasten the bundle sideways (horizontally) underneath a windowsill, rain gutter, or the roof overhang of the school building. The bundle must be in a sunny location. With luck, bees may eventually move into this artificial hive and set up housekeeping. If placed near a window, students can observe the actions of "their hive" over an extended period of time.

Bugs

Introduction

Bugs are everywhere! In fact, bugs are the most common creature in the entire world (there are more than one million species of insects). They may be as large as the enormous Goliath Beetle of Africa or as small as a tiny mite, which is smaller than the period at the end of this sentence.

Bugs (insects) all hatch from eggs and they all have three body parts: head, thorax, and abdomen. Bugs have no skeleton (they are known as invertebrates), but most have an exoskeleton that protects their bodies. Most insects have two sets of eyes and a chewing or sucking mouth. They are a favorite food of many birds, reptiles, some mammals, and other insects.

Research Questions

1. What happens to a caterpillar when it comes out of its cocoon?

2. Name four bugs that can do harm to humans.

3. Which bug is the fastest flyer?

4. What does a mosquito eat and how does it do it?

5. How can bugs make life easier for humans?

Web Sites

http://www.insectworld.com

This Web site offers a rare view of some of the biggest, the smallest, and the most bugs. The site also has general knowledge to help children learn the basics of bugs. (S: 4–6)

http://www.pbrc.hawaii.edu/~kunkel/wanted/

This site profiles some of the World's Most Wanted bugs – those that irritate us and those that harm us. A light-hearted look at some pesky creatures. (S: 4–6; T: 4–6)

http://www.minnetonka.k12.mn.us/grv/insect.proj/insects.html

Kids from around the country report of their "buggy" discoveries. A super site for any series of insect lessons. (S: All)

http://www.comnet.ca/~defayette/newinsects/intro.htm

At this site kids learn how to put together an insect collection from a leading entomologist. Lots of information here. (S: 4–6)

Literature Resources

Canizares, Susan & Chanko, Pamela. (1998). *What Do Insects Do?* New York: Scholastic.
This book has excellent close-up pictures of all different types of insects.

Canizares, Susan & Reid, Mary. (1998). *Where Do Insects Live?* New York: Scholastic.
This book contains great pictures showing where insects live. It also provides good descriptions of how bugs live.

Carle, Eric. (1994). *The Very Busy Spider*. New York: Scholastic.
This story is about the day of a spider and what happens to him during the day.

Carle, Eric. (1995). *The Very Lonely Firefly*. New York: Philomel Books.
A firefly is born and flies through the night searching for other fireflies.

Carle, Eric. (1993). *The Very Quiet Cricket*. New York: Scholastic.
A cricket encounters several different animals and cannot make a sound for any of them. One day he meets another lonely cricket and finally can talk.

Markle, Sandra. (1998). *Creepy, Crawly, Baby Bugs*. New York: Scholastic.
This book shows pictures of baby bugs. It gives some facts about them and how they survive.

Reid, Mary & Chesser, Betsy. (1998). *Bugs, Bugs, Bugs!* New York: Scholastic.
Excellent pictures of all the parts of bugs are included in this book. Readers are provided with up-close illustrations of parts of a bug.

Activities and Projects

1. Provide students with some clay and an assortment of pipe cleaners in various sizes and colors, toothpicks, or straws. Ask students to make an insect of their choice, using a picture from one of the sites above as a guide. The clay can be used to represent the bodies and the pipe cleaners, straws, or toothpicks the legs and antennae. Provide an area where the insects can be displayed. Ask students to label their insects by placing a small piece of paper beside each with its name and the student's name.

2. Obtain a medium-sized, wide-mouth jar that you can secure by placing a piece of netting or nylon stocking over the opening and holding it in place with a rubber band. Then take a nature walk outside to look for insects. The jar can become the habitat for an insect that the students find. Once the insect is caught, be sure to put a twig, leaves, and other materials appropriate for that particular insect's environment in the jar and put the cover over the top. Allow students to observe the insect for a few days, record their findings, and then carefully return it to its original environment.

3. Ask students to select an insect whose movement they can demonstrate. (For example, for a bee, they could extend their arms and buzz around the room; for a caterpillar, they could slither on the floor.) Ask other children to guess what the insect is. The child who correctly guesses gets to act out the next movements.

4. Provide students with an assortment of magazines that contain pictures of insects. Encourage them to bring in old magazines from home. Ask the students to make a class collage by pasting pictures of different insects on an insect graffiti wall.

5. Invite an entomologist to visit the class. Explain to students that an entomologist is someone who studies insects. Many entomologists have collections of insects. Ask the entomologist if she or he has a collection and would be willing to share it with the class. Note: Many museums have collections of insects that might be available for use in a classroom.

Butterflies and Moths

Introduction

Butterflies and moths are part of the family *Lepidoptera*, meaning wings of scale. Although often confused, there are several differences between the two. For example, when a moth goes through its metamorphosis it does so in its silk cocoon. These cocoons are usually found on the ground, many times at the base of a tree. Butterflies, however, go through their change in what is known as a chrysalis, which can be found on leaves. Another interesting difference is in the way they hold their wings when they land. A butterfly usually has its wings closed, but the moth lands with its wings open.

Both insects have four wings that are covered in scales. Both taste with their feet and smell with their antennae. Their bodies have distinct parts: head, antenna, proboscis, thorax, and abdomen.

Research Questions

1. What are the differences between a butterfly and a moth?

2. How does a caterpillar change into a butterfly?

3. What is the migration of the Monarch butterfly?

4. What are the different parts of a butterfly/moth?

Web Sites

http://www.fmnh.org/butterfly/
At this site students can learn all about butterflies at the Field Museum. (S: 4–6)

http://www.npwrc.usgs.gov/resource/distr/lepid/bflyusa/bflyusa.htm
The butterflies of North America are profiled on this informative site. Lots of data for any butterfly unit. (T: 4–6)

http://www.enchantedlearning.com/subjects/butterflies/allabout/
This site is subtitled "All About Butterflies"—and it truly lives up to its name. A great collection of valuable data and information. (S: 4–6; T: All)

http://library.thinkquest.org/27968
This is a fascinating site with some wonderful pictures and drawings. The text goes into great detail about the different body parts, predators, and life cycles of butterflies and moths. Also included are a special teachers' section and a glossary of new terminology. There is tons of information on this site, all of which is supported by detailed pictures and drawings. (S: 4–6, T: All)

http://mgfx.com/butterfly

Voted "best site" (on butterflies) in 1998, this is a great resource for teachers. On this Web site other schools have listed activities and projects they have done. There are current articles on butterflies, the latest research, and ongoing projects. There is also a list of children's books. (T: All)

http://www.mesc.usgs.gov/butterfly/butterfly.html

Here students will find answers to frequently asked questions. This site also provides students and teachers with other Web links and references. In addition, there is a picture of the life cycle of butterflies that can be downloaded and printed for younger students to color. (S: 4–6, T: All).

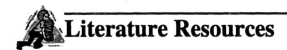 # Literature Resources

Bunting, Eve. (1999). *The Butterfly House*. New York: Scholastic.

This is a story of a little girl who, with the help of her grandfather, builds a house for a butterfly larva. The girl watches the larva develop into a beautiful butterfly and finally sets it free.

George, Jean Craighead. (1993). *The Moon of the Monarch Butterflies*. New York: HarperCollins.

This is a beautiful story with pictures to match. This story follows the spring migration of a butterfly back to her birthplace.

Lavis, Bianca. (1992). *The Monarch Butterflies*. New York: Dutton Children's Books.

This is a factual story that takes the reader through the different stages of a butterfly. There is also a section about tracking the migration of the Monarch from Mexico.

Still, John. (1991). *Amazing Butterflies and Moths*. New York: Knopf.

This book deals with the differences between butterflies and moths. There is also an interesting section on myths about butterflies and moths.

Whalley, Paul. (1988). *An Eyewitness Book: Butterfly and Moth*. New York: Knopf.

This book takes the reader through the courtship and egg laying of the butterfly and moth, the developing caterpillars, progression to pupa, the pupa stage, and finally the emerging creature.

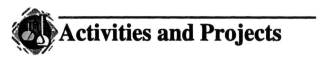 # Activities and Projects

1. Cut large sheets of paper into a simple butterfly shape. Then ask students to write a brief paragraph that begins, "If I were a butterfly, I . . . ." Allow students to share their stories and then compile them into a class booklet.

2. Create a butterfly field in your classroom by hanging pictures of different butterflies around the room. Have the students "catch" a specific number of butterflies, then use their resources to identify those butterflies. They should be sure to note where they are found, whether or not they migrate, and other interesting facts.

3. Some people collect butterflies. Try to locate someone with a butterfly collection who will bring it into your class to share. If this is not possible, use one or more of the Web sites or literature selections above that contain illustrations of butterflies. Allow time for students to look at the different kinds of butterflies. Discuss the differences and similarities between the butterflies.

4. As a follow-up to activity 3, collect the appropriate materials and plan a creative art time in which children can make butterflies. Demonstrate how they can make butterflies by putting a pipe cleaner around the middle of a sheet of tissue paper. The butterfly can then be decorated, if desired. Another method is to shave old crayons onto wax paper, lay another sheet of wax paper over it, and press with an iron set on low heat (use caution with iron). Then mount the melted crayon under a butterfly-shaped mat opening. Display the butterflies.

5. Cut egg cartons in half, lengthwise. Ask students to paint the egg cartons. When they are dry, have students make faces on one end, then insert pipe cleaners for feelers, to make a caterpillar.

6. Butterflies can be grown in the classroom by obtaining a "Butterfly Garden" from Nasco Co. (901 Janesville Ave., Ft. Atkinson, WI 53538, 1-800-558-9595).

Cats

Introduction

They are furry, smart, and cuddly. Some have long hair and others have short hair. Their size varies along with the color of their fur. Cats can be found anywhere in the world. There are wildcats and domesticated cats. Cats have been celebrated in song and dance and have been revered by people since the dawn of civilization (cats were even mummified and buried with Egyptian kings and queens).

Cats communicate by body language, roaring, and purring. They prey on many things, from small mice and sparrows (domesticated cats) to wild antelope and zebras (wildcats). They come in a wide variety of sizes, shapes, and colors. They are as varied as nature itself.

Research Questions

1. What kinds of cats purr? How does the purring sound occur?

2. Why did ancient Egyptians worship cats?

3. What year was the Year of the Cat in China?

4. What is the purpose of a cat's tail?

5. When a cat jumps or fall, how does it always land?

Web Sites

http://www.acmepet.petsmart.com/feline/
At this Web site students can become aware of cat care and the needs of cats. There is also information about veterinary decisions and surgical procedures for cats. Everything students need to know about having a cat as a pet can be found on this site. (S: 4–6)

http://www.canuck.com/iseccan
The international society for endangered cats has a Web site to educate people on the preservation of small wildcats. There are slide shows of cats along with information on adopting cats that have been abandoned. Fact sheets are also provided about endangered cats. (T: All)

http://www.lam.mus.ca.us/cats/
This is a great Web site for kids and teachers. There are cat facts along with a history of both domestic and wildcats. A small section on activities for families with cats and cat care is also provided. (S: 4–6, T: All)

http://www.paranormalatoz.com/cats.html
This site examines how and why cats occur in myths. These animals are commonly associated with witchcraft, and the stories behind those myths are presented here. (S: 4–6)

Literature Resources

Carle, Eric. (1987). *Have You Seen My Cat?* New York: Simon & Schuster.
This book offers a look at different places around the world and the cats that exist there. Creative illustrations of all kinds of cats from leopards to panthers to tigers are presented.

DePaola, Tomie. (1979). *The Kids' Cat Book.* New York: Holiday House.
This book provides detailed descriptions of the different breeds of domestic cats, including specific characteristics of each breed. Historic information about felines from Rome, Egypt, and England and basic cat care ideas are also discussed.

Kraus, Robert. (1987). *Come out and Play, Little Mouse.* New York: Mulberry.
The cunning ways of a cat preying on a mouse are interpreted, using the days of the week.

Tildes, Phyllis Limbacher. (1995). *Counting on Calico.* Watertown, MA: Charlesbridge.
The author uses numbers to describe cats, with corresponding facts about their characteristics.

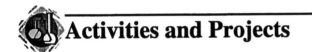

Activities and Projects

1. Invite the class to create a Cat Fact display on an empty wall or bulletin board. Encourage students to find and cut out or print out pictures of cats, both domestic and wild, using the Internet sites listed and various magazines. Basic facts can be recorded on a sheet of paper cut out in the shape of a paw. The various "paws" can be attached to the Cat Fact display.

2. Ask the students to imagine that they are cats. Have them create imaginary diaries in which they record the events and happenings in one day of their cat lives. What did they see? What did they think about? What did they eat? Where (and for how long) did they sleep? Provide opportunities for students (cats) to share their respective diaries.

3. If possible, invite the parents of one or more of your students to bring a family cat into the classroom. Students may wish to consult one or more of the Web sites above to record interesting information and data about their selected "visitor" (breed, habits, diet). Depending on the "attitude" of the "visitor," youngsters may be able to examine the cat.

4. If possible, invite a veterinarian into your classroom to discuss how to treat cats that come into a clinic. What are some of the diseases of cats? How long do cats live? What are some tips that will help ensure contented cats? How can cats be trained?

Cows

Introduction

Cows are ruminants, which means they chew their cud. This results from the cattle swallowing partially chewed food. This food is then brought back up to the mouth for chewing. In dairy cows, the grass they eat produces milk. A dairy cow produces milk when her first calf is born. She continues to give milk for nine to ten months but gives less and less as the months progress. Farmers keep their cows calving throughout the year to ensure continuous milk production.

There are many types, or breeds, of dairy cattle. Most of the breeds originated in Europe and came to America during early colonial days. Some breeds make more milk than others do. One breed, Jersey, produces milk that is richest in butterfat, used to make cream and butter.

Research Questions

1. What is the process milk goes through before it is seen in a grocery store?

2. Describe different breeds of dairy cattle and reasons that make them good milk producers.

3. How many stomachs does a cow have?

4. What does it mean when a cow "chews its cud," and what is the process?

5. List five foods that would be unavailable if we did not have cows producing milk.

Web Sites

http://www.pbs.org/wgbh/nova/madcow
This is a more in-depth page, appropriate for older students. Questions about bovine spongiform encephalopathy, otherwise known as Mad Cow Disease, are answered. The subject of food safety is also discussed. (S: 4–6)

http://www.allcows.com/
Just about everything you would want to know about cows can be found at this site including the "cow of the month," photos, and detailed information. (S: 4–6; T: All)

http://www.gl.umbc.edu/~dschmi1/cows/index.html
Poetry, songs, clip art and dozens of meaningful and meaningless data about cows is on this site. This is amazing! (T: All)

http://www.gl.umbc.edu/~dschmi1/cows/sounds.html
Sounds of cows in various stages of rest and activity can be found on this site. Lots of fun here. (S: All)

Literature Resources

Aliki. (1992). *Milk: From Cow to Carton*. New York: HarperCollins.
   This book shows the process of milk production from the cows grazing to the milking process and then to the dairy.

Gibbons, Gail. (1985). *The Milk Makers*. New York: Atheneum.
   This book shows how milk is made. The route the milk takes from the cow to the store for people to buy is explained.

Older, Jules. (1998). *Cow*. Watertown, MA: Charlesbridge.
   This book takes a humorous approach to cow information. Fun facts about cows and milk are discussed. Definitely a "must-have" book for any classroom.

Potter, Tessa. (1990). *Cows*. Austin, TX: Steck-Vaughn.
   This book describes the importance of cows on the farm. Several reasons why humans need cows are discussed.

Activities and Projects

1. If possible, visit a local dairy farm or a commercial dairy to view a cow being milked, both by hand and by machine. If possible, videotape the process so that it can be reviewed in the classroom. Create a Venn diagram comparing both milking methods. Invite the farmer to discuss caring for the cows. Upon returning to the classroom, ask the students write a journal entry about their trip to the dairy.

2. After viewing Big Dave's Cow Page, have students create their own cow poetry or a song to share with the class. The songs or poetry should be written on chart paper to be used in the classroom. The songs or poetry can be taught to the class and later recited during a "cow festival" (see number 4).

3. The students may wish to make their own homemade ice cream. Following is a recipe:

Materials/Ingredients: 1 gallon freezer bag, 1 pint freezer bag, 2 cups (approx.) of cracked ice, 6 tablespoons of salt, 1 tablespoon of sugar, 1/2 teaspoon of vanilla, 1/2 cup of whole milk.

Directions: Put the ice into the large freezer bag. Pour the salt over the ice in the bag. Set this bag aside. Pour the milk into the small freezer bag. Add the sugar and vanilla to the milk. Mix the ingredients thoroughly (the bag can be squished by hand for 20–30 seconds). Remove some of the air from the small freezer bag and seal it tightly. Place the small freezer bag inside the large freezer bag. Seal the large freezer bag. Place the large freezer bag on a flat surface and turn it over and over (by the corners) for approximately five minutes. Carefully open the large freezer bag and remove the small freezer bag from it. Open the top of the small freezer bag and spoon out the ice cream.

Variations: 1) Use chocolate milk instead of whole milk. 2) Add chocolate chips, coconut sprinkles, etc. 3) Add flavors other than vanilla (peppermint, cinnamon). 4) Add different food colors (how about blue ice cream?).

Tips: 1) Always use whole milk. 2) Always use name brand freezer bags.

4. Have a classroom "cow festival" in which the students take part in various cow activities. During this festival the students can consume the homemade ice cream from the previous activity. The students can be invited to recite their cow poetry and songs for the class. The cow festival would be used as a culminating activity for a cow unit.

Dinosaurs

Introduction

Ask any child to name her or his favorite subject in science, and most will name "dinosaurs" as the one topic they always enjoy. It may be because dinosaurs were so large (although, in fact, most dinosaurs were no larger than a modern day chicken), or it may be because dinosaurs are portrayed as being ferocious (although, in fact, most dinosaurs were herbivores), or it may be because they have been the "stars" of so many movies. Whatever the reason, children of all ages enjoy studying and learning about these ancient creatures.

Although comic strips and motion pictures would have us believe otherwise, it's important for students to know that dinosaurs died out 65 million years before humans ever appeared on the face of the Earth. What we know about dinosaurs has been learned through painstaking research and intensive fieldwork in almost every corner of the world. For many people, the study of dinosaurs extends beyond the interests of childhood into a lifetime of fascinating discoveries and incredible explorations.

Research Questions

1. How long ago did dinosaurs live?

2. Who are some of the scientists who study dinosaurs?

3. How can you distinguish between meat eaters and plant eaters?

4. What do you think may have been responsible for the extinction of dinosaurs?

5. What was the heaviest dinosaur? The smallest dinosaur?

6. What is a paleontologist?

Web Sites

http://dinosaurs.eb.com/dinosaurs/index2.html

This site is presented by Encyclopedia Britannica and is loaded with interesting facts about dinosaurs. Upon entering the site the user can follow the ever-changing views about dinosaurs through the great-dinosaur-debate timeline. Links for related books and Web sites are also provided. (S: 4–6)

http://www.cotf.edu/ete/modules/msese/dinosaur.html

This site provides viewers with a variety of factors that may have played key roles in the disappearance of dinosaurs. Children can travel around the site and examine various theories that attempt to explain why dinosaurs became extinct. (S: 4–6, T: All)

http://www.EnchantedLearning.com/subjects/dinosaurs/Dinotopics.html

This site is designed for users of all ages and abilities. It is set up as an index, and the user can simply choose an underlined topic to learn more about it. This site is also full of teaching tips and dinosaur related activities, which make it ideal for use in almost any learning environment. (S: All, T: All)

http://www.isgs.uiuc.edu/dinos/dinos_home.html

Dino Russ's Lair provides students with a number of helpful links for everything from dinosaur eggs and exhibits to dinosaur tracks. Dino Russ, otherwise known as Russell J. Jacobson, is a geologist with the Illinois State Geological Survey. He provides the user with various sites to visit, both real-time and online, and is available to answer questions via e-mail or clear phone. (S: 4–6)

http://www.ucmp.berkeley.edu/diapsids/dinosaur.html

This site provides the user with some interesting information about the life and times of the dinosaurs. Common myths about dinosaurs are dispelled at this site, and a number of dinosaur-related links are presented. Users can also learn about a variety of others things, including fossil records and the life history of specific dinosaur groups. (S: 4–6)

Literature Resources

Aliki. (1990). *Fossils Tell of Long Ago*. New York: HarperCollins.

This is a great introduction to the formation and creation of fossils, highlighted by easy to understand illustrations.

Cole, Joanna. (1994). *The Magic School Bus in the Time of the Dinosaurs*. New York: Scholastic.

Ms. Frizzle's class has turned their entire classroom into Dinosaur Land for Visitor's Day. They receive an invitation to participate in a dinosaur dig, so before their visitors arrive they hop into the magic yellow school bus and head for adventure. The class does more than participate in the dig; they go back in time and visit the dinosaurs before they become extinct.

Farlow, James O. (1991). *On the Tracks of Dinosaurs*. New York: Watts.

Not only does this book examine several different types of dinosaurs, it also goes into great detail about how fossils are formed and discovered.

Gillette, J. Lynett. (1994). *The Search for Seismosaurus, the World's Longest Dinosaur*. New York: Dial Books for Young Readers.

This book begins with the discovery of fossils at a mesa in New Mexico and takes the reader through the search, discovery, and study of this enormous dinosaur.

Hopkins, Lee Bennett. (1987). *Dinosaurs*. San Diego: Harcourt Brace.

Eighteen delightful poems give youngsters fresh perspectives on and insights into the world of dinosaurs.

Lambert, David. (1989). *Dinosaurs*. New York: Warwick.

This well-written book presents general information about dinosaurs. It includes some activities related to specific dinosaurs.

Sattler, Helen. (1990). *The New Illustrated Dinosaur Dictionary*. New York: Lothrop.

It's all here: everything any dinosaur nut would want to know about 350 dinosaurs and other related creatures.

Simon, Seymour. (1990). *New Questions and Answers About Dinosaurs*. New York: Morrow.
    Scientists are learning more about dinosaurs every day. This book presents readers with the most up-to-date information.

Activities and Projects

1. Prior to the introduction of this unit, use string to measure out height and length of various dinosaurs. You may wish to use some of the following measurements:

Dinosaur	Length	Height
Tyrannosaurus Rex	32 feet	14 feet
Brachiosaurus	67 feet	27 feet
Stegosaurus	28 feet	13 feet
Plateosaurus	20 feet	7 feet
Camptosaurus	18 feet	8 feet
Velociraptor	8 feet	3 feet
Protoceratops	8 feet	3 feet

    Line up the class by height and choose the student in the center of the line to be "average." Trace this person on heavy butcher paper to get a pattern. Go out on the playground and roll out the string for a dinosaur. Have the students guess how many bodies long and high that dinosaur is. Record the estimates and then use the pattern to obtain actual measurements. Do this for all the dinosaurs. Ask students to compare the sizes.

2. Ask students to work in small groups to create a large wall mural showing life when the dinosaurs existed. The mural can be drawn on heavy butcher paper and decorated with paints, crayons, construction paper, or other art materials selected by the students. Be sure there are no humans depicted on the murals.

3. Invite a professor from a local college to make a short presentation on dinosaurs. Encourage students to prepare a list of questions beforehand to ask the visiting speaker.

4. Ask students to poll other students in the school about their favorite dinosaurs. The information can be collected and displayed on large wall charts.

5. Ask students to create a testimonial on herbivores versus carnivores. Their journal entries can focus on the attributes of various dinosaurs and why some attributes might be more desirable than others.

6. Provide small groups of children with piles of chicken bones (boil the bones in a solution of water and vinegar and dry thoroughly). Ask each group to arrange the bones in their original configuration. Encourage students to discuss any problems they have in putting a chicken skeleton back together, even though most of them know what a chicken looks like. Talk about the difficulties scientists have in putting dinosaur skeletons back together, particularly because no human has ever seen a live dinosaur.

Dogs

Introduction

Dogs have been friends of humans ever since the dawn of recorded history. They have been our pets, they assist us in our work (drug enforcement, rescue work, tracking), and they have been the focus of countless stories, both real and fictional. Often portrayed as "man's best friend," dogs are one of the most common creatures in almost every country and every culture.

Students also may be surprised to learn about wild dogs, the packs of marauding carnivores that inhabit the savannas and grasslands of Africa and prey upon other animals. These animals have elaborate social structures and a complex "society" that rivals anything that humans have created.

Dogs are as much a part of our lives as we are of theirs. Students will enjoy some of the investigations and explorations about dogs listed below.

Research Questions

1. Why do people enjoy dogs?

2. What is the most popular breed of dog?

3. What is the largest breed? What is the smallest?

4. Where did dogs originate?

5. How have dogs been used throughout history?

6. What are some famous dogs?

Web Sites

http://apl.discovery.com/working_dogs/working_dogs.html
At this site you'll be able to discover lots of information about working dogs from around the world. (T: 4–6)

http://www.thirteen.org/extraordinarydogs/
Extraordinary dogs from around the world are profiled on this interesting site. (T: All)

http://www.EnchantedLearning.com/subjects/mammals/dog/index.shtml
Wow! Tons of information and loads of interactive activities make this a superior site. (S: All)

http://www.petstation.com/dogs.html#TOP
This Web site takes a look at the different breeds of dogs. There are pictures of various breeds as well as descriptions of specific breeds. (S: 4–6)

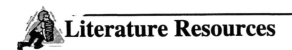

Literature Resources

Clutton-Brock, Juliet. (1991). *Dog*. New York: Knopf.

This book is a "mini museum" about dogs. It offers firsthand knowledge about taking care of dogs. A good book for all ages.

Posell, Elsa. (1981). *Dogs*. Chicago: Children's Press.

Everything you need to know about how to train dogs is here. The book also helps you see which breed is best for you. It would be suitable for any age. A great tool for resources.

Activities and Projects

1. Invite a veterinarian to visit your class. Have students generate a list of questions beforehand. After the visit, encourage small groups of students to gather the information together into a series of informative brochures or newsletters that can then be distributed throughout the school or placed in the school library.

2. Invite students to take a field trip to the local animal shelter. While there, students can observe how many dogs are there. Discuss why it is important to keep the dog population down and the role of animal shelters in those efforts. After completing the trip, invite students to make a pamphlet providing information on adoption procedures of the animal shelter.

3. Ask the students to make an ABC book of dogs. Give each student in your class a specific breed of dog that represents a different letter of the alphabet. Then encourage students to find information on that breed by using selected literature and Web sites. Gather the pages together into an attractive book and donate it to the local public library.

4. Ask each student to observe a dog for a day. Have students report on the activities of their observed dogs. What characteristics are common to all dogs? What characteristics are specific to a particular breed of dog? What do dogs do that other animals cannot do? What was the most humorous event? Plan time to discuss any commonalties or unusual occurrences with students.

Dolphins

Introduction

Dolphins have always been favorites among humans. Sometimes confused with porpoises, dolphins are marine mammals (they actually are small-toothed whales) that live in the ocean. The majority of dolphins (21 out of the 31 species) live along the coastlines of Australia. They communicate underwater by using a variety of sounds and whistles.

Despite their popularity, many dolphins are in danger. Tuna fishing in the Pacific has killed many dolphins since the 1960s, and after numerous protests, some tuna companies have changed their practices so that they can declare their product "dolphin-safe." The destruction of dolphin habitat, however, is the main cause for the dolphin population decrease. Heavy pollution of the waters that serve as their habitat is a serious problem for dolphins.

Research Questions

1. What is one way we can help to protect the dolphins?

2. How do dolphins make sounds underwater?

3. What is the difference between a dolphin and a porpoise?

4. Why do dolphins perform a behavior called "spouting" or "blowing?"

5. What are some ways in which dolphins can help people?

6. What is the largest dolphin and how much does it weigh? The smallest?

Web Sites

http://www.dolphinresearch.org.au/index.html

The Dolphin Research Institute, Inc., provides children with a wealth of information about dolphins. At this site students can learn about different species of dolphins and their location on Earth, their behaviors, specific threats to dolphins, and how they personally can help protect dolphins. (S: 4–6)

http://www.natureexplorer.com/WD/WD1.html

Here's an incredible Web site all about whales and dolphins. Loads of factual data and information can be found here. (S: 4–6, T: All)

http://www.cetacea.org/index.htm

Loads of information about whales, porpoises, and dolphins can be obtained from this valuable site. (T: All)

http://neptune.atlantis-intl.com/dolphins/

Lots of photos of dolphins and whales can be found at this site – perfect for any classroom. (S: All, T: All)

http://www.seaworld.org/bottlenose_dolphin/k3activitydol.html

Provided by Sea World and Busch Gardens, this site gives teachers a specific lesson to use in the classroom, "Dolphin Documentary," in which the students create their own movie. This lesson can also be adapted for other grades and subject areas. The Web site includes links to other dolphin sites as well. (T: K–3)

http://www.divinedolphin.com/connections.htm

This site focuses on the human/dolphin connection and relationship. People (including students) have submitted their experiences with dolphins. Many photos are also located in this interesting Web site, and the students can learn about other people's experiences.

 # Literature Resources

Cerullo, Mary M. (1999). *Dolphins: What They Can Teach Us*. New York: Dutton.

Striking photographs highlight the author's text on ways in which dolphins help people and vice versa. Along with general dolphin facts and information, Cerullo includes ways in which dolphins can help people.

Fowler, Allan. (1997). *Friendly Dolphins (Rookie Read – About Science)* Danbury, CT: Children's Press.

Geared more toward younger children, this book describes the physical characteristics and behavior of dolphins and several other marine mammals.

Pascoe, Elaine. (1998). *Animal Intelligence: Why Is This Dolphin Smiling?* Woodbridge, CT: Blackbirch Marketing.

This book describes scientific research on dolphin/human communication. Written for older kids, it includes dolphin facts.

Stoops, Erik D. (1996). *Dolphins*. New York: Sterling.

Over 100 color photos accompany a wealth of information about dolphins. The many visuals make it appropriate for younger readers as well as older readers.

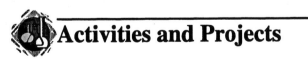 # Activities and Projects

1. Divide the students into several different groups and invite each group to pick a specific species of dolphin. Ask them to accumulate information about their species of dolphin, such as where it lives, what it eats, and what behaviors it exhibits, by using a variety of resources in the classroom and school library (the Internet, books, teachers, magazines). Ask the students to use the information they found to create a "mini-mural" (the size of a piece of posterboard) depicting the dolphin in its habitat, along with a written description. Hang the "mini-murals" around the classroom and allow the students to question each other about the information they gathered.

2. Encourage the children to write to several of the following conservation organizations requesting information about dolphins and how they can help to save the dolphins in their habitats.

    Dolphin Research Institute
    P.O. Box 1245
    Frankston, Victoria
    Australia 3199

    American Cetacean Society
    P.O. Box 1391
    San Pedro, CA 90733-1391

    National Marine Fisheries Service
    Alaska Fisheries Science Center
    7600 Sand Point Way NE
    Seattle, WA 98115

    Review the information the students received together and encourage the children to create an information center in the back of the classroom. Ask them to include their mini-murals as well as the pamphlets and literature they received from the organizations. Invite other classes to view the information center and encourage the children to share their knowledge about dolphins with others.

3. Ask the students how they communicate with each other when they want something, then write their answers on the board. Some of the answers might by talking, pointing, signing, gesturing, and so forth. Play a tape of various dolphin sounds and explain to the children that these sounds are how dolphins communicate. Discuss some of the purposes for these sounds (identifying their "name," where they are in the water, for finding food, etc.). After reviewing the information located in the Web site http://nmm101.afsc.noaa.gov/education/cetaceans/cetacea.htm, ask the children to create a "Dolphin Dictionary" listing the sounds a dolphin makes and their behaviors (tail flapping, etc.) and explaining why these habits exist.

4. Encourage the children to share any experiences they have had in caring for an animal, whether it is their own pet, a stray, or a neighbor's pet. Ask them to name the different responsibilities associated with caring for an animal and create a semantic web on the board using their responses. Ask the children to create a semantic web depicting the different responsibilities associated with taking care of a dolphin by looking in magazines, books, on the Internet, in the school library, and so forth. Topics to explore include what dolphins eat, how they get exercise, or what happens if they get sick. Encourage the children to share their webs with a partner and to expand upon their own webs if they need to. Ask the students to create a book using the information in their webs, explaining how to take care of a dolphin and the various associated responsibilities (encourage them to include illustrations along with the text). Donate their completed books to the school library for other children and teachers to view.

Eagles

Introduction

Eagles are located on every continent in the world except Antarctica. There are 59 species and four different major groups: booted eagles, fish eagles, giant forest eagles, and snake eagles. The United States has two species of eagles: the bald eagle, which is a fish eagle, and the golden eagle, which is a booted eagle. The bald eagle is especially important because it is our national bird and only resides in North America. It is important for students to learn more about the bald eagle and other eagles because some are endangered and may not be around in the future if more is not done to protect them.

Research Questions

1. What two species of eagles reside in North America?

2. Why are bald eagles endangered?

3. At what age do eagles start to fly?

4. How do parents care for their young?

5. Why is the bald eagle our national symbol?

Web Sites

http://www.nu.com/eagles/eagles.htm
This Web site takes a look at a nest in western Massachusetts that used to have bald eagles in it. It is interesting because the nest is camera-equipped and actually shows a picture of the bald eagles, which still visit regularly, in this nest. The site gives details about this nest site and a second new site at which wildlife experts may place a second camera. (S: 4–6)

http://www.eagles.org/all.html
All About Eagles is an interesting Web site that talks about the four major groups of eagles. It mainly focuses on the two species of eagles that reside in the United States, what they look like, what their young look like, and how they live. This is a great Web site for teachers and students to learn about and see these two types of eagles and their young. (S: All, T: All)

http://www.eagles.org/eagleday.html
This is an excellent Web site for students and teachers to learn why the bald eagle was selected to be the national bird and why bald eagles are so important to our culture and history. It encourages teachers and students to write letters for the establishment of an "American Eagle Day." (S: All, T: All)

Literature Resources

Mckinley, Maura. (1997). *Eagle Feathers*. Austin, TX: Steck-Vaughn.

This wonderful contest-winning book was written by a 10-year-old girl. It is about a Native American family that relies on eagle feathers for an important part of their culture and the adventure that takes place in getting them.

Morrison, Gordon. (1998). *Bald Eagles*. Boston: Houghton Mifflin.

This book provides students with a close-up look at a family of bald eagles and the stages that the new baby goes through. Most pages provide sidebars that tell the students educational facts and show pictures of how babies develop and what they look like. Also, there is a page that locates and names each part of the exterior and interior parts of the eagle's body.

Patent, Dorothy. (1984). *Where the Bald Eagles Gather*. New York: Clarion.

This great book provides excellent information and pictures about eagles. It talks about the two species of eagles that are found in North America, where they gather, and how they live. It also talks about how they are tracked, what we know as a result of tracking, and why, in some areas, bald eagles are endangered.

Activities and Projects

1. Discuss the importance of the bald eagle to our nation and talk about the history of the bald eagle. Invite students to log on to http://www.eagles.org/eagleday.html. Encourage students to write a letter to the organization telling why it is important to have an "American Eagle Day." Make a book of all the letters and send it to this organization. As a class, keep up on this issue to see if an American Eagle Day is established.

2. Discuss the different stages that eagles go through in their lives. Put students into groups and assign each group a stage of an eagle's life. Encourage students to use books and the Internet to find out about their assigned stage. Ask students to draw a picture of what the eagle looks like at that stage and have them make a poster or collage of what the eagle does at this stage. Put these pictures and posters in order along a wall in the room, showing the stages step by step so students can get a better sense of the significance of each stage.

3. Play examples of classical or instrumental music for the students. What type of music best represents the flight of an eagle? Is there an artist who best captures the spirit of an eagle in flight? What instrument or combination of instruments best depicts the flight of an eagle?

4. Ask students to take on the role of an eagle. Have them prepare a daily diary as though an adult eagle or a baby eagle was writing it. What events take place during the course of a single day? What things does the bird see? What things does it hear? Where does the eagle travel, and who or what does it meet in its travels? Be sure to provide sufficient opportunities for students to share their diaries in a large group format.

Elephants

Introduction

There are two types of elephants in the world. The African elephant, which lives in central and southern Africa, is the world's largest land animal. A bull elephant can weigh up to 15,000 pounds and may stand 13 feet high at the shoulder. African elephants also have very large ears, often up to six feet in length from top to bottom.

The Asian elephant, which lives in India and several Southeast Asian countries, is smaller than its African relatives. An adult bull may weigh up to 12,000 pounds and stand about 10 feet tall. In many parts of the world elephants are endangered as a result of excessive poaching and weak game laws. Several conservation and animal welfare organizations are working to protect dwindling populations of elephants.

Research Questions

1. What is the difference between African and Asian elephants?

2. How old can an elephant live to be?

3. How long is the gestation period (the time it takes to develop in the womb) of elephants?

4. How much water does each elephant consume in one day?

5. Why are elephants endangered?

6. How do elephants communicate with each other?

Web Sites

http://www.birminghamzoo.com/animals
This site, sponsored by the Birmingham Zoo, offers a look at a variety of animals, including the Asian elephant. After entering the page designated for Asian elephants, students are presented with a number of interesting facts about the great animal. The user can also follow the links to enjoy pictures of the elephants housed at the zoo. (S: All)

http://www.discovery.com/area/nature/elephants/elephants.html
Discovery Online takes a look at elephants found in Amboseli National Park, Kenya. It is considered to be one of Africa's most beautiful places, and in the Amboseli ecosystem elephants still roam freely in coexistence with humans. This site also examines several reasons why elephants are endangered. (S: 4–6, T: 4–6)

http://www.pbs.org/wnet/nature/echo/html/body_intro.html

In this site, presented by PBS, teachers and students are introduced to researcher Cynthia Moss. Along with her family, Cynthia Moss has spent nearly a quarter of a century studying elephants. Not only does this site present interesting facts about such topics as elephant communication, it also includes contests and educational activities. (S: 4–6, T: 4–6)

http://www.si.edu/organiza/museums/zoo/hilights/Webcams/molerat1/elecam/ elecam10.htm

The National Zoo in Washington, DC offers live video feed that allows the user to view pictures of the elephants in 20-second intervals. The viewer can travel around the site to learn interesting facts about elephants, as well as other animals housed at the zoo. "Elephant Cam" runs from 6:30 A.M. until 5:30 P.M. eastern standard time and offers various educational displays and demonstrations. (S: All, T: All)

 # Literature Resources

Fredericks, Anthony D. (1999). *Elephants for Kids*. Minnetonka, MN: Creative Publishing.

This book provides readers with lots of interesting and little-known facts about the largest animal. The story of the elephant is told through the eyes of a 10-year-old child, Kwasi, whose family moved to the United States from Kenya. The elephant is Kwasi's favorite animal, and he helps to present the reader with exciting information.

Hoffman, Mary. (1983). *Elephant*. Milwaukee, WI: Raintree Children's Books.

This book takes the reader through a day in the life of an elephant. Not only does this book provide the reader with valuable information, it also makes studying elephants interesting and exciting.

Le Tord, Bijou. (1993). *Elephant Moon*. New York: Doubleday Books for Young Readers.

Elephant Moon is a heartwarming tale of the magnificent elephants living in Africa. These creatures are being killed for their ivory at a rate of 200 elephants per day. This book tells of the peaceful lives elephants lead, and the types of activities the herd takes part in daily.

Overbeck, Cynthia. (1981). *Elephants*. Minneapolis, MN: Lerner.

Elephants discusses the largest land animal on earth. This book provides the reader with various types of information about the ways in which elephants live. The reader learns about how elephants interact and what is being done to protect the environment where the elephants reside.

Pringle, Laurence. (1997). *Elephant Woman*. New York: Atheneum Books for Young Readers.

Elephant Woman is the story of elephant researcher Cynthia Moss. She is able to identify more than 900 African elephants simply by sight. This book describes her life, discussing her family, her schooling, and her career. The book takes the reader through Cynthia's journeys working with elephants, discovering their lives, and attempting to save the magnificent creatures.

Redmond, Ian. (1993). *Elephant*. New York: Knopf.

Elephant is an informative book in the Eyewitness Books series. It provides the reader with some insight into the secret lives of elephants. This book takes a look at both living and deceased relatives on the elephant family tree.

Tsuchiya, Yukio. (1988). *Faithful Elephants*. Boston: Houghton Mifflin.

This is a touching story of what happened at the Ueno Zoo in Tokyo during World War II. Bombs were falling on Tokyo throughout the day. Zoo officials were afraid of what would happen if bombs were to hit the zoo and powerful elephants were released into the city. To prevent this from happening, the zookeepers decided to use poison to put the animals to death. A touching and dramatic story.

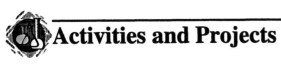

Activities and Projects

1. Suggest that students write letters to the Office of Endangered Species, U.S. Fish and Wildlife Service, Department of the Interior, Washington, DC 20240, to obtain information on the current status of elephants. Students may also wish to address some letters to various conservation groups (World Wildlife Fund, National Wildlife Federation) to obtain the latest information on the status of elephants in the wild. When the information is received, ask students to create special posters to inform the public about the status of elephants worldwide.

2. Place students in small groups and ask them to research various elephant legends and tales in different cultures or countries. Students should duplicate stories and gather them together into a bound book (e.g., "Elephant Legends of Kenya") .

3. Invite students to log on to the Web site http://www.pbs.org/wnet/nature/echo/ html/body_intro.html. Ask them to read *Elephant Woman*. After they have learned about Cynthia Moss, have students assemble a book about her life, her work, and her discoveries about elephants in Amboseli National Park in Kenya. Encourage students to share their completed project with students in other classes.

4. Invite a zoologist or biology professor from a local college or university to visit your class and share information about elephants. Provide an opportunity before the visit for students to generate an appropriate list of questions to pose to the visitor. If possible, videotape the presentation and invite students to evaluate the videotape for accuracy (based on the information they collected from the sources above). Plan time after the visit for students to discuss the information shared.

5. Ask students to assemble a collection of "Amazing Elephant Facts" to include in a class-made booklet or brochure. Using the resources above, students can identify some of the amazing details about elephants and their lives. For example:

   Elephants can run at speeds up to 35 mph for short distances.

   Elephants walk on their tiptoes.

   Elephants may live to be more than 70 years old.

   An elephant's trunk has more than 150,000 muscles.

   An elephant can lift up to 600 pounds with its trunk.

   The longest elephant tusk on record measured 11 feet, 6 inches long.

   An adult elephant needs to eat between 300 and 400 pounds of food a day.

Frogs

Introduction

Frogs are tailless amphibians that have protruding eyes, strong, webbed hind feet and smooth, moist skin. Many frogs are aquatic, but some live in trees, on land, or in burrows. Frogs can be found in all regions of the world, including dry deserts, humid rainforests, and backyards. Most frogs eat insects or small arthropods, but some eat other frogs as well as rodents and reptiles.

From egg, to tadpole, to adult, the life cycle of this amphibian is intriguing to children of any age. The annual breeding of frogs usually takes place in freshwater. Eggs are laid in numbers as high as several thousand. The eggs float off in clusters and some attach to water plants or sink. A tadpole hatches within a few days to a week. The continuation of metamorphosis happens within two months to three years. During this metamorphosis the lungs develop, limbs appear, and the tail is absorbed.

Research Questions

1. What are the differences between frog and toads?
2. Describe the life cycle of a frog.
3. What are the different types of frogs?
4. What is the habitat of the poison dart frog?
5. What is the purpose of a frog's sticky tongue?
6. What are some natural enemies of frogs?

Web Sites

http://www.exploratorium.edu/frogs
This is a great Web site designed for older children. Online exhibits, easy activities, and cultural frog myths are some of the exciting things children can access from this page. (S: 4–6)

http://cgee.hamline.edu/frogs/
Teachers, students and families are all connected in this impressive study of frogs. (S: All, T: All)

http://www.seagrant.wisc.edu/Education/madisonjason10/frogs.html
Quizzes, data, games, research information and more abound at this interesting and delightful site on frogs. (S: All, T: All)

http://www.si.edu/folkways/frogmain.htm
If students want to hear the sounds of different species of frogs from throughout North America this is the place to be. (S: All, T: All)

Literature Resources

Burns, Diane L. (1997). *Frogs, Toads, and Turtles*. Minnetonka, MN: NorthWord Press.
This book provides in-depth explanations of various types of frogs, toads, and turtles. A brief overview of frogs in general is presented. Detailed descriptions of different species of frogs are included.

Gibbons, Gail. (1993). *Frogs*. New York: Holiday House.
This book provides a step-by-step description of the life cycle of a frog. A description of a frog's anatomy is also included, along with a frog's role in nature and its natural enemies. The difference between a frog and toad is explained in this book.

Julivert, Maria Angels. (1993). *The Fascinating World of Frogs and Toads*. New York: Barron's Educational Series.
This educational series describes frogs and toads in great detail. The anatomy, life cycle, and habitat of different types of frogs are discussed.

Parker, Steve. (1999). *It's a Frog's Life—My Story of Life in a Pond*. Pleasantville, NY: Reader's Digest Children's Books.
This story is told from a frog's point of view as it deals with the daily ups and downs of environmental conditions. The different point of view makes this book very enjoyable.

Activities and Projects

1. Have the students use the resources provided to find information on the habitat of frogs. Allow the students to create this environment in an aquarium. After the aquarium is complete, purchase a few tadpoles to raise in the classroom. Have the students create a baby book for the tadpoles, writing down lengths, weights, habits, feeding routines, growth changes, and so forth. Put the baby book in the classroom library upon completion.

2. After reviewing some of the listed resources, have each student create a book from a frog's point of view. The story should contain information about a day in the life of a frog. The book should also include facts learned from class discussions, literature, and outside resources. These stories are an excellent way of assessing the students' knowledge of frogs. The students may present their books to the class.

3. Divide the class into groups. Ask each group to find information about frogs in different cultures. Each group should prepare their information for a classroom presentation. The presentation should be organized in the form of a play, from either the point of view of the frog or of a person.

4. If possible, have an adult frog and an adult toad in the classroom. The class should create a Venn diagram describing the similarities and differences they observe between the frog and toad. Display the diagram in the classroom. As students read more about both toads and frogs, they should add this information to the Venn diagram. Weekly, review the additions in a class discussion, encouraging students to ask questions or comment on the facts.

5. Have students use the Internet and literature resources above to compile a book of "Amazing Frog Facts." The following facts may help get them started:

    The first frogs swam in prehistoric ponds nearly 170 million years ago.

    The goliath frog of central Africa is the world's largest frog, nearly 1 foot long.

    The glass frog of South America has transparent skin: You can see through its skin and watch its heart beat.

    The barking tree frog sounds just like a dog when it croaks.

    Frogs, like other amphibians, absorb water through their skin.

    Frogs must close their eyes to swallow.

    Some species of frogs can leap 40 times their length. Human long-jumpers can only leap about four to five times their height.

Gorillas

Introduction

With the exception of chimpanzees, the gorilla is the closest animal relative to humans. Gorillas are forest dwellers native to Africa. The gorilla is a stocky, powerful ape with black skin and hair, large nostrils, and prominent brow ridges. It lacks hair on its face, hands, and feet, and the chests of the older males are bare. Although gorillas are thought to be ferocious, studies indicate that they are unaggressive and shy unless disturbed.

Due to human activities and the deterioration of their habitat, gorillas are an endangered species. Farming, grazing, lumbering, and illegal hunting are the human activities that have forced gorillas into endangerment. Today, some gorillas can still be seen in their natural habitats. The majority of gorillas can only be seen at zoos or reserves in an artificial habitat.

Research Questions

1. What do gorillas eat?

2. Can gorillas be trained? If so, what can they be trained to do?

3. What types of habitats are home to gorillas?

4. What are the two major similarities shared by gorillas and humans?

5. What are the sizes of an average full-grown male and female gorilla?

Web Sites

http://www.seaworld.org/gorilla/gorillas.html
This Web site is full of easy to read facts concerning the classification, habitat, diet, reproduction, babies, and longevity of gorillas. Topics such as how the gorillas use their senses and communicate are also discussed. (S: All)

http://www.gorillafund.org/005_gorilla_frmset.html
The Dian Fossey Gorilla Fund International Web page focuses on the life of the mountain gorilla. Dian Fossey and her work are also documented. Adoption information is available on this page. (S: 4–6)

http://www.discovery.com/cams/gorillas/gorilla.html
This site is great for children! The "Gorilla Cam" allows the viewer to see two baby gorillas growing up in the Children's Zoo Nursery at the Oklahoma City Zoo. Students can get pictures of the babies, vote on names for them, and find out how they are cared for. (S: K–3)

Literature Resources

George, Jean Craighead. (1998). *Gorilla Gang*. New York: Disney Press.
This book describes the natural actions of gorillas in their natural habitat. The antics of gorillas with others in their tribe are also described.

Lewin, Ted & Lewin, Betsy. (1999). *Gorilla Walk*. New York: Lothrop, Lee and Shephard.
This is a true story of the authors' trek to find gorillas in their natural habitat. This book is very descriptive of environmental conditions as well as the gorilla actions within their own group. The trip took place in 1997 in the Impenetrable Forest in Southern Uganda.

Patterson, Dr. Francine. (1985). *Koko's Kitten*. New York: Scholastic.
This is a true story of a gorilla named Koko, who was trained to use sign language by the author. This story describes Koko's affection for a kitten and shows the language abilities of gorillas.

Redmond, Ian. (1995). *Eyewitness Books: Gorilla*. New York: Knopf.
This book explains every aspect of gorillas in great detail. The habitat of gorillas is also described.

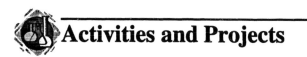

Activities and Projects

1. The class can adopt a gorilla through the Dian Fossey Gorilla Fund (see the Web site above). Display the information received about the adopted gorilla in the classroom. The students can guess how the money sent is used for the gorillas. Using the Web site provided, find out how the money is really used.

2. Divide the class into groups. After reading *Gorilla Walk*, invite the groups to create their own skits describing their trek to find mountain gorillas. The skits can be shared with another class. The skits should focus on the habitat of mountain gorillas, as well as their communication skills.

3. Encourage students to create a classroom Gorilla Awareness Campaign. Ask them to create a list of ways to convey information, such as pamphlets, posters, and news broadcasts. The students, working in groups, can develop appropriate promotion and "advertising" campaigns within the classroom as well as throughout the school. What organizations or agencies would be most appropriate to gather necessary information, and how will that information be shared?

4. Discuss the habitats of gorillas. How do the natural environments of gorillas compare with the artificial habitats in zoos and wild animal parks? If possible, invite students to visit a local zoo and obtain information about how gorillas are maintained in that environment. How similar is the artificial environment to the gorilla's natural environment? What are some of the major differences? What are the implications for the physical and/or emotional well-being of gorillas in a zoo-like environment? Students should consult the resources listed above or contact zoos directly for the necessary information.

Hawks

Introduction

Hawks belong to the *Accipitridae* family, which also include eagles. Worldwide, there are about 240 species, of which about 24 breed in North America. This varied group of birds ranges from the very large eagles to small hawks not much larger than a robin.

All hawks are predators, with hooked bills and sharply pointed talons. Some hawks have short, broad tails and wide, rounded wings adapted for soaring as they search for prey. Others have short, rounded wings and long, narrow tails that allow them to dart and twist among dense branches in search of prey. Well-known hawks include the sharp-shinned hawk, Cooper's hawk, the red-shouldered hawk, the broad-winged hawk, and the red-tailed hawk.

Research Questions

1. What does a hawk look like?

2. What is in the diet of hawks?

3. How are hawks and eagles similar?

4. What are some of the threats to the hawks' environment?

5. What is the life expectancy of a hawk?

Web Sites

http://www.desertusa.com/aug96/du_hawk.html
Within this Web site there are facts concerning raptors and their classifications. Also included is detailed information about the red-tailed hawk and its life cycle. (S: 4–6)

http://www.raptor.cvm.umn.edu/raptor/rfacts/broadw.html
This site describes in detail the broad-winged hawk, including identifying characteristics, location, habitat, nesting, feeding habits, and conservation status. (S: 4–6)

http://www.raptor.cvm.umn.edu/raptor/rfacts/nharr.html
This site describes in detail the northern harrier hawk, including identifying characteristics, location, habitat, nesting, feeding habits, and conservation status. (S: 4–6)

http://www.raptor.cvm.umn.edu/raptor/rfacts/sharps.html
This site describes in detail the sharp-shinned hawk, including identifying characteristics, location, habitat, nesting, feeding habits, and conservation status. (S: 4–6)

http://www.raptor.cvm.umn.edu/raptor/rfacts/sharpts.html
This site describes in detail the rough-legged hawk, including identifying characteristics, location, habitat, nesting, feeding habits, and conservation status. (S: 4–6)

Literature Resources

Arnold, Caroline. (1997). *Hawk Highway in the Sky*. San Diego: Gulliver Books.
Full-color photographs illustrate the details of the magnificent birds. This book depicts the research done by Hawk Watch International, which watches many raptors fly overhead at Goshute Mountain Nevada and researches their migratory procedure.

Baylor, Byrd. (1976). *Hawk, I'm Your Brother*. New York: Aladdin Paperbacks.
This is the story of little boy named Rudy. His only dream is to fly like a hawk over Santos Mountain. Rudy finds an unusual way to make his dream come true.

Bushnell, Jack. (1996). *Sky Dancer*. New York: Lothrop, Lee & Shephard.
Jenny has an encounter with a red-tailed hawk. The hawk mesmerizes her, and she becomes concerned when she hears of a neighbor who wishes to kill the hawk for killing his hen. What can Jenny do to protect this wild creature?

Matteson, Summer W. (1995). *Hawks for Kids*. Minnetonka, MN: NorthWord Press.
This book provides detailed information about hawks as well as incredible photographs.

Activities and Projects

1. Ask students to contact a nearby wild animal park, game preserve, zoo, animal rescue association, or raptor center to obtain relevant literature, brochures, pamphlets, or flyers. Once they have collected all of the literature, ask students to create an informational brochure for adults on the preservation of raptors, including hawks.

2. Invite students to investigate several of the Web sites listed above. Encourage them to assemble a fictitious diary on a day in the life of a hawk, based on the results of their inquiries. What does the hawk see? What does the hawk eat? Where does the hawk travel? Plan opportunities for students to discuss any similarities and/or differences in their diaries.

3. Ask students to create an attractive display of hawk-related information for the school library or a school display case. Encourage students to discuss the vital information that should be included in the display and how the display will sensitize students as well as school visitors to the life cycle of hawks, with particular reference to the endangerment of selected species.

4. Students may enjoy creating a wall mural of a hawk scene using selected illustrations and photos from the literature listed above. Obtain some newsprint and work with students to create an oversized painting. Discuss the additional plants and animals that should be in the scene.

Lions

Introduction

Lions are the most social members of the cat family. Males are usually 20 to 35 percent larger than the females. Lions typically band together in groups known as prides, each of which consists of five to fifteen adult females and their offspring, and one to six adult males.

Lions range in weight from 260 to 520 pounds. They usually hunt cooperatively, with the females doing most of the work. When hunting, the adult females will fan out and surround the prey, slowly stalking it. Victims are killed by using a short burst of speed from an ambush. Only then will the males come in to take their share.

Research Questions

1. Are lions an endangered species?

2. Where do most of the world's lions live?

3. How long do lion cubs stay with their parents?

4. Why do lions live in large groups?

5. How old do lions live to be?

Web Sites

http://www.primenet.com/~brendel/lion.html
The Cyber Zoomobile provides students with lots of information and lots of insights into these big cats. (S: 4–6)

http://www.sazoo-aq.org/lion.html
This site is a good source for background information about African Lions. (T: 4–6)

http://lionresearch.org
This Web site describes research on lions in Africa. There are a number of activities that children can do to learn more about lions. (S: 4–6)

http://Papanack.com/white_lions.htm
This Web site explores four cubs that were born as white lions. There are a lot of pictures for children to look at and there is a time line of the cubs' development. (S: All)

http://wkWeb4.cableinet.co.uk/alic/

The home page for the Asiatic Lion Information Center contains lots of information. There are pictures, general information, survival threats, and other links that are related to lions. A good Web site to find general information on lions and information on efforts to save the lion. (S: 4–6, T: All)

Literature Resources

Arnold, Carolyn. (1995). *Lion*. New York: Morrow.
   Young readers are introduced to two lion cubs. Colorful photos and exciting text make this book a sure winner.

Denton, Kady Macdonald. (1995). *Would They Love A Lion?* New York: Kingfisher.
   Anna takes on many different animal forms until she decides to become a lion. This book is suited for younger children.

Llewellyn, Claire. (1999). *I Didn't Know That Only Some Big Cats Can Roar*. Brookfield, CT: Copper Beech.
   A collection of random facts and loads of illustrations make this book a good introduction to the world of big cats.

Parsons, Alexandra. (1990). *Amazing Cats*. New York: Knopf.
   This book is an encyclopedia on all types of big cats. This is a great tool for all children.

Saign, Geoffrey. (1999). *The African Cats*. New York: Watts.
   This book is a combination of dramatic wildlife color photographs and lively, informative text. A great reference tool!

Simon, Seymour. (1991). *Big Cats*. New York: HarperCollins.
   This is a photo essay on seven varieties of big cats. This book is designed for children ages four through eight.

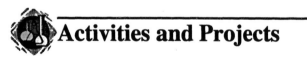

Activities and Projects

1. Discuss with students reasons why lions live in prides. Have students make charts or graphs of the benefits and disadvantages of living in large groups, using the Internet resources and literature listed above. Ask students to research other animals that live in large groups. Do the same advantages/disadvantages apply to those animals as to lions?

2. Ask small groups of students to create a time line that illustrates the life history of a typical lion. Encourage children to mark and illustrate selected events in the life of a lion (male or female), using the resources above. Post a strip of newsprint along one wall of the classroom and invite students to record the events for all to see.

3. Work with the school's music teacher to select several instrumental pieces that might represent various activities in a lion's life (e.g., stalking a victim, sleeping in the shade of a tree, carrying a cub to safety, etc.). Play these selections for students and ask them to close their eyes and imagine a lion engaging in the selected activities. Provide opportunities for students to discuss their mental images with each other.

4. Students may be interested in designing a Venn diagram or other similar chart comparing the life of a common house cat with that of a lion. What activities are similar? What activities are different?

Sharks

Introduction

Sharks are part of a class of fish known as *Chondrichthyes*. Fish in this class all have a skeleton made of cartilage (the same material in your nose and ears). This is different from most other fish, whose skeletons are made of bone. However, just like bony fish, this class of fish has jaws, paired fins, and paired nostrils. Another recognizable feature of these fish is their torpedo shape and their five to seven pairs of gill slits.

Sharks are well adapted to life in the sea, particularly life as predators. Most sharks are countershaded, with a dark back that, when seen from above, blends in with the dark depths of the ocean. They also have white bellies that, when seen from below, blend in with the sunlight streaming down from the surface. Several species also have a distinctive array of spots and stripes, which further help them blend in with their surroundings.

Research Questions

1. What is the largest shark in the world?

2. How deep in the ocean do most sharks live?

3. How many teeth can sharks have?

4. What do sharks eat?

5. What is the world's most dangerous shark (to humans)?

Web Sites

http://enchantedlearning.com/subjects/sharks/
All About Sharks provides students with easy to read facts about sharks. Included are size, diet, habitat, migration, evolution, teeth, and more. This site contains colorful animated pictures with labels. (S: All)

http://www.flmnh.ufl.edu/fish/sharks/sharks.htm
Florida Museum of Natural History allows students to find links that contain stories and facts about shark attacks. There are also links to books about sharks. (S: 4–6, T: All)

http://www.seaworld.org/Sharks/pageone.html
Sharks and Their Relatives lets older students find information about sharks' habitat, characteristics, behavior, anatomy, reproduction, and more. (S: 4–6, T: All)

http://users.bart.nl/~jkoetze/

This incredible Web site has loads of fascinating information about various species of sharks (including the great white). Students can e-mail scientists, look up information on any shark, and link up with other Web sites. (Don't miss the accompanying music on this site.) (S: 4–6 T: All).

 # Literature Resources

Chinery, Michael. (1996). *Shark*. Mahweh, NJ: Troll Associates.
   Stories and information about the fierce, fast-moving animals of the sea are included here. The whale shark is the largest fish and can smell its prey.

Gibbons, Gail. (1992). *Sharks.* New York: Holiday House.
   This is an easy to read book about different types of sharks. The large labels and colorful pictures allow students to explore the interesting world of sharks.

Llewllyn, Claire. (1999). *The Best Book of Sharks*. New York: Kingfisher.
   Students can take a journey to the world of sharks in this book. They can go deep under the sea and explore the characteristics, life cycle, and behaviors of sharks.

Markle, Sandra. (1996). *Outside and Inside Sharks*. New York: Simon & Schuster Children's Publications.
   Find out how sharks swim, hunt, and eat in this book. What do their bones, skin, and teeth look like? Find out with close-up pictures.

Rothman, Michael & Ryder, Joanne. (1997). *Shark in the Sea*. New York: Morrow.
   This is a scary but fun story about sharks as predators. What do they eat? How do they find their prey? Explore and find out.

Simon, Seymour. (1995). *Sharks*. New York: HarperCollins.
   Students can enjoy interesting facts and pictures of sharks. Read about and explore the world of the scariest fish in the sea.

 # Activities and Projects

1.   Ask students to assemble a book of "Amazing Shark Facts." Small groups of students should use the resources listed above to gather important and incredible information about sharks and their lives and create a book that can be donated to the school library. Some amazing facts to consider could include:

   Almost seventy percent of a shark's brain is used for the sense of smell.

   Sharks can hear sounds in water that are more than a half mile away.

   Sharks are considered the first living creatures to develop teeth.

   Sharks can detect one drop of blood in 100,000 gallons of water.

   Sharks have a two-chambered heart; humans have a four-chambered heart

   Fifty percent of all sharks are less than three feet long.

   Sharks may lose up to 30,000 teeth in their lifetime.

2. Invite children to write to one or more of the following environmental agencies and request information on the endangered status of selected shark species.

   National Wildlife Federation
   8925 Leesburg Pike
   Vienna, VA 22184

   Friends of Wildlife Conservation
   New York Zoological Society
   185 St., Southern Blvd.
   Bronx Zoo
   Bronx, NY 10460

   When the information arrives, invite students to put together an informational brochure about the plight of sharks in selected places in the world. Why should we protect certain species of sharks?

3. After students have collected sufficient data from the resources above, ask them to create an original story from the perspective of a shark. They may wish to detail a day in the life of a shark, as though the shark were relating the story. What did the shark observe? What did it experience? What other creatures did the shark encounter? What did it eat? Be sure to provide opportunities for students to share their stories with each other.

4. Invite students to log on to the Web site http://users.bart.nl/~jkoetze/. After youngsters have had an opportunity to gather appropriate data, ask them to design a brochure addressing many of the myths and superstitions people have about sharks. Where did these beliefs come from? How did they get started? Why are people so afraid of all species of sharks?

Snakes

Introduction

There are more than 2,700 species of snakes in the world. They can be found on every continent, except Antarctica. Interestingly, there are no snakes in Ireland, Iceland, or New Zealand.

Snakes are distinctive because they possess an elongated body without limbs, external ear openings, or eyelids. Some are active by day; others are quite active at night. They can be found living in trees, on the ground, or in water. Depending on the species, snakes live at elevations ranging from sea level to well above 10,000 feet. All snakes are carnivorous and, for the most part, they swallow their prey whole. They shed their skins periodically throughout their lifetimes. Some snakes are egg-layers; others bear their young alive. There are only 17 venomous species of snakes in the United States.

Research Questions

1. From what prehistoric animals are snakes considered to be descended?

2. What is the average life span of a snake?

3. Why are snakes cold-blooded?

4. What is the world's most poisonous snake (to humans)?

5. What is the world's most common snake?

Web Sites

http://www.rattlesnakes.com
This is a site for anyone who is interested in learning more about rattlesnakes. It covers everything about rattlesnakes, from fangs to coil and strike positions. (S: 4–6, T: All)

http:///worldkids.net/critters/reptiles/rattle.htm
Filled with facts about rattlesnakes, this site can be used by kids and adults alike to learn many facts about this type of snake. (T: All, S: 4–6)

http://www.kingsnake.com/mamba/index.html
This site is devoted to mambas. On this site is a link to Frequently Asked Questions about mambas. Teachers will find this site useful for answering questions their students will have about mamba snakes. (T: All)

http://www.nwf.org/nwf/intlwild/mamba.html
This site is the National Wildlife Federation's site about black mambas. It will answer almost all of the questions one can have about black mambas. (S 4–6, T: All)

http://unmuseum.mus.pa.us/bigsnake.htm
This site, Big Snakes, is devoted to sharing information about anacondas. Much information is presented, and it is easy enough for older children to access and understand. (S 4–6, T: All)

http://www.wf.net/~snake/index.html
On this site are links to sites about many types of snakes, including rattlesnakes, moccasins, copperheads, coral snakes, and anacondas. There are also links to sites about snake care and handling, what to do about snakebites, field safety tips, and a questions and answers page. (S 4–6, T: All)

http://www.geom.umn.edu/~jpowell/corn.html
This site is about corn snakes, which reside primarily in the southeastern United States. General information and care, as well as a photo of a corn snake, are accessible from this site. (S: All)

Literature Resources

Cole, Joanna. (1981). *A Snake's Body*. New York: Morrow.
Cole examines the unique features of a python's body. She tells how snakes get around without legs.

Jonell, Lynne. (1998). *I Need a Snake*. New York: Putnam.
This fictional story is about a little boy who wants a snake for a pet. When his mother says no to this idea he uses his imagination and finds "snakes" in all sorts of places.

Julivert, Maria Angels. (1993). *The Fascinating World of Snakes*. New York: Barrons.
This book shows several different varieties of snakes during their various stages of growth and development. It also shows that snakes live in many different climates and in most parts of the world.

Lavies, Bianca. (1993). *A Gathering of Garter Snakes*. New York: Dutton.
This book tells about the life of an 18-inch, red-sided snake from Manitoba, Canada. The reader will discover all about the communal dens where more than 10,000 snakes live together, how they mate, migrate, hunt, give birth, and shed their skins.

Markle, Sandra. (1995). *Outside and Inside Snakes*. New York: Aladdin.
Markle describes what snakes' bodies look like on the inside as well as the outside. In addition, the pictures illustrate to the reader how snakes hatch from their eggs, hide, and shed their skin.

Activities and Projects

1. Discuss the handling and care of snakes with your class. Ask them to speculate on what snake owners might feed their pets, where they should keep their pets, and so forth . Invite a snakekeeper into your class to speak to your students about the care and handling of a snake. This expert can be from a local zoo, reptile farm, or animal conservatory. Ask this expert to discuss with the class their thoughts and opinions on

snake care. Ask the snake expert to bring in some snakes for the class to handle and look at. Afterward, ask the children to draw a picture or write a story about one thing that they learned from the snake expert. Follow up by having the children write a thank-you letter to the visitor and include any drawings that the children would like to give to your guest.

2. Ask each student in your class to select one species of snake. Encourage each student to become an "expert" on that species, using the resources listed above. Each "Snake Expert" should be encouraged to assemble a brief brochure or leaflet that includes pertinent information about the selected species. Print out these brochures using appropriate software and then display them in an attractive format in the school library.

3. Ask students to put together a "Snake Newspaper" (e.g.. "The Slithering Serpent News") that presents interesting facts and observations about snakes in a newspaper format. Tell students to use the same sections as the local newspaper (e.g., sports—how fast snakes can travel; fashion—illustrations of colorful snakes worldwide; food and health—the different diets of selected species). Assemble the newspaper using a word processing program and print it out for distribution to family and friends.

4. Ask students to compile a profile of where a snake might live, using the knowledge that they have gained from the various resources. They should keep in mind that many different types of snakes like many different types of environments. Take a field trip around your town or school to look for local snake habitats. Ask children to draw a map of the area surveyed and mark on the map possible snake habitats as well as the types of snakes that would live in the habitats they found. Ask your students to pretend they are snakes living in your city or town. Ask them to keep a snake journal about the life of a snake in the area you live in, writing about their daily life from a snake's point of view: what they eat, where they go, what they do for fun, and so forth.

5. Discuss the differences between venomous and non-venomous snakes. Ask the class to guess whether there is a danger of venomous snakes in the area where you live. Identify the venomous snakes in your area and where they can be found on a class-designed map. Invite local emergency medical personnel to discuss caring for a snake-bite wound, making sure to specifically discuss care for bites from snakes you may have in your area.

6. If practical or feasible, go to a local pet store and purchase a pet snake for your class-room. Invite students to decorate their snake's new habitat with appropriate materials (check with the pet store personnel). Delegate snakekeeping responsibilities to your students. Ask students to keep a daily journal of the snake's progress and chart your snake's growth and how much it eats. Observe what happens to the snake's skin as it grows.

Spiders

Introduction

Spiders are the largest group of arachnids in the world. There are more than 35,000 species worldwide, including about 3,000 in North America. Spiders can be found almost everywhere: under rocks, in grass, on plants, in tree branches, in underground caves, and even in the water.

They are easily recognized by the four pairs of segmented legs. Most species have eight simple eyes, although some have fewer and some have none. Below the eyes are two small jaws that end in fangs. Venom is produced in glands and empties through a duct in the fangs. This venom is used to paralyze or kill prey. There are usually six fingerlike silk glands, called spinnerets, located beneath the abdomen. But not all spiders spin webs: Some live in burrows, and others have no retreats whatsoever.

Research Questions

1. How does a spider spin its web?
2. What are the differences between spiders and insects?
3. What do spiders catch with their webs?
4. Why do spiders molt?
5. What is the largest spider in the world?
6. How do spiders kill their prey?
7. How do spiders protect themselves?

Web Sites

http://www.discovery.com/exp/spiders/spiders.html
This Web site is filled with facts and vibrant pictures of different species of spiders, giving students lots of valuable information about these creatures. (S: 3–6)

http://www.letsfindout.com/subjects/bug/rfispsta.html
On this site, students will learn all the differences between spiders and insects. It is a complete and thorough guide. (S: 4–6)

http://www.desertusa.com/july97/du_bwindow.html
Everything youngsters would want to know about black widow spiders can be found on this site. Cool! (S: 4–6)

http://www.ufsia.ac.be/Arachnology/Arachnology.html

This thorough and complete guide to arachnids will provide you with tons of information and more hyperlinks than you'll ever be able to use. (T: All)

Literature Resources

Carle, Eric. (1984). *The Very Busy Spider*. New York: Philomel Books.
    This celebrated book recounts a spider's interactions with all of the other farm animals as the spider spins its wonderful web.

Crewe, Sabrina. (1998). *The Spider*. Austin, TX: Steck-Vaughn.
    Illustrated with color photographs, this simple text describes the life cycle of the black widow spider.

Halpern, Jerald. (1998). *A Look at Spiders*. Austin, TX: Steck-Vaughn.
    An ideal first book for young readers, this volume provides basic information and details about the lives of spiders.

Llewellyn, Claire. (1997). *I Didn't Know That Spiders Have Fangs*. Brookfield, CT: Millbrook Press.
    Lots of random information and a profusion of colorful illustrations make this an interesting first book on spiders.

Markle, Sandra. (1999). *Outside and Inside Spiders*. New York: Aladdin.
    With large colorful photographs, the author makes a clear distinction between spiders and insects and offers some amazing information.

McAuliffe, Bill. (1998). *Black Widow Spiders*. New York: Grolier.
    Just about everything the young scientist would want to know about these creatures can be found in this book.

Morris, Dean. (1988). *Spiders*. Milwaukee, WI: Raintree Children's Books.
    This book gives the student the opportunity to learn factual information about spiders, accompanied by great illustrations.

Scarborough, Kate. (1997). *Spider's Nest*. New York: Time Life.
    This super book is filled with eye-popping illustrations and incredible information.

Activities and Projects

1. After students have completed some research on the Web sites listed above, challenge them to weave their own webs. Provide individuals with a ball of string and ask each to weave a spider's web based on an illustration from one of the selected sites. Students will undoubtedly discover that the task is not as easy as it looks. Provide opportunities for students to discuss some of the difficulties they encountered. How are spiders able to overcome those difficulties?

2. Have the students create their own spiders, using pipe cleaners, pompoms, and wiggle eyes. Cut the pipe cleaners into four-inch lengths. Each child receives four of the pieces of pipe cleaner, 1 three-inch pompom, and a set of wiggle eyes. Directions: Twist the four pipe cleaners together, making a star shape. Glue the pompom in the center. Bend the legs of the spider. Glue on the wiggle eyes. Attach the spider to a pencil, using an elastic thread.

   Provide opportunities for students to display their "spiders" in the classroom.

3. Provide students with an opportunity to collect a variety of interesting facts and fascinating data about spiders. Encourage students to assemble that information into a brochure, especially designed for students in a grade lower than yours. Plan time to discuss the way the facts should be presented as well as the language that should be used.

4. Create a classroom spider web on a bulletin board in the classroom. Encourage students to cut out illustrations or photos from old magazines (depicting spiders and their habitats) that can be posted or placed on the classroom web. As students continue their studies of spiders, encourage them to add additional information as warranted.

Tigers

Introduction

Tigers, the great cats of Asia, are the largest member of the cat family. The tiger is one of the big, or roaring, cats and is rivaled only by the lion in strength and ferocity. Thought to have originated in northern Eurasia and to have moved southward, the tiger's present range extends from the Russian Far East through parts of China, India, and Southeast Asia.

There are seven or eight generally accepted species of tigers. Three are believed to be extinct, another is near extinction, and another three are on the endangered species list. The tiger is primarily hunted for sport and for fur.

Size and the characteristic color and striped markings of the tiger vary according to locality and race. The tiger has no mane, but in old males the hair on the cheeks is rather long and spreading. The tiger inhabits grassy and swampy districts and forests. It hunts by night and preys on a variety of animals, including deer, wild hog, and peafowl. In warm regions, tigers produce young at any time of the year; in cold regions they bear their cubs in spring. The average life span of a tiger is about 11 years.

Research Questions

1. How many different subspecies of tiger are there?

2. What species of tiger are believed to be extinct and endangered?

3. What is the rarest type of tiger?

4. Why are tigers poached?

5. What is the significance of a tiger's stripes?

Web Sites

http://www.primenet.com/~brendel/tiger.html
This site is a thorough description of tigers. Students can learn about the eight different subspecies of tigers, tigers in the wild, and the evolution of tigers. They are also invited to read about the different characteristics of a tiger, such as their hunting skills and the reasons for their stripes. (S: All, T: All)

http://www.lam.mus.ca.us/cats/P18/
This Web site is dedicated to the endangered tigers. Students can get exact statistics on world tiger populations and learn how serious the possibility of their extinction is. There is an easy to read map for students to view the scattered and scarce populations of tigers. (S: 4–6, T: All)

http://www.tigerlink.com/read@tigers.html
Learning All About Tigers contains lots of information about these creatures. A great resource tool for all students. (S: All)

http://www.cptigers.org/animals/tiger.html
The Carnivore Preservation Trust has lots of data for students on this informative site. (S: All)

http://www.geocites.com/RainForest/5685/nofrindex.html
This is one of the best Web sites about tigers. It describes every subspecies of tiger, such as the white tiger, Caspian tigers, and Siberian tigers. Students can learn the habits, markings, and hunting style of each type. Students are also provided with an in-depth, detailed list of tiger facts, tiger appearance, biology, and some typical body measurements of a tiger. (S: 4–6)

Literature Resources

Bailey, Jill. (1990). *Save the Tiger: Earth's Endangered Creatures*. Austin, TX: Steck-Vaughn.
Akbar, a tracker for a tourist lodge, works with would-be poachers and those involved in Project Tiger to protect the diminishing number of tigers in his part of India.

Butterfield, Moira. (1997). *Fast, Strong, and Striped: What Am I?* Austin, TX: Steck-Vaughn.
Readers can learn basic information about the physical characteristics, behavior, and habitat of the African elephant, brown bear, and the Bengal tiger in this book.

Higgins, Maria. (1998). *Cats: From Tigers to Tabbies*. New York: Crown.
Higgins presents information about the behavior of both wild and domestic cats.

Irvine, Georgeanne. (1995). *Blance and Arusha: Tales of Two Big Cats*. New York: Simon & Schuster.
The San Diego Zoo is the setting for short biographies of two rare inhabitants, a white tiger and a cheetah. The circumstances of their arrival at the zoo, facts about their breeds and about other big cats, and information about endangered species are also included.

Activities and Projects

1. Have small groups of students assemble a series of informational brochures on the life cycle of a specific species of tiger, using the Web sites listed above. Inform students that these brochures will be distributed through a local zoo or wild animal park and should be designed to offer the public important information about the identified tiger as well as data concerning its endangered status and preservation, if appropriate.

2. Ask small groups of students to each select one of the literature sources and one of the Web sites listed above. Encourage them to read the information on each resource and then prepare a Venn diagram that compares and contrasts the data. What resource was most complete? What resource was most useful? What resource provided the most interesting information? Provide opportunities for students to share the results of their investigations with other members of the class.

3. Ask the class to prepare a "Tiger Preservation Manifesto." Initiate a discussion on the current plight of selected tiger species around the world. Why are some species being systematically eliminated? What efforts are governmental agencies making to curb the decline in tiger populations? What are some laws that can be passed to prevent the extinction of selected species? Ask students to gather the results of their discussions as well as any data collected from Web sites to prepare a statement that condemns tiger poaching and advocates the passage of strict laws.

4. Ask each youngster to assume the role of a tiger. Have students move in a manner similar to the way tigers move. How can they simulate the movements of a tiger? What challenges do they face? Provide opportunities for students to discuss any similarities or differences between the way humans move and the way tigers move through the wilderness.

Turtles and Tortoises

 Introduction

What is the difference between a turtle and a tortoise? Tortoises pull their heads into their shells by retracting their necks into a curve. Turtles hide their heads by bending their necks sideways.

Turtles and tortoises came into being about 200 million years ago. They range in size from the box turtle's six inches to the leatherback turtle's eight feet. Some are carnivorous, but most are omnivorous. Turtles can live for more than 100 years. However, many are becoming endangered due to a lack of nesting grounds from shore development and by drowning in fishing trawls. Many of their habitats are being diminished due to river channeling, swamp draining, and highway construction.

 Research Questions

1. What are some differences between turtles and tortoises?

2. How do reptiles survive on land? In the sea?

3. Why are some turtle species at risk of extinction?

4. What are their shells used for?

5. How long can sea turtles hold their breath?

 Web Sites

http://www.tortoise.org/

Students can find articles full of information about both creatures at this site. They can click to hear the sound of tortoise calls. Links to related books and pictures are included. (S: 4–6, T: All)

http://www.turtles.org/dive.htm

Students can enter the real lives of Peter and Goofyfoot by viewing pictures of them and reading about how they surface for air. These sea turtles enjoy being on the reef but sometimes have to struggle for survival. (S: All)

http://www.nmfs.gov/prot_res/turtles/leathtur.html

Lots of information about leatherback sea turtles can be found on this site. A good resource for students (S: 4–6, T: 4–6)

http://www.micronet.net/users/~turtles/pondfolder/kidspage/questions.html

This site has lots of questions (and answers) that kids typically ask about turtles. A great resource for any turtle-related unit. (S: All)

http://www.desertusa.com/june96/du.tort.html

Students can discover facts about how tortoises survive in the desert. This site provides pictures with information about their dry habitat, range, and behavior. (S: All)

Literature Resources

Burns, Diane L. (1997). *Frogs, Toads, and Turtles*. Minnetonka, MN: NorthWord Press.

Through colorful illustrations, students can learn basic facts about both turtles and tortoises. Are all these creatures reptiles? Do they live in water or on land? Students can explore their world.

George, William T. (1989). *Box Turtle at Long Pond*. New York: Greenwillow Books.

Students can enjoy the story of the daily life of a turtle that lives by the pond by reading this book. Follow the turtle as he wakes, eats, walks, and encounters others.

Guiberson, Brenda A. (1996). *Into the Sea*. New York: Henry Holt.

A little sea turtle crawls over sand to begin a life in the ocean. Children can join the journey as the sea turtle grows and meets other sea creatures. Colorful and realistic illustrations.

Hirschi, Ron. (1994). *Turtle's Day*. New York: Cobblehill Books.

Beginning readers can learn the basic facts about turtles and view photographs. Why is the shell important? What do turtles eat? Explore how a turtle searches for food and uses the sharp beak to eat.

Lewin, Ted. (1999). *Nilo and the Tortoise*. New York: Scholastic.

Children will love to be a part of Nilo's adventures with his new friend. Nilo finds a turtle and cares for it and feeds it. He wants to keep it as a pet, but should he return his friend to where he belongs?

Papastavrou, Vassili. (1992). *Turtles and Tortoises*. New York: Bookwright Press.

Particularly suited for older children, this book explains turtles and tortoises at risk in the wild. Students will discover endangered turtles and tortoises and some reasons that they are endangered. What can people do to help?

Ruiz, Andres Llamas. (1997). *Reptiles and Amphibians: Birth and Growth*. New York: Sterling.

Older students can research facts about reptiles in this book. They will discover the metamorphosis and habitat of turtles. From egg to turtle, students will explore the growth and behaviors of these interesting creatures.

Activities and Projects

1. Ask the students to use string or yarn to measure out the length of various turtles:

Turtle	Length
Loggerhead Sea Turtle	31–48"
Eastern Box Turtle	4–8 ½"
Musk Turtle	3–5 ½"
Wood Turtle	5–9"
Eastern Painted Turtle	4–10"
Snapping Turtle	8–18 ½"
Spotted Turtle	3 ½–5"

    Divide students into small groups. Supply each group with rulers, one piece of measured string, and two-inch blocks. The students will determine what turtle their string represents and then how many blocks it would take to equal the length of their turtle. Encourage the students to share their findings with the class.

2. Invite the students to write to the Turtle and Tortoise Preservation Group:

    5812 S. Coleman
    Oklahoma City, OK 73179

    Encourage them to ask questions about what type of turtles and tortoises are endangered and why. They should ask about how they, as a class, can help.

3. Ask the students to create a Venn diagram using the topics turtles and tortoises. In small groups, have the students use the Internet and literature resources to write characteristics under each topic. Once the diagram is complete, ask the students to orally explain the similarities and differences between turtles and tortoises.

4. Contact the biology or zoology department at a local college or university. Ask to be put in touch with a zoologist or herpetologist. Make arrangements for a visit to the campus so that children have an opportunity to talk with and ask questions of a "turtle expert." Prepare youngsters ahead of time by encouraging them to prepare a set of questions to ask the expert. After the trip, ask students to select one or more of the following projects based on the information they learned:

    1. Ask a group of students to create a newsletter or newspaper describing the trip.

    2. Encourage students to design a brochure on important points learned during the visit. The brochure can be distributed to other classes in the school.

    3. Have students put together a news broadcast about what was learned during the visit.

Whales

Introduction

Whales are magnificent creatures that roam the oceans of the world. Many children believe that whales are just like all of the other fish in the sea, but whales are actually mammals. Whales share many of the same characteristics of other mammals. Students will be surprised to find that not all whales are the same. They vary greatly in size and appearance. It is also important for students to learn that many species of whales are endangered. With the help of these Web sites, books, and activities, students will learn about four different types of whales: beluga whales, killer whales, sperm whales, and humpback whales. They will also learn why whales are being hunted, and what they can do to preserve them.

Research Questions

1. Why are humpback whales an easy target for whale killers?

2. Which whale is the largest?

3. How long can sperm whales stay underwater?

4. Do all populations of whales sing the same songs?

5. Why are whales becoming extinct?

Web Sites

http://oceanlink.island.net/
Students can discover a ton of answers to tons of questions at this super site. A great resource for student reports. (S: All)

http://www.seaworld.org/killer_whale/killerwhales.html
This information site from Sea World has tons of information on the killer whale, laid out in an outline form. On this site, students can learn about the adaptations that these whales have made to survive in an aquatic environment, communication and echolocation, and the common causes of death of these creatures. A film clip of Shamu, the famous killer whale, is included on this Web page. (S: 4–6)

http://whale.wheelock.edu
This is an exciting Web site for students who want to gain more in-depth information about whales and want to engage in a variety of hands-on activities concerning research about whales. Students can actually track whale movements and migration patterns via this Web site. (S: 4–6, T: All)

http://www.pacificwhale.org/

This site is great for teachers because it provides the latest research and facts on whales. You can subscribe to a newsletter via e-mail to immediately get this new and exciting information. There are also many activities that you can engage your students in on this page, such as adopt a whale, ask a scientist, and artwork contests. (T: All)

 # Literature Resources

Asimov, Isaac. (1992). *Why Are Whales Vanishing?* Milwaukee, WI: Gareth Stevens Children's Books.

This book discusses the different reasons why whales are dying out and what people are doing to save them. Included at the end of this book are more books to read and organizations that you can write to obtain more information on what you can do to help the whales.

Braithwaite, Althea. (1988). *Whales.* New York: Longman

This Save Our Wildlife book discusses the life journey of the humpback whale. Information on topics such as their tail markings and their unique eating patterns is included. The simple language of this book makes it an easy read for beginners.

Conklin, Gladys. (1974). *Journeys of the Gray Whale.* New York: Holiday House.

The "Moby Dick Parade," the migration of the California gray whale along the Pacific Coast, is introduced in this book. Information on the birth, feeding, and behaviors of these whales is also included in this book.

McGovern, Ann. (1979). *Little Whale.* New York: Four Winds Press.

This book tells the story of what happens in the first five years of a humpback whale's life, including its behaviors and habitat. The end of the book contains an author's note discussing the meaning of *extinction* and the reasons why whales are still being killed today. New vocabulary words are also located at the end of the book.

Patent, Dorothy H. (1993). *Killer Whales.* New York: Holiday House.

There are great photos in this book! All aspects of the killer whale are explained in this book, with a photograph and caption to explain each aspect, including the different family groups, or "pods," that killer whales belong to. This is a great book for visual learners!

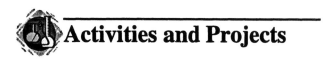 # Activities and Projects

1.   Invite students to write to one or more of the following organizations requesting information on how many whales still exist and how they can help save the whales.

   American Cetacean Society
   P.O. Box 2639
   San Pedro, CA 90731

   The Whale Protection Fund
   1725 DeSales
   Washington, DC 20036

Pacific Whale Foundation
101 N. Kihei Road
Kihei, HI 96753

When the information arrives, invite students to create an "advertising campaign" that would alert other students or the general public to the plight of various species of whales.

2. Divide students into several groups and assign a whale to each group. Ask each group to conduct necessary research (using library books, encyclopedias, cetacean experts, a high school biology teacher, etc.) to create a tabletop diorama of that species of whale in its natural habitat. Ask students to compose a written description of their whale to accompany the diorama. Provide opportunities for students to share their dioramas with others.

3. This simple activity that will demonstrate how a baleen whale obtains its food.

    Materials: a sink filled with cold water, a packet of dry vegetable soup, and a kitchen strainer

---

Directions:

  a. Fill a sink with cold clear water.

  b. Open and sprinkle the packet of vegetable soup over the surface of the water. (Students will note that the soup does not sink, but rather floats on the surface.)

  c. Ask one student to hold the kitchen strainer in one hand and skim it slowly over the surface of the water.

  d. Ask students to note how the vegetable pieces are caught in the strainer and how the water passes through the wire mesh of the strainer.

The strainer is able to "capture" the various vegetable pieces in its "bowl." The pieces are caught and the water passes through. If the strainer is lifted out of the water it will contain a wide variety of "food."

Baleen whales sift their food in much the same way as the students did with the strainer. However, their food isn't floating on the surface, it swims through the water. The baleen combs allow a whale to swim through a school of its dinner, strain the water from the plant or animal life, and eat what remains on its baleen. This is a very efficient form of eating as long as there is a sufficient quantity of food in the water. For example, one blue whale needs to eat about 4 tons of krill *every day* to survive. That's a lot of food to strain from the water!

4. This activity will help students appreciate the lengths of various types of whales throughout the world.

    Materials: A ball of yarn, scissors, a yardstick.

    Directions:

    a. Measure the height of selected students. Cut pieces of yarn according to those heights. Lay the strings of yarn outside (on the sidewalk, in the backyard, or on the driveway).

    b. Measure other pieces of yarn according to the lengths of the whales listed below:

Porpoise	8 feet
Dolphin	8 feet
Pilot whale	22 feet
Killer whale	30 feet
Grey whale	45 feet
Humpback whale	50 feet
Right whale	60 feet
Sperm whale	60 feet
Blue whale	100 feet

    c. Lay the various pieces of yarn side by side. How do various students compare with the lengths of common whales around the world?

5. As a class, adopt a whale using the package you can order at http://www.pacificwhale. org/. The students will learn about the life history of their whale, receive a newsletter on updates of sightings of their whale, and learn the latest whale news. A whale-watching guide is also included with this package. It only costs $35, which should be no more than $2 each from your students.

6. Students can track specific whales using a program called S.T.P. (Satellite Tagging Program) using the Web site http://www.pacificwhale.org/. This is an exciting way for students to learn about the migration pattern of a specific whale species.

Cells

 Introduction

Cells are found in all living things. From plants to viruses, we encounter cells every day that "build" living things, both big and small. Every different type of cell has a different job and function. Red blood cells transport oxygen around the different parts of the body. White blood cells kill off germs and infection that invade the body and make you sick. In addition to animal cells, children also encounter plant and bacteria cells every day.

 Research Questions

1. How many different types of cells are there, and where are they found?

2. How do cells get their food?

3. By what process does a cell divide?

4. What are the jobs of three different cell structures?

5. Which cells does the human body use to fight disease?

 Web Sites

http://www.cellsalive.com/toc.htm
This is one of the best Web sites about cells and their many functions. Video clips are provided on this site about the stages of cell division that a cell goes through. Included on this site is video footage of protozoa cells, diseased cells, and healthy cells. (S: 4–6, T: All)

http://www.brainpop.com/health/basicsandcells/cells/index.asp
Kids can learn all about cells and the basic of the human body through Web movies at a fabulous site. (S: All)

http://www.chavez.cps.k12.il.us/thumphrey/documents/pages/cellsite/PAGES/cell.html
What is a cell? At this site fifth- and sixth-grade students from a school in Chicago explain the basics of cells and what they do. (S: 4–6)

http://www.kapili.com/biology4kids/
Biology for Kids offers lots of information for students and teachers alike on various elements of the human body. (S: 4–6, T: 4–6)

Literature Resources

Haslam, Andrew. (1997). *Make It Work! Body*. Chicago: World Books.

A great diagram of a human cell that children can recreate outside of the classroom is included in this book. Functions of the different parts of the cell shown are also explained.

Llamas Ruiz, Andres. (1996). *Cycles of Life: The Life of a Cell*. New York: Sterling.

This is a marvelous resource on the life of an animal cell and a plant cell. It is a great book for children to read to learn about the life of a cell.

Roca, Nuria and Marta Serrano. (1995). *Invisible World: Cells, Genes, and Chromosomes*. New York: Chelsea House.

This is a wonderful source of information about the cell, inside and out. This book explains how cells relate to their environments, reproduce, gain energy, and function as units of two or more to form other organs in both the animal body and plants.

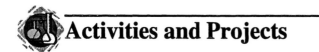

Activities and Projects

1. Have students break up into four small groups. Each group should then read one of the books or log on to one of the Web sites above and become a group of "experts" on a particular type of cell (plant or animal). Have each group devise a cell dictionary, which can later be compiled with the other groups' dictionaries and stored as one big class dictionary. The dictionaries can contain photographs, picture illustrations, definitions put in the students' own words, and, if possible, places where entries can be seen or observed. (Methods for observation, such as a microscope slide, may also need to be included.)

2.. Have each group create pamphlets about two or more types of cells. Sample pamphlets should be available for the groups to refer to when deciding the style in which they would like to create their pamphlets. For example, they can choose to arrange their pamphlets like a medical pamphlet, a travel brochure pamphlet, or an instructional pamphlet. These pamphlets should then be made available to the entire class for future use as a reference material about cells.

3. Discuss the process of mitosis (cell division) with the class. Include a basic definition. Invite students to log onto the Web site http://www.cellsalive.com/toc.htm. Allow students to observe the healthy cell dividing. They may play with the time-lapse frames to better understand the actions a cell goes through to divide. Ask the students to chart the progress of the cell's division and to draw pictures of the cell dividing at various stages. Have the students then watch the cancer cell undergo mitosis. Again, ask the students to keep a log of the process, draw pictures, and play with the time-lapse frames.

4. Ask students to stand in one large circle. (This activity works best in a large, open space such as a field or the gym.) Have the students work together to cross to another side of the area you are using. Explain to the class that they are representing an animal cell. Have the class divide into two equal circles (first division in mitosis). Try to have the same approximate ratio of boys to girls in each circle. Explain that the class now

represents two daughter cells. Continue to divide the circle until every child is representing one cell. Ask the class "How many times did the cell have to divide before it formed eight cells?" Discuss what the students learned from this process.

5. Obtain as many microscopes, plastic microscope slides, iodine solution, and slide covers as possible from a local high school or biology lab. Provide toothpicks for the class, making sure that their tips are not too sharp. Have students work in pairs or groups of no more than three. First each child should take a piece of masking tape and a pen/marker and label the slide with her or his name. Instruct the students to select one person from their group to take the toothpick and gently rub it around the inside of her or his cheek. Have the students then wipe the toothpick on the slides. Add a drop of iodine to each slide and place the slide covers on top of the samples. Let the samples sit for 24 hours. Then have the children look at the cells their bodies are made of under the microscope. Point out that the cell membrane, which outlines and protects the cell, appears to be darker due to the iodine. Also explain that the dark "dot" within their cell is the cell nucleus, or "brain." Allow students to reflect on their observations within their groups and then silently record their observations in their lab notebooks. Also allow children to discuss their discoveries with the entire class. Add onto the semantic web what your students have learned.

6. The average life span of a red blood cell (RBC) is approximately 120 days. A cell will die before that time if it is deprived of oxygen. To stay alive, a cell needs to be supplied with oxygen about every four minutes. (In one minute your body replenishes its RBCs with oxygen approximately 15 times. This equals a minimum of 900 times a day and 6,300 times a week that your body supplies oxygen to an RBC for that cell to live out its life span.) Ask your students to figure out the minimum number of times in a day, and in a week, they must feed their RBCs with oxygen by respiration. Teach the students how to find the respiration of a partner by counting the number of times in one minute that their partner's chest cavity expands. Have students do this twice for a four-minute period to gain an average of how many respirations their partner had in four minutes. Starting on a Monday, have the students take their partner's respiration rate several times during the day (in the morning, before/after lunch, and in the afternoon) and record their rates on graph paper. Have the students note whether exercise, time of day, and activity can affect respiration rates. Explain that each time the lungs expand they are sending oxygen to all the cells in the body. Have the students infer whether their partner's body is going to keep a cell alive for 120 days. Discuss how students arrived at their conclusions.

Endangered Species

Introduction

They roam across the savannas of Africa. They slip and slide through the swamps of the southern United States. They patiently chew on the stalks of bamboo plants in the jungles of China. What are they? They are the dwindling herds of white rhinos, the small clusters of American crocodiles, and isolated enclaves of pandas of the world. They are threatened, they are endangered, and they are all fighting a daily battle for survival.

It is unfortunate, but one of the most significant factors in the endangerment (and extinction) of animals around the world is humans. But it is also important to note that humans have the capacity to save and protect the reduced schools, dwindling herds, and waning colonies of many animals around the world. For example, consider these facts:

- Worldwide, there are more than 4,500 animal species on endangered species lists.

- The Endangered Species Act of 1973 is designed to protect over 900 species.

- Many scientists estimate that 99 percent of all the species that have ever lived on the Earth are now extinct.

- Some scientists predict that during the twenty-first century, three or four species may vanish *every hour!*

Imagine a world without many of the animals we take for granted. What will future generations know about some of the most amazing and incredible animals of the planet if the animals no longer exist? Sadly, some animals may only be found in the pages of a book.

Research Questions

1. What is the single most significant factor in the endangerment of animals?

2. Where are most of the world's endangered animals located?

3. What steps are being taken to save endangered animals?

4. What is the world's most endangered animal?

5. What laws are used to protect endangered animals?

Web Sites

http://www.sprint.com/epatrol/ep-endangered.html

Here students can learn about endangered species in different parts of the world. They are provided with pictures and descriptions of each animal. They can learn about the endangered species of North America, South America, Europe, Africa, Asia, Australia, and Antarctica. (S: K–3, T: K–3)

http://www.seaworld.org/endangered_species/edintro.html

This site explains what *endangered* means and how these species can be helped. Students can obtain profiles on endangered species and see what organizations work to help these animals. (S: 4–6, T: All)

http://tqiunior.advanced.org/5802/

Here students can learn about different types of endangered species. They can read about where they live, what they eat, their habits, and why they are endangered. (S: 4–6, T: 4–6)

http://www.worldwildlife.org

Here students can learn about endangered species. They can learn about breeding, what they eat, and physical characteristics. They can also learn about how the World Wildlife Fund is trying to save these animals. (S: 4–6, T: All)

http://library.advanced.org/25014/english.index.html

Here students can learn about the endangered species of the year 2000. They can obtain detailed information on individual species and also learn how to help them. (S: 4–6, T: 4–6)

Literature Resources

National Wildlife Foundation. (1997). *Endangered Species: Wild and Rare*. Philadelphia: Chelsea House.

This book highlights several species that are considered to be in danger. It provides information about how these animals can be helped. Activities are included throughout the book to keep students interested and involved.

Patent, Dorothy. (1997). *Back to the Wild*. San Diego: Harcourt Brace.

This book introduces the breeding and reintroduction of large mammals. The animals included are the red wolf, black-footed ferret, golden lion tamarin, and leaping lemurs. The book explains how this technique may work in some cases and not in others.

Stone, Lynn. (1984). *Endangered Animals*. Chicago: Children's Press.

In this book children can learn why animals are endangered and about extinction. They can also learn about the different endangered animals and where they are from. Most important, it describes different ways to help save the animals.

Activities and Projects

1. Ask the students to read *Back to the Wild*. Also encourage them to explore the endangered species Web sites. Give a ball of yarn to a student and ask her or him to share something that she or he has learned about an endangered species. Then, holding onto the end of the string, the student should pass the yarn to another student, who will do the same, only she or he must share something about an animal that has not already been said. Continue until the ball of yarn is done.

2. Provide students with copies of old magazines. Have them work in small groups to cut out pictures, illustrations, and photographs of selected endangered animals around the world. Encourage students to create an oversize collage on one wall of the classroom profiling these animals. Be sure to have students note the large number of different animal species portrayed on the mural.

3. Focus on a different group of animals each day (e.g., Monday, insects; Tuesday, fish; Wednesday, mammals). Each day, include stories, songs, student-created skits, trivia, games, and environmental concerns related to the subject animals. Invite a speaker from the community or local college to discuss current issues relating to these animals.

4. Ask each student to select a single endangered animal. Students should pretend that they are writing a newspaper obituary for their selected animal. They can do the necessary research on the Web sites listed above. Provide the obituary section of your daily newspaper for students to use as reference for writing their articles. Decorate a section of the bulletin board to look like a section of the newspaper and hang the animal obituaries there. Students can include an illustration of each animal.

Flowering Plants

Introduction

The flower is a special part of a plant that produces new plants of the same kind. Most flowers live for a short time and then parts of a flower become a fruit. The fruit has seeds in it and the seeds produce the new plant.

Most flowers have four parts: sepals, the thin, leaflike parts on the outside of the flower; petals, usually larger than the sepals and brightly colored to attract insects; stamens, the male part of the flower that produces sperm; and pistils, the female part of the flower that produces ovules, which will later become seeds.

Research Questions

1. Name at least three different methods of pollination.

2. What are the parts of a flower?

3. What are the functions of each part of the flower?

4. List at least five flowering plants that grow in the region of your choice.

5. What is phototropism?

6. How big is the largest flower in the world?

Web Sites

http://www.ucmp.berkeley.edu/anthophyta/anthophyta.html
This site provides teachers with a basic introduction to flowering plants. (T: 4–6)

http://aggie-horticulture.tamu.edu/wildseed/tamuhort.html
This site has pictures and growing information for many different kinds of wildflowers. (T: 4–6)

http://www.arnprior.com/kidsgarden/
Kids Valley Garden has loads of information for budding gardeners. (S: All)

http://tqjunior.advanced.org/3715/index.html
Don't miss this site, entitled Plants and Our Environment, presented by the Hinkle Creek Elementary School's fourth grade. It could also be called Everything You Ever Wanted to Know About Plants. Such topics as what a flower is, spreading seeds, how a plant grows, photosynthesis, pollination, monocots and dicots, germination, and dour environment are covered. Truly an in-depth look at flowering plants plus much more. (S: All)

Literature Resources

Bruchac, Joseph. (1995). *Native Plant Stories*. Golden, CO: Fulcrum.
This book represents the retelling of a collection of Native American stories. The focus of the stories is the relationship between humans and the plant world.

Busch, Phyllis. (1977). *Wild Flowers and the Stories Behind Their Names*. New York: Scribner.
This book tells stories about how certain flowers got their names. It also gives the scientific name and then the other popular names. For instance, the red dot in the middle of Queen Ann's lace is said to be a drop of blood from when Queen Ann pricked herself making lace.

Ganeri, Anita. (1992). *Plants*. New York: Franklin Watts.
This book contains illustrations accompanied by exploratory text to provide information about various types of plants.

Gibbons, Gail. (1991). *From Seed to Plant*. New York: Holiday House.
This book shows the stages in which a seed grows into a plant. Illustrations and diagrams show parts of a plant and give an explanation of what the part does. This book also describes a fun project for growing beans in which a child can watch how a plant grows from a seed.

Kalaman, Bobby. (1997). *How a Plant Grows*. New York: Crabtree.
This book provides a wonderful description of the life of a plant. It takes children on a journey showing different kinds of plants and their functions. It also includes a glossary to explain unknown words to children.

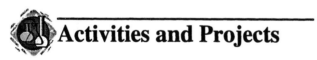

Activities and Projects

1. Start a K-W-L chart by having students list what they know about flowering plants. Next, have students generate a list of things that they would like to know about plants. As a means of answering some of the unknown facts, invite a plant expert to speak to the class about flowering plants Following the visit, complete the chart, noting what the students have learned.

2. Students can explore and communicate to others about the types of flowering plants that grow where they live by completing an Internet survey. Information for the survey can be obtained by using either the Internet sources or books from the library. Internet sources can include state agencies that govern wildlife protection. Information needed for the survey includes one type of local endangered species for both animals and flowering plants. Other information needed will be the name of a local popular plant and types of food that local endangered animals eat. To complete the survey go to http://tqjunior.advanced.org/3715.index.html.

3. Obtain seeds from a local plant nursery or seed catalog. Invite students to start the seeds in the classroom. Later, the seedlings can be transplanted in the spring to a schoolyard garden plot. This can be done schoolwide to create a school beautification project. Students should observe the growth process on a regular basis and keep a log or journal of their observations.

4. Ask students to create a three-dimensional model of a flower. Encourage youngsters to "manufacture" their own replica of a flower using materials such as clay, papier mâché, or a flour and water mixture. Have students add labels for each of the flower parts to their models and display the completed objects in a school display case or in the library.

5. Fill an empty shoe box with potting soil. Ask youngsters to plant six to ten flower seeds very close together at one end of the box. Ask them to plant another set of six to ten seeds at the other end, spaced apart from each other. Water the soil thoroughly, being careful not to wash it away from the seeds. Set the box in a sunny location and continue to water as necessary. Have students record the number of seeds that sprout at either end of the box. Plan time to discuss the need for flowering plants to have adequate space around them to carry out their life processes.

Food Chains and Food Webs

Introduction

A frog eats a mosquito, a snake eats the frog, and an eagle eats the snake. This is an example of just one of the many food chains in nature. Each organism in an environment is dependent upon one or more other organisms for its survival. The elimination of one species of organism from an environment may have a significant impact on other species. All plants and animals, including humans, can diagram their dietary needs using a food chain or a food web. A food chain or web is the schematic diagram of what each living organism eats.

Research Questions

1. How does a food chain or food web help us to better understand a living organism?

2. What do *herbivore, carnivore,* and *omnivore* mean? How are they related to food chains and food webs?

3. Which items tend to be at the beginning of a food chain, and which are at the end?

4. Make a food chain or food web for yourself.

5. What problems may occur if an element is eliminated from the food chain? What are some of the reasons that this may happen?

 ## Web Sites

http://edu.leeds.ac.uk/~edu/technology/epb97/forest/azfoodcw.htm
    The A to Z of Food Chains and Webs is an all-inclusive site with loads of valuable information. (S: 4–6, T: All)

http://www.kapili.com/biology4kids/eco/index.html
    Students can learn all about ecosystems at this site. Lots of information about food chains and food webs. (S: 4–6)

http://www.alienexplorer.com/ecology/e37.html
    This site is student-friendly, with a lot of factual information about food chains. (S: 4–6, T: All)

 **Literature Resources**

Barré, Michel. (1998). *Animals and the Quest for Food*. Milwaukee, WI: Stevens Publishing.
This text comments on the hunters and prey of the animal kingdom. The ways in which animals obtain food, digest food, and eat food are also examined.

Geraghty, Paul. (1989). *Over the Steamy Swamp*. San Diego: Harcourt Brace Jovanovich.
A hungry mosquito starts a food chain in a steamy swamp, as each hungry animal both preys and is preyed upon.

Godkin, Celia. (1993). *Wolf Island*. New York: Scientific American Books for Young Readers.
When a family of wolves is removed from the food chain on a small island, the other animals living there feel the impact on the island's ecology.

Kalman, Bobbie. (1998). *What Are Food Chains and Webs?* New York: Crabtree.
Food chains and food webs are discussed simply in this book. Both herbivores and carnivores are discussed. Energy, food production, and decomposition of various ecosystems are commented on also.

Lauber, Patricia. (1995). *Who Eats What?* New York: HarperCollins.
The concepts of food chains and food webs are explained. The ecological link between humans, animals, and plants is explained.

Penny, Malcolm. (1988). *Hunting and Stalking*. New York: Bookwright.
This book explains what makes a good predator, the difference between the animals of the night and the day, and other special features used by predators and prey.

Shahan, Sherry. (1995). *Barnacles Eat with Their Feet: Delicious Facts About the Tide Pool Food Chain*. Brookfield, CT: Millbrook Press.
This book describes the physical characteristics and eating habits of plants, crustaceans, and other sea creatures that make their home in the tide pools.

 **Activities and Projects**

1. Ask students to gather or identify things outside that may be a potential food source or need a food source (e.g., sun, tree, acorn, bees). Have the students work with a partner to choose one of the items to make a food web. Encourage the children to include at least four other items on the food chain. For example, if the bee were chosen, the chain would include items such as:

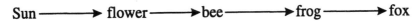

Sun ⟶ flower ⟶ bee ⟶ frog ⟶ fox

Each group should have a turn to write their web on the chalkboard. The class will help to further enhance the web. When each web is discussed, invite each group to put their web on tagboard with illustrations. Display the food webs on a classroom wall entitled "What's for breakfast, lunch, or dinner?"

2. Ask students to choose a plant or animal that interests them, then research their organism using Web sites, books, film strips, and so forth. Have them create a food chain or web and discuss it with you, then write a story, with appropriate illustrations, which incorporates the information.

3. Invite the students to create a food web or chain that they are directly linked to. For example, students can cut pictures out of magazines and place them in the order in which they may be eaten. An example would be a picture of grass, then a cow eating grass, then a human being eating a hamburger. A story should accompany the food web or food chain explaining why the student chose this food chain or web.

4. With a partner, students should pick three animals in the same food chain, excluding humans. For example, an insect, a bird, and a cat. Have the students determine whether each animal is an herbivore, a carnivore, or an omnivore. Students must create a habitat that their food chain would be found within. Each group should create a habitat in a shoebox or any other type of box. Have each group display the finished project around the room and explain the food chain to the class.

5. Have students create their own food chains. They should start by diagramming their chains on a piece of paper. The students should enjoy actually creating a three-dimensional representation of their chains, as follows: On a 1 1/2-by-4-inch piece of construction paper they should place a picture of each element of their food chain (from a magazine, the Internet, or by drawing it). Invite them to link each strip together. Similar elements on the food chain should be joined together to create a food web. The class may want to agree ahead of time on the colors of paper that represent the different kingdoms (e.g., plants may be red, orange, and yellow; animals may be black, blue, and purple). The color representation could even be broken down further, or it could be completely bypassed.

Habitats

Introduction

Basically defined, a habitat is an area in which different kinds of plants and animals live. The rainforest is a habitat. The desert is a habitat. The plants and animals that live in the rainforest habitat probably could not live in the desert habitat because each plant or animal has adapted to the environment in which it lives. In essence, every habitat has its own unique ecosystem.

Ecosystems are places in which plants and animals live side by side and help each other survive. For example, plants produce oxygen that animals need to breathe. When animals exhale, they produce carbon dioxide, a gas plants need to survive. Animals eat plants as well as other animals. In many ways, all life on Earth is interconnected, and what affects one organism may have an effect on many other organisms.

Research Questions

1. What are the key ingredients necessary for a habitat?

2. What effect do humans have on a habitat?

3. Which habitat is the most diverse?

4. What types of habitats are found in the United States?

Web Sites

http://tqjunior.advanced.org/6225/index.html
Biomes in Our Modern Environment was created by the Rogers Public School. This student-created site contains information on all six biomes. Information describing the grasslands, the tundra, the taiga, tropical rain forest, temperate forest, and the desert is presented. (S: K–3)

http://www.nwf.org/nwf/kids/cool
Take a Cool Tour of Water, Wetlands, Endangered Species, and Our Public Lands is sponsored by the National Wildlife Foundation. The site provides kids with information on the description of a wetland, as well as its functions. Additionally, information about the connection between wetlands and wildlife is presented. (S: 4–6)

http://www.nwf.org/habitats/schoolyard/basics/provide.cfm
This site is entitled School Yard Habitats. The basics of any habitat—food, water, cover, and places to raise young—are presented and can lay the basis for this or other habitat activities. (T: All)

http://www.kaytee.com/discovery/habitats/
    This site defines a habitat in addition to focusing on four of our 12 ecosystems. The interdependency among organisms that live in the prairie, urban areas, temperate forest, and wetlands is described. (S: 4–6)

Literature Resources

Buller, Laura & Taylor, Ron. (1990). *Habitats and Environments*. New York: Cavendish.
    Filled with many wonderful projects and experiments to explore different habitats of different animals, this book includes instructions on building a butterfly farm, bird feeder, forest, and pond.

Dewey, Jennifer. (1974). *Animal Architecture*. New York: Harcourt Brace Jovanovich.
    This book shows the many structures animals build to live in. Animal Architecture gives illustrations of animals and their houses such as a bird and a nest, a spider and its web, and bees in their hive.

Gibbons, Gail. (1993). *Caves and Caverns*. San Diego: Harcourt Brace.
    This book takes students on an exploration of caves and caverns. Students are shown how cave formations are made. Kids are led to discover the life in and around caves and caverns.

Parker, Philip. (1994). *Your Living Home*. New York: Thomas Learning.
    This book explores the world of animals that make their homes in or around humans. A description of each animal from mites to mice is accompanied by illustrations. Children are given experiments to reinforce the facts that are provided. The "Did You Know" section includes interesting facts about certain kinds of animals.

————. (1994). *Your Wild Neighborhood*. New York: Thomas Learning.
    This book introduces students to the wildlife they will encounter in their neighborhoods, whether they live in a city or a rural area. Interesting facts are given in the "Did You Know?" sections. Experiments accompany each section of this book.

Parker, Steven. (1988). *Pond and River*. New York: Knopf.
    This book explores ponds and rivers and the animals that live there. Rivers and ponds are busy habitats for many plants and animals. These plants and animals help each other survive, and children can discover how they do it.

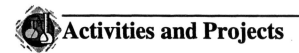

Activities and Projects

1. If possible, take students on a habitat walk. Explore some of the local habitats in your area, such as a deciduous or coniferous forest, grassland, marsh, beach, desert, wetland, local park, or schoolyard. Ask students to take a notebook along on the walk to record their observations. Activities on the walk could include student drawings of the site and a listing of all the known species of living and the nonliving things. Have students deduce how the living and nonliving things are dependent on each other. If possible go on a second habitat walk that explores another type of environment. Students may wish to repeat the above procedure. As a class, complete a comparison and contrast between the two habitats using a Venn diagram.

2. Have students work in groups of three to research the elements necessary for a habitat, using Internet sources such as www.nwf.org/habitats.schoolyard/basics/provide.cfm. Each team should use long sheets of paper, construction paper, colored paper, scissors, glue, and markers to create a three-dimensional mural illustrating a habitat of their choice that contains all of the elements. Each element should be labeled.

3. After students learn about habitats, have them choose the "house" they would most want to live in. Invite students to state reasons for their choice. Ask them to explain what they would need to build one to fit their needs. Encourage them to draw a picture of how they would decorate their habitat.

4. Take students on a walk around the school grounds. Ask them to bring a notebook so they can list all of the different animal homes they see. Make sure they pay attention to hidden homes such as termites in a dead tree. Compile all of the findings and have the students make a large poster of what they saw around the schoolyard. Display the poster in the school.

Invertebrates

Introduction

The most common types of animals on Earth are unique because they are spineless. From spiders to jellyfish, these interesting creatures fascinate children. There are more than 1 million known species of invertebrates and only about 40,000 species of vertebrates.

Nearly all the major types of invertebrates had come into being by about 500 million years ago. They all still lived in the sea. Some, such as worms and jellyfish, had soft bodies. Others, such as starfish and snails, had hard outer skeletons. The most advanced early invertebrates were trilobites. These were flat shellfish that crawled along the bottom of the sea. Trilobites were related to later invertebrates such as crabs, shrimp, spiders, and insects.

Research Questions

1. What is the difference between invertebrates and vertebrates?

2. Are all invertebrates soft-bodied?

3. Can invertebrates live in water and on land?

4. Are all insects invertebrates?

5. Why are invertebrates so common?

6. Why are many invertebrates becoming endangered?

Web Sites

http://nyelabs.kcts.org/tv/98_12/eg75.html
Bill Nye presents facts about invertebrates such as worms, squid, clams, flies, and more. Students can find the answers to their questions and view pictures. This site also includes experiment ideas. (S: All)

http://www.aqua.org/animals/species/jellies/whatis.html
Students can discover fun trivia facts about jellyfish at this site. They will also explore the life cycle and why these creatures sting. (S: 4–6, T: All)

http://www.selu.com/bio/wildlife/gallery.html#Invertebrates
Students can click on any invertebrate to read about its characteristics and view a picture. From the Brazilian cockroach to the zebra longwing butterfly, students can look at close-up pictures of these interesting invertebrates. (S: All)

http://www.cyhaus.com/marine/inverts.htm

At this site students can view invertebrates that live in the water. They will learn about how these invertebrates adapt to their environment. Students can find out what phylum each invertebrate belongs to and whether or not it has an exoskeleton. (S: All)

 # Literature Resources

Fredericks, Anthony D. (1996). *Weird Walkers*. Minnetonka, MN: NorthWord Press.

Millipedes, snails, starfish, and hydras are all weird walking invertebrates. Some walk in the water and some on land. In this book students can view illustrations and read fun facts about these fascinating creatures.

Greenberg, David T. (1997). *Bugs!* Boston: Little, Brown.

From playmates to lunch, children will love to find out how much fun bugs can be. Whether they like them or hate them, children will enjoy exploring the humorous ways to investigate the bugs' world.

Landau, Elaine. (1991). *Interesting Invertebrates: A Look at Some Animals Without Backbones*. New York: Watts.

From sponges to oysters, these invertebrates have interesting characteristics and a variety of habitats.

Landau, Elaine. (1999). *Jellyfish*. New York: Grolier.

In this book students can explore the unique features, habitats, and other facts about jellyfish. Why do they sting people? Enjoy the colorful photos of these slimy invertebrates.

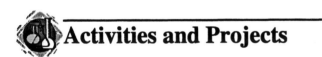 # Activities and Projects

1. Divide students into small groups to choose their favorite invertebrate, using the supplied Web sites and literature resources. Each group of students should discuss their creature and use the sources to find habitat, scientific names, species, evolution, reproduction, and other facts about their creatures. Each group will present their findings to the class orally.

2. Provide the students with a few earthworms. Encourage the students to observe their behavior. How do they move? How do they behave? What are some of their physical characteristics? Are the characteristics of earthworms similar to those of any other animal? Are those characteristics similar to other invertebrates?

3. Invite an entomologist to visit the class. Ask the entomologist to bring in insects that the students will be able to touch and view. Explain to the class that an entomologist is a person who studies insects. The entomologist should explain to the students why and how she or he studies insects.

4. Ask students to create a Venn diagram comparing invertebrates and vertebrates. What are their similarities? What are their differences? Plan opportunities for students to discuss their findings.

5. Provide students with the following statements. Inform them that one fact is incorrect in each of the examples. Ask students to circle the incorrect part and then write in the correct fact (answers are provided).

The arthropods are a large group of invertebrates. They have a hard inner skeleton known as an exoskeleton. (They have a hard *outer* skeleton.)

Other features of this group include jointed legs and a segmented body. Groups of arthropods include spiders, insects, and worms (include spiders, insects, and *centipedes*).

The largest group of arthropods is the insects. They have three pairs of legs and six body sections (*three* body sections).

The antennae enable an insect to smell and feel. They are usually joined at the thorax (joined to the *head*).

When an insect outgrows its exoskeleton, it sheds it. This is known as molding (is known as *molting*).

Plant Parts

Introduction

Flowering seed plants have six basic parts. The root holds the plant firmly in the ground, takes in water and minerals from the soil, and conducts them to the stem. The stem produces the leaves and holds them up to the sunlight. It also conducts water and minerals from the roots to the leaves and carries the food from the leaves to the roots. The leaves make the food that the plant needs to survive. They let carbon dioxide into the plant while releasing oxygen into the surrounding atmosphere. The flower is that part of the plant that produces seeds from which new plants can grow. The fruit is the protective covering for the seed. The seed is the part of the plant that can grow into a new plant.

Research Questions

1. Why are roots important to a plant?

2. What function does the stem serve?

3. Why are leaves considered an important part of a plant?

4. What are some examples of fleshy fruits?

5. What is the world's largest seed?

Web Sites

http://tqjunior.advanced.org/3715
This site explains how plants grow and reproduce. It also explains about each part of the plant. There is a diagram of a plant and sections to choose from such as spreading seeds, growth, pollination, germination, photosynthesis, and monocots and dicots. (T: 4–6)

Literature Resources

Gibbons, Gail. (1991). *From Seed to Plant*. New York: Holiday House.
This book shows different kinds of plants and the different function of each part of each plant. There are many labeled diagrams of the parts and explanations of what they do.

Gutnick, Martin. J. (1976). *How Plants Make Food*. Chicago: Children's Press.
A girl named Brenda does experiments with plants to show us the different functions of the plant parts. The book describes what plants really need to survive.

Heller, Ruth. (1992). *Plants That Never Bloom*. New York: Grosset & Dunlap.
    This easy-to-read rhyming book describes which plants do not bloom and where they live. The plants that are focused on are moss, liverworts, ferns, seaweed, mushrooms, algae, and lichen.

Julivert, Maria Angles. (1993). *The Life of Plants*. Philadelphia: Chelsea House.
    This book introduces all the parts of a plant and their functions. Photosynthesis, pollination, reproduction, and respiration are described. Experiments are also included.

Selsam, Millicent E. & Hunt, Joyce. (1978). *A First Look at the World of Plants*. New York: Walker.
    A living thing that is not an animal is a plant. This book describes what a plant is and illustrates the plant parts. It is a very easy-to-read rhyming book. There are very simple and easy to understand illustrations.

Activities and Projects

1. Provide students with three glasses of water, each with a different quantity of sugar mixed in (1 tablespoon, 3 tablespoons, and 5 tablespoons). Mix some food coloring in the water and place a celery stalk in each glass. Ask students to measure how long it takes for the colored water to rise three inches in each celery stalk. Does the amount of sugar in the water affect the rate at which the water rises in the stem of the celery? Invite students to make projections about other plants.

2. Put three bean plants on the windowsill of your classroom. Cover one with light cellophane, one with dark cellophane, and leave one uncovered. Provide the plants with equal amounts of water. Invite students to note any differences in growing rates among the three plants. Did the color of the light getting to a plant affect its rate of growth?

3. Show students photos or slides of various plants with different root structures, for example, plants with broad, expansive root structures; plants with short, stubby root structures; and plants with massive, deeply penetrating root structures. Ask students to speculate about the condition of the soil or the amount of rainfall in the area in which each plant grows.

4. Ask students to develop an experiment that would test the ability of different root systems to absorb water. Which type of root system takes in the most water? Do the roots determine how much water is taken in, or do the nutrients in the water determine the rate of osmosis?

5. Ask students to create a classroom garden. Several different sites can be constructed, such as in milk cartons, in a plot of land on the school playground, or in the classroom. Have students grow several different plants using various soil types, light factors, and nutrients, What effects do these factors have on the condition of the leaves, roots, and stems?

6. Provide students with a varied collection of vegetable seeds. Ask small groups of students to classify and categorize the seeds (large, small, smooth, rough, brown, white, red, etc.). Are there any physical features that might be advantageous to the germination of a seed? What does a seed need for germination?

Plant Processes

Introduction

The plant process most of us are familiar with is *photosynthesis,* the means whereby a plant makes it own food. It does this by trapping sunlight and changing it into a form of chemical energy. That chemical energy is combined with carbon dioxide in the air to make a special kind of sugar that is transported to all parts of the plant. Through photosynthesis plants release much of the oxygen we breathe. *Transpiration* is the process by which a plant transports water throughout its system. Plants typically lose water through cells in their leaves. This loss of water pulls up more water from the roots. *Respiration* is the process whereby plants use oxygen to break down sugar into carbon dioxide and water. This action also releases energy from the sugar—energy the plant's cells need to do their work. Another process of plants is *fertilization,* or when a sperm cell joins with an egg cell to form a seed. Each seed has a seed coat, an embryo, and stored food.

Research Questions

1. What is photosynthesis?

2. What enables a plant to turn sunlight and carbon dioxide into food?

3. How do plants reproduce?

4. How do seeds grow into trees?

5. What role do animals play in the plant world?

6. Why are plants so important?

Web Sites

http://tqjunior.advanced.org/3715
This site is written for kids by kids. The information is great for students but is also useful for teachers. There are also games and activities for the students to do while visiting the site. (S: 4–6, T: All)

http://www.esf.edu/pubprog/brochure/leaves/leaves.htm
This site focuses on why leaves change color and what the plant is going through during this process. The information presented is simple yet detailed. It describes the chlorophyll breaking down due to the change in seasons. The site also goes into some detail about why some plants do not lose their leaves. (S: 4–6, T: 4–6)

http://www.ifmt.nf.ca/mi-net/enviro/photo.htm
Students who visit this site will find an interactive diagram of photosynthesis. By clicking on each component students are able to access more information about it. Factual information is presented in a clear and simple way. (S: 4–6)

http://www.ucmp.berkeley.edu/glossary/gloss3/photosyn/index.html
This site was designed by college students and explains photosynthesis in technical terms. It provides formulas and is a good site for teachers who want to know the technical aspects of photosynthesis. It is very detailed and provides a glossary of terms. (T: 4–6)

Literature Resources

Ardley, Neil. (1991). *The Science Book of Things That Grow*. New York: Harcourt Brace.
This is a super book with lots of information about plants. A great classroom resource.

Fredericks, Anthony D. (1995). *Simple Nature Experiments with Everyday Materials*. New York: Sterling.
This is a fantastic collection of nature activities that encourage students to become actively engaged in the dynamics of nature. Loads of hands-on projects and activities!

Ganeri, Anita. (1993). *What's Inside Plants*. New York: Peter Bedrick Books.
This is a very cool book that shows the reader the insides of plants, or cutaways. By showing these cutaways the author shows the student the different parts of a plant and its functions.

Heller, Ruth. (1992). *The Reason for a Flower*. New York: Grosset & Dunlap.
This book has great pictures! Heller shows the reader, through the use of many, many pictures, what a flower's purpose is. Great drawings, too. Both combined with the easy to follow text make it a nice book for students. It's a little young for an older fifth- or sixth-grader, but it is ideal for third and fourth grades.

Johnson, Sylvia. (1986). *How Leaves Change*. Minneapolis, MN: Lerner.
This is a lower level book that describes why and how leaves change colors. It takes the reader through the four seasons and notes the differences to the tree and its leaves. This is a very good book to introduce children to the plant processes.

Rafferty, Kevin. (1989). *Kids Gardening: A Kid's Guide to Messing Around in the Dirt*. Palo Alto, CA: Klutz Press.
This is a superior resource jam-packed with super activities and lighthearted explorations of the natural world.

Ross, Bill. (1995). *Straight From the Bear's Mouth: The Story of Photosynthesis*. New York: Simon & Schuster.
This story was written to introduce children to the photosynthesis process. It details simple concepts like "the sun is energy" and "the plants need energy for photosynthesis."

Activities and Projects

1. Obtain two similar potted plants (of equal vigor and height). Ask students to select 20 leaves on one plant. Ask students to smear a thin layer of petroleum jelly on the tops of 10 leaves and the bottoms of 10 other leaves (on the same plant). Place both plants on a windowsill and water and fertilize as necessary. After several days invite students to observe the two plants and note any differences. What happened to the leaves with petroleum jelly on the top? What happened to the leaves with petroleum jelly on the bottom? What can this tell us about some of the processes of plants?

2. Obtain two similar potted plants (of equal vigor and height). Water and fertilize the plants as necessary. Ask one student to place a large, clear cellophane bag over the top of one plant, securing it around the pot with a rubber band (The bag should be as air tight as possible around the plant.) Place the plants on a windowsill. After several days ask students to note what happens inside the bagged plant. Students may wish to occasionally remove the bag from that plant and measure the amount of water that is transpired by the plant. Be sure to keep both plants adequately watered.

3. Ask students to consult library books to determine how seeds travel. Encourage students to construct a large chart with the words "water," "wind," "animals," and "other" printed across the top. Ask students to record the names of plants in one or more of the categories on the chart. They may want to specifically look at plants such as the milkweed, dandelion, coconut, thistle, and sugar maple. What devices do some seeds have that help them in being transported to new areas?

4. Following is an experiment that will help students learn about what seeds need to begin growing.

Materials: Thirty-six radish seeds, six plastic sandwich bags, paper towels (cut in half), water, candle wax, marker

Directions: Ask students to moisten pieces of paper towel and place them in the bottom of sandwich bags as directed below. Drop six radish seeds in each bag (leave the bags open). Label each bag with a number and then finish setting up each bag as follows:

Bag 1: paper towel, water, no light (put in a drawer or closet), room temperature.

Bag 2: paper towel, water, light, room temperature.

Bag 3: paper towel, no water, light, room temperature.

Bag 4: no paper towel (seeds floating in water), light, room temperature.

Bag 5: paper towel, water, no light, keep in refrigerator or freezer.

Bag 6: paper towel, no water, no light, room temperature, seeds covered by candle wax

Ask students to record the date and time they began this activity and check each of the bags twice daily for any changes.

Eventually, students will note that the seeds in Bag 1 and Bag 2 begin to germinate. There may be some minor change in the seeds in Bag 4. Discuss with them the fact that seeds need favorable temperature, adequate moisture, and oxygen to germinate. Light is not needed for germination.

Seeds

Introduction

A seed is the part of a plant that grows into a new plant of the same kind. All seeds have three parts: a seed coat (the covering of the seed that protects it), stored food (which helps the young plant grow until it can make its own food by photosynthesis), and the embryo (the tiny young plant inside the seed).

To grow, seeds need the right temperature, air, and room to grow. Seeds do not need sunlight when they first begin to grow because they are able to live off their stored food.

Research Questions

1. Where do seeds come from?

2. What is meant by germination rate?

3. How long can seeds be stored?

4. How do seeds grow?

5. How do seeds travel?

Web Sites

http://www.greendealer.com/seeds/HowtoGrowSeed.html
This is an extremely informative site. Detailed information is included regarding the seed itself, the germination process, soaking a seed with a hard shell, the effects of heat, light, fertilizers, and controlling disease. (S: 4–6, T: All)

http://www.creditcharge.com/sesbania/strat.html
Within this Web site is an insightful array of information about when the seeds should be planted, germination, and the stratification process in planting seeds. (T: All)

http://www2.bianca.com/shack/closet/germinating.html
This site has information about the germination process of a seed. It also investigates the planting process and the results that you should be seeing once you have planted something. (S: 4–6, T: All)

 # Literature Resources

Gibbons, Gail. (1991). *From Seed to Plant*. New York: Holiday House.

The illustrations in this book are terrific as it follows the steps of creating seeds and the process for the seeds to be produced from a flower and how the seeds are scattered around the Earth. There is an experiment in the back of the book on how to raise bean plants using black construction paper and a glass jar so the students can see the experiment.

Henry, Peggy. (1992). *The Great Mystery of Seeds for Kids*. Los Angeles: NK Lawn and Garden.

This is an extremely informative book about the many different tricks to successfully planting seeds, from where they come from to planting seeds indoors and outdoors. There are helpful hints on gardening and using the tools properly as well and hints on special types of seeds and the care necessary for them to grow.

Hughes, Monica. (1996). *A Handful of Seeds*. New York: Orchard Books.

Growing up on a farm is much different than living in a big city. After her grandmother dies, Concepcion is forced to move to a big city. Her grandmother had always taught her to save the seeds for the next planting, so Concepcion had her handful of seeds to bring to the city.

Jordan, Helene J. (1992). *How a Seed Grows*. New York: HarperCollins.

This simple text introduces the procedures for planting a seed and caring for it as it grows, as well as discussing the importance of sunlight, water, and other nutrients.

Krauss, Ruth. (1988). *The Carrot Seed*. New York: HarperCollins.

Terrific colorful illustrations for the young reader are used in this story about a little boy who plants a carrot seed, even though everyone has told him that it will not grow. He carefully tends to his seed and a carrot appears.

Lauber, Patricia. (1981). *Seeds, Pop, Stick, and Glue*. New York: Crown.

Realistic pictures in this book show plants on the move by attaching themselves to animals or people or being carried by the wind and water.

Pascoe, Elaine. (1997). *Seeds and Seedlings*. Brookfield, CT: Blackbirch Press.

This is an informative book on plant processes from seed to flower and growing plants from seeds. A section investigates what seeds need for growth, how important seed leaves are, whether plants know up and down, if plants can grow around obstacles, and if fertilizer is a helpful agent.

Petie, Harris. (1976). *The Seed the Squirrel Dropped*. New York: Prentice Hall.

In this book is the story of a cherry tree, with blossoms and fruit that develop from a seed that the squirrel dropped. It is rhythmic text.

Saunders-Smith, Gail. (1998). *Seeds*. Minneapolis, MN: Capstone Press.

This is a perfect book for younger readers, easily readable and having illustrations of different kinds of seeds and how seeds are planted.

Selsam, Millicent. (1957). *Play with Seeds*. New York: Morrow.

The contents of this book are extremely informational. It covers the plant processes from seaweed to seed plants, a flower to seeds, how a seed travels, experimentation with seeds, and the uses of seeds.

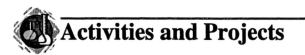

Activities and Projects

1. Following is an experiment to show students how to raise bean plants:

   a. Find a clean glass jar. Take a piece of black construction paper and roll it up.

   b. Slide the paper into the jar and fill the jar with water.

   c. Wedge the bean seeds between the black paper and the glass. Put the jar in a warm place.

   d. In a few days the seeds will begin to sprout. The root will grow down and the shoots will grow up.

   e. The plants will eventually need to be transplanted to a larger pot. Fill the larger pot with dirt.

   f. Carefully remove the small plants from the glass jar. Place them in the soil, covering them up to the base of their shoots.

   g. Water them and watch them grow.

2. To establish whether plants know up from down, do the following activity:

   a. Cut a piece of construction paper long enough to wrap around a jar and just wide enough to fit between the base and neck of the jar.

   b. Roll the construction paper loosely. Slide it into the jar and press it out against the sides.

   c. Mist the paper with water to dampen it.

   d. Put seeds between the jar sides and the paper, spacing them around the jar. Place some right side up and some on their sides and some bottom up. Press the damp paper against the side of the jar.

   e. Put the jar in a warm, bright place and do not let the paper dry out.

   f. After the seeds sprout, watch to see which way the roots and shoots are growing. Then turn the jar upside down and wait a few days.

   g. Have the students do a writing activity to describe the results and the reasons for those results.

3. Conduct the following experiment with the students to establish if fertilizer helps seedlings grow:

   a. Take two sponges and wet them thoroughly, then sprinkle grass seed over them.

   b. Place the sponges in dishes in a warm bright spot.

   c. Keep the sponges moist with water; once the seeds sprout, continue to add water to the saucers. Once a week add fertilizer to one saucer.

   d. Have the students record the results and whether they think there is a benefit to using fertilizer.

4. Distribute a lima bean, a sheet of paper, and a magnifying glass to each student or group. Ask students to examine their seeds. Tell them to look closely at their seeds and draw what they see on their papers. Soak the seeds in water overnight. The next day ask students to examine the seeds again, carefully and closely. Instruct students to look for any changes. Discuss the changes they observe. Ask students to gently open the seeds along their natural openings—the seam (stress how gently this must be done). Ask students to discuss what they see inside and have them to draw what they see. Encourage students to discuss changes in the two drawings.

Trees and Forests

 ## Introduction

For many years there was a belief that this country's supplies of trees was inexhaustible. Over the past 200 years, much of the forested land in this country was cleared for lumber or farming. Only in recent years have we begun to understand that wholesale destruction of forests has serious consequences for plants, animals, and people. This unit can help students become more aware of the value of trees and the need for preserving this nation's forest land.

 ## Research Questions

1. How can you tell how old a tree is?

2. What are three products or crops that come from trees?

3. Why is sunlight important to trees?

4. What is the difference between a simple leaf and a compound leaf?

5. How can you measure the height of a tree?

 ## Web Sites

http://www.alienexplorer.com/ecology/topic27.html

This Web site lets students investigate forests and trees such as pine, hemlock, white spruce, and sugar maples. (S: 4–6)

http://www.mobot.org/sets/temp/index.html

This Web site discusses temperate deciduous forests, where they are located, animals that live there, and why leaves change color in the fall. A section also includes the names of different leaves and pictures of them. (S: 4–6)

http://edu.leeds.ac.uk/~edu/technology/epb97/forest/aztrees.htm

The A to Z of Trees provide students and teachers with a compendium of data on trees around the world. (S: 4–6, T: 4–6)

http://www.ucmp.berkeley.edu/seedplants/conifers/conifers.html

Introduction to the Conifers offers information on these trees about which many students have misperceptions or misinformation. (T: 4–6)

Literature Resources

Arnosky, Jim. (1992). *Crinklefoot's Guide to Knowing the Trees*. New York: Bradbury.

This book is great for children, describing various aspects of trees, such as different types, their uses in the forest, and how to tell how old they are.

Burnie, David. (1988). *Trees*. New York: Knopf.

This book discusses various types of trees, the growth of trees, pollination, and inhabitants of trees, among other topics.

Collard, Sneed. (1994). *Green Giants*. Minnetonka, MN: NorthWord Press.

This is a wonderful look at some of the giants of the plant world. Lots of information and delightful photography highlight this book.

Locker, Thomas. (1995). *Sky Tree*. New York: HarperCollins.

This impressive book combines the beauty of the four seasons with the life cycle of a single tree. This is a "must have" book for any classroom.

Markle, Sandra. (1993). *Outside and Inside Trees*. New York: Bradbury.

This book explores the various parts of a tree, including the bark, the trunk, the roots, and the leaves.

Reed-Jones, Carol. (1995). *The Tree in the Ancient Forest*. Nevada City, CA: Dawn Publications.

Using a cumulative format, the author tells many stories about the creatures that inhabit the branches, leaves, and roots of a forest tree. A super read-aloud book.

Viera, Linda. (1994). *The Ever-Living Tree: The Life and Times of a Coast Redwood*. New York: Walker.

This book follows the growth of a sequoia tree and events happening in the world around it. From the times of Alexander the Great and the Great Wall of China to gold being discovered in America and men walking on the moon, the development of one tree is explored.

Activities and Projects

1. Trees for Life (1103 Jefferson, Wichita, KS 67203) is an organization that uses its profits to plant fruit trees in underdeveloped countries. For a fee of $.50 per student, the organization will send you seeds, individual cartons for planting, and a teacher notebook. The type of tree they send will depends on the state in which you live, because they only send trees that are native to your region. Students should enjoy watching their seeds sprout and finally grow into seedlings.

2. Ask each student to select a tree on the school grounds and to "adopt" that tree for the length of the school year. Take pictures of each tree, have students make bark rubbings, and have them write down observations of animal or plant life in and around the

tree. Encourage students to observe their "adoptees" on a regular basis (once a week, for example) and to maintain a journal of their observations, predictions, and experiments throughout the school year. If the tree is very young, have students create a "baby album" for their tree.

3. Discuss the importance of recycling newspapers as a significant way of saving trees. Explain that approximately every four-foot stack of newspapers equals the wood from one tree. Designate one corner of your room or hallway as a newspaper recycling center. Ask students to save newspapers and stack them in the designated area. Once a week, measure the stack of newspapers and record the measurement on a chart, placing a figure of a tree on the chart each time four feet of newspapers is collected.

4. Invite students to write to the National Arbor Day Foundation (100 Arbor Avenue, Nebraska City, NE 68410) and request a copy of "The Conservation Trees" brochure. This brochure explains how trees help the environment. Ask students to draft a similar document that would apply to the trees in your particular area of the country.

5. Invite an employee of a local garden center or nursery to visit the classroom and discuss the types of trees that are native to your area of the country. What are some planting techniques? How should trees be cared for? Why are some trees easier to grow than others? Ask students to collect the responses to those and their own questions in an informative brochure or leaflet that could be distributed at the garden center or nursery.

Vertebrates

 Introduction

Vertebrates are animals with backbones. They use their bones for support, protection of internal organs, and structure. They also use their bones for protection and defense. Types of vertebrates include human beings, mammals, fish, dinosaurs, birds, and reptiles.

In humans, there are more than 200 bones in the skeletal system. These bones support the body and protect vital organs from damage. The skeleton also provides a place for muscles to be attached, thus making it possible for the body to move, breathe, and eat.

 Research Questions

1. What is the largest vertebrate? The smallest?

2. How are vertebrates classified?

3. What is the importance of animals having a backbone?

4. What is the largest bone in the human body?

 Web Sites

http://www.ucmp.berkeley.edu/mammal/mammal.html
This site allows users to discover all about mammals. Here students and teachers can click on the different groups of mammals, including marsupials, eutheria, multituberculata, and monotremata, to find out more about these animals. In addition, the site contains an audio introduction to mammals from *The Encyclopedia of Mammals*. (S: 4–6, T: All)

http://www.sbnature.org/curator3.htm
At the Ask a Curator site, students can pose questions about vertebrates to working scientists at the Santa Barbara Museum of Natural History and get responses in return. (S: 4–6)

http://birdsource.cornell.edu/index.html
This site provides students with everything they need to know about birds. Here they can get tips on bird watching and learn how they can work to protect the birds of the world. Finally, students can look up information on any type of bird they can imagine. (S: All)

http://www.yucky.com/body/
This site is a true "kids' site." On it are various facts about the human skeletal system as well as other fascinating information that kids will be researching for hours. (S: All)

Literature Resources

Burton, Maurice. (1985). *The World of Science: Warm-Blooded Animals*. New York: Facts on File.

In this book Burton does everything from explaining what a mammal is to talking about specific details concerning many different kinds of mammals. In addition, he talks about the skeletal makeup of these vertebrates.

Cole, Joanna. (1982). *A Bird's Body*. New York: Morrow.

This book discusses the anatomy of birds, including the fact that they have a backbone. In addition, Cole explains why birds are able to fly.

Cole, Joanna & Wexler, Jerome. (1978). *A Fish Hatches*. New York: Morrow.

This story describes the life of a trout, one of many vertebrates, from the time its egg was laid until it is grown.

Lauber, Patricia. (1994). *Fur, Feathers, and Flippers: How Animals Live Where They Do*. New York: Scholastic.

Lauber does an excellent job of bringing all of the many creatures in this book to life. The way that she talks about the homes of these animals makes you feel you are right there with them.

Roy, Ron. (1986). *Big and Small, Short and Tall*. New York: Clarion.

Roy compares the largest and smallest of several different kinds of animals. Included in these comparisons are dogs, sharks, birds, snakes, and more.

Segaloff, Nat & Erickson, Paul. (1990). *Fish Tales*. New York: Sterling.

This book describes the characteristics, habitat, and behavior of all kinds of fish.

Selsam, Millicent E. & Hunt, Joyce. (1978). *A First Look at Animals with Backbones*. New York: Walker.

This book provides an introduction to the major groups of this category: fish, amphibians, reptiles, birds, and mammals. The information and diagrams are spectacular.

Silverstein, Dr. Alvin, Silverstein, Virginia & Silverstein, Robert. (1996). *The Kingdom of Life: Vertebrates*. New York: Twenty-First Century Books.

This book explains how animals are classified and what a vertebrate is. There is in-depth information on a variety of vertebrates.

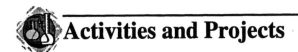

Activities and Projects

1. Explain to your class that vertebrates are animals that have backbones and invertebrates are animals that do not. Discuss reasons why vertebrates might have bones and the functions that these bones serve. Have your students brainstorm the types of animals that are vertebrates and invertebrates. Use a Venn diagram to categorize these animals into vertebrates and invertebrates. Using the knowledge gained, create a classroom semantic web about vertebrates. Display this web in a prominent area where the children will have easy access to it. Allow students to come back to the web for revision and easy reference. Ask students where human beings belong on the Venn diagram and why.

2. Divide the students into groups of three or four. Ask each group to think of a place or a habitat where animals live. Provide the students with a large sheet of paper and have them draw a mural of this particular habitat. Ask them to include all of the animals that live in this habitat. Then ask the students to find information about these animals, using the books in the classroom and the library, as well as Internet sites. Have them write a brief introduction to each animal and whether or not it is a vertebrate. Display these murals in the hallway so that others can learn about different vertebrates that live in a variety of places.

3. Assign students to work in small groups of three or four. Ask each group to create a picture dictionary of vertebrates. Groups can be broken up into sections of the alphabet for ease. Get copies of magazines that have animal pictures, such as *National Geographic* and *Animal Planet.* Have the students cut and paste these pictures onto paper that can later be bound together to form a classroom vertebrate dictionary. Allow students to add new animals to this dictionary as they are discovered to be vertebrates. They should include a short description of each animal. Place this dictionary in the reference section of your classroom library and let students refer back to it as often as needed.

4. Have students select one of the animals from the vertebrate dictionary that your class has created. Each student should write an autobiography, pretending to be the animal selected. The autobiography should include animal name, class, and kingdom as well as areas where the animal is found, its diet, and its recreational activities. All autobiographies should include cover illustrations. Children may need to refer to trade books and Internet sources for this project. When they are completed, invite the child to share their autobiographies with the class. Display the autobiographies for the class and remember to allow the children to refer back to them in the future.

5. Ask students to think about how different vertebrates interact with one another. Then have the students form groups of four or five students each. Ask the groups to choose several vertebrates that interact together. Next, have each group member decide which one they would like to discover more about. Supply the students with books, Internet access, and magazines and allow them time to gather information about their animals. Then ask each group to write a skit about how their animals interact. They may wish to use a variety of art materials to create masks, costumes, and backgrounds for their skits. After rehearsing these skits, allow each group to perform for the class.

Chapter 5

Physical Science

From the time we get up in the morning until we climb back out of bed the next morning, our lives are influenced by a countless variety of scientific laws and principles. Although we may give little thought to the soap floating in the bathtub, the static electricity in the carpet, or the mechanical can opener on the kitchen counter, they are all governed by basic tenets of science. The need to understand the forces that regulate our lives underscores the importance of physical science.

In this section your students will be able to investigate simple machines and examine the laws of physics as they apply to electricity, forms of energy, and magnetism. Students will also explore heat and light and the influence these energy forms have on our daily lives.

Understanding our world means understanding the forces that influence it. As students explore the dimensions of their physical world through the processes of science, their curiosity will be aroused and their interest stimulated. In turn, they will develop a deeper appreciation for the physical principles and precepts of nature and learn to work in harmony with these concepts.

Electricity

Introduction

Electricity is the flow of electrons. When an electric current is flowing through a material the electrons move from atom to atom inside the material. This is known as *current electricity*. Typically, current electricity flows in a circuit. There are three parts to a simple electric circuit: a source of electricity, such as a dry cell or electric generator; a path along which the electric current can travel, such as a copper wire, and an appliance that uses the electricity, such as a bell or light bulb.

In an electric circuit, the current flows from the source of electricity along one path to the appliance, passes through the appliance, and then returns through a second path to the source of the electricity. When all three parts of the circuit are connected so that an electric current is flowing, the circuit is said to be closed. When any of the three parts of the circuit are disconnected so that the current is not flowing, the circuit is said to be open.

Research Questions

1. What are some ways electricity is used?

2. What are some safety tips to remember when using electricity in your home?

3. How does electricity get to your house?

4. What is static electricity?

Web Sites

http://www.brainpop.com/science/electricity/electricity/index.weml
Brainpop is a fun Web page with a movie and a quiz. A great resource for any classroom. (S: K–3)

http://tqjunior.thinkquest.org/6064/main.html
The Shocking Truth About Electricity will provide students with a wealth of information and teachers with loads of data for any unit. (S: 4–6, T: 4–6)

http://www.thinkquest.org/php/lib/site_search.php3
A great Web site that lists twenty-nine electricity-related sites can be found here. A super resource for students and teachers. (S: 4–6, T: All)

Literature Resources

Flaherty, Michael. (1999). *Electricity and Batteries*. Brookfield, CT: Copper Beech.
This delightful introduction to electricity for younger readers includes plenty of projects for home and school.

Gibson, Gary. (1996). *Understanding Electricity*. Brookfield, CT: Millbrook Press.
Interesting activities are provided in this book as an introduction to the basic principles of electricity.

Glover, David. (1995). *Batteries, Bulbs, and Wires*. New York: Kingfisher.
Loads of super activities and projects fill the pages of this book. Perfect for younger students.

Leary, Catherine. (1998). *Awesome Experiments in Electricity and Magnetism*. New York: Sterling.
Lots of interactive and dynamic experiments using electricity are included in this delightful resource.

Parker, Steve. (1992). *Electricity*. New York: DK Publishing.
Electricity explains the history and discovery of electricity. Also discussed is how electricity is used, from electrical charges to power plants. Communication with and without the use of electricity is also shown.

Riley, Peter D. (1999). *Electricity*. Danbury, CT: Watts.
The scientific principles of electricity are discussed in this book. Experiments are also provided.

Walley, Margaret. (1997). *Electricity and Magnetism*. New York: World Book.
Experiments and activities in this book introduce the basic principles of electricity and magnetism. A truly outstanding resource for *every* classroom.

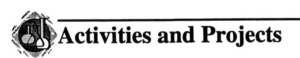

Activities and Projects

1. Provide each student with an already inflated balloon. Ask the children to rub the balloons vigorously against their heads, then stick the balloons on a wall. If done correctly, the balloons should "magically" hang on the wall. At the conclusion of this activity, ask the students to write down in their journals their reactions and ideas about why the balloons stuck to the wall.

2. Invite a lineman from the local electric company to discuss safety when dealing with electricity. At the conclusion of the presentation, ask the students to promote electrical safety by creating posters and brochures about the topic. These safety fliers can be placed around the school as well as in the community.

3. Divide the class into groups. Have each group brainstorm ideas about what electricity might be used for in the future. When the groups have their ideas they should then create dioramas in shoe boxes demonstrating their ideas. At the completion of the projects, each group should present their "future inventions" to the class.

4. Discuss conductors and insulators with the class. Have the students create a list of both conductors and insulators, then ask them to find pieces or parts of the items on the lists. These items may include, but are not limited to, rubber, wood, metal, and plastic. As the students bring the items to class, have them place them in designated areas of the classroom. Upon completion of the piles, ask the students to make a class collage or display of the items.

Forms of Energy

Introduction

Energy is the ability of matter to move other matter or to produce a chemical change in other matter. Scientists divide energy into six different forms: Mechanical energy is the energy produced from all kinds of machines. Heat energy is the energy produced by the moving molecules in a substance. Electrical energy is the energy produced by electrons moving through a substance. Wave energy is the energy that travels in waves. Two examples of wave energy are sound energy (which is produced when matter moves back and forth, or vibrates, rapidly) and radiant energy (which includes light rays, X-rays, radio waves, infrared waves, ultraviolet rays, cosmic rays, and radiant heat). Chemical energy occurs when a chemical reaction takes place and new substances are formed. Nuclear energy comes from the nucleus of the atom when the atom splits in two.

Energy can be changed from one form to another. However, in all these changes the energy is not destroyed, but changed in form instead. The Law of Conservation of Energy says that energy is neither created nor destroyed, but only changed from one form to another.

Research Questions

1. What is the difference between potential and kinetic energy?

2. What is solar energy?

3. What form of energy is most used in the United States?

4. What is the Law of Conservation of Energy?

5. How many different forms of energy do you have in your house?

Web Sites

http://www.eren.doe.gov/erec/factsheets/rnwenrgy.html
At this site, Learning About Renewal Energy, renewable energy is defined and explained. Solar, photovoltaic, geothermal, and biomass energy are also explained. (S: 4–6)

http://www.eren.doe.gov/solarnow.html
This site is entitled The Solar Now Project. The history of solar energy is explained, along with renewable energy, and the overall energy system. (S: 4–6, T: 4–6)

http://www.eren.doe.gov/roofus

Roofus's Solar and Efficient Neighborhood is an excellent site for younger children. On the site a dog, Roofus, uses his dog house to explain energy. He explains how to conserve energy and what energy actually is. (S: K–3, T: 3–K)

http://www.miamisci.org/af/sln/

The Atoms Family examines in great detail energy conservation, potential energy, kinetic energy, and different forms of electricity. (S: 4–6, T: All)

http://www.mos.org/sln/toe/toe.html

Theater of Electricity includes a picture gallery and a video gallery of electricity for students to explore. The history of electricity, safety with electricity, and other information about electricity can be found at this site. (S: 4–6, T: All)

http://www.pbs.org/wgbh/pages/amex/three/timeline/index.html

The Timeline of Nuclear Technology is just that. It is a great site for children to find concrete facts about when the Atomic Energy Act was developed or when various atomic plants were built. (S: 4–6, T: 4–6)

 # Literature Resources

Asimov, Isaac. (1983). *How Did We Find out About Solar Power?* New York: Walker.

Asimov describes what the sun's energy has been used for from the times of the Romans and Greeks up to the present day. The possibilities of energy in the future as discussed as well.

Harlow, Rosie & Morgan, Sally. (1995). *Energy and Power*. New York: Kingfisher.

This text includes a very informative and simplified description of the various forms of energy. For each type of energy experiments are suggested.

Johnston, Tom. (1988). *Energy: Making It Work*. Milwaukee, WI: Gareth Stevens.

This book examines how one form of energy converts into another and alternative energy sources that may lie in the future.

Parker, Steve. (1997). *Science Works! Energy*. Milwaukee, WI: Gareth Stevens.

This book presents the uses of energy in its various forms.

Rickard, Graham. (1991). *Water Energy*. Milwaukee, WI: Gareth Stevens.

Rickard discusses one of the oldest forms of alternative energy, waterpower, and the ways of using it.

 # Activities and Projects

1. Invite students to access http://www.sprint.com/eputrol/epenergy.html and to answer the following questions: What can we do differently to conserve energy in this room? How do we know that we are wasting energy in this room? Then have students design a poster promoting energy conservation.

2. Ask students to investigate, using the Internet and literature sources, various ways energy is produced and used (e.g., hydroelectric power, solar power). After the students complete their investigations, have them create posters illustrating and describing the various forms of energy.

3. Invite students to contact one or more of the following organizations to ask for information on renewable energy, energy conservation, or any other aspect of energy usage. After the students receive their information, have them assemble it in a scrapbook.

> The Energy Efficiency and Renewable Energy Clearinghouse
> P.O. Box 3048
> Merrifield, VA 22116
>
> National Renewable Energy Laboratory
> Center for Science Education
> 1617 Cole Boulevard
> Golden, CO 80401
>
> Renew America
> 1400 16th Street, NW, Suite 710
> Washington, DC 20036

4. Plan time to discuss the difference between potential (stored) and kinetic (the energy a body has because it is moving) energy. Ask students to look for common examples of kinetic energy in their everyday lives. Have them construct an oversized poster of the entire collected example. Plan time to discuss the various ways kinetic energy is illustrated.

5. Write the six different forms of energy on the chalkboard and ask students to list examples of how each form is used. Then ask students to provide examples of how energy can be changed from one form to another.

Heat

Introduction

Heat energy is the energy produced by the moving molecules in a substance. The faster the molecules move, the more heat energy the substance has, and the hotter the substance becomes. Children, like adults, often confuse two similar terms: *heat* and *temperature*. Heat refers to energy in motion. In other words, heat is the total amount of energy in the moving particles of an object or substance. Temperature is a measure of how hot something is; that is, it is a measure of the amount of heat an object has.

Heat moves through solid objects by a process known as conduction, the movement of heat from one molecule to the next. Some objects, such as those made from metal, conduct heat better than others, such as those made of wood. Heat also moves through the air and water through a process known as convection: when heat rises and sinks in moving currents.

Research Questions

1. What is the difference between heat and temperature?

2. How is heat transferred from one thing to another?

3. What is an example of conduction?

4. What is an example of convection?

Web Sites

http://www.eren.doe.gov/solarnow/solarnow.htm
   At this site children can learn about solar energy and how to store and use it in their lives. Instructions on how to make a solar oven are included. Students will learn several different energy terms and become more aware of the various uses of solar energy. (S: 4–6)

http://www.unidata.ucar.edu/staff/blynds/tmp.html#Heat
   This site fully explains the distinction between heat and temperature. It is an ideal resource for classroom teachers. (T: 4–6)

Literature Resources

Olesky, Walter. (1986). *Experiments with Heat*. Chicago: Children's Press.

In this clear, concise book the author explains the concept of heat to the young learner. Each section ends with an experiment that the reader can conduct that clearly illustrates the idea of the section. The difference between heat and temperature is also explained.

Whyman, Kathryn. (1986). *Science Today: Heat and Energy*. New York: Gloucester Press.

This book focuses on heat as a form of energy rather than as temperature. Whyman starts off by explaining what energy is, and then segues into how heat is a form of energy. The book then discusses temperature and includes a clear color illustration of where heat and energy can be found in a person's home.

Wood, Robert. W. (1998). *Heat Fundamentals: Funtastic Science Activities for Kids*. New York: Chelsea House.

This hands-on book teaches such difficult concepts as conduction, convection, evaporation, and cryogenics through easy-to-follow experiments. Wonderfully illustrated, these experiments are simple to do.

———. (1990). *Physics for Kids: 49 Easy Experiments with Heat*. New York: Tab Books.

The focus of this book is how heat can be transformed into work through producing electrical and mechanical energy. Students will learn about the potentials and limitations of heat by doing these fun experiments: how heated air can crush a can, how heat affects wind currents, and even how to make a heat monitor.

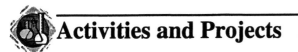

Activities and Projects

1. To measure temperature, have students work in groups of two to make water thermometers. Each group will need to fill a small soda bottle almost to the top with water. Have each group add some food coloring so they can see the water easily. The students should dry off the bottle opening and then put a straw halfway into the bottle, then stop up the bottle opening with clay, making sure that the water is about halfway up the straw. Tell the students to leave their water thermometers in the sun for an hour, then with a marker mark off the water level on the straw. Next have the students leave their water thermometers in a refrigerator for one hour, then mark the water level on the straw again. Finally, have the students measure the difference between their two marks, then on the straw mark off some even measurements between the two marks. It is important that the students distribute these marks evenly. Now the students can tape an index card to one side of their straws and label their markings. These numbers will not be a true indicator of either the Fahrenheit or Celsius scale, but they will do for the classroom. Ask the students to use their water thermometers to measure the heat of the air several times a day and keep a chart of the temperature readings for one week. At the end of the week the students should share their readings with the class.

2. To introduce the effect that heat has on creating wind you will need a lamp without the shade, talcum powder, a pencil, a piece of paper, and scissors. Turn on the lamp and allow it to heat up for a minute. Then sprinkle the talcum powder just above the light bulb. Ask the students what they see and why they think it is happening. For the second part of the experiment, cut a spiral out of the piece of paper. Balance the spiral on the point of the pencil, but be careful not to make a hole in the paper. Now hold it over the warm light bulb. Again, ask the students to describe what is happening to the spiral. It should be spinning because the air is warmed by the heat coming from the light bulb and because warm air rises. This is also the reason why the talcum powder rose.

3. Using the information at the Web site http://www.eren.doe.gov/solarnow/solarnow. htm, make a solar-powered oven with your class. For a snack you can make English muffin pizza or s'mores. Remember that this solar-powered oven cooks at a maximum of 275 degrees Fahrenheit and takes about two times as long as a regular oven does to cook.

4. Ask students to use a series of thermometers to measure the temperature of the classroom in various locations (in the corner near the ceiling, along the floor of one wall, inside a closet). Talk with students about why the temperature in a single room may vary by several degrees. Discuss with students the process of convection, in which air tends to move in currents from the top to the bottom and back up to the top of a room again. You may want to have students blow a series of bubbles in various locations in the classroom to determine the "existence" of air currents.

Light

Introduction

Turn on a flashlight and you see light. Flip a switch and you light your home. Look outside at night and see lights everywhere. By definition, light is a visible form of energy. White light, the most common form of light, is actually a combination of all the colors of the rainbow (red, orange, yellow, green, blue, indigo, and violet). Both white light and the colors of light in it are referred to as the visible spectrum.

People see colors because of what happens when light hits different colors. Objects absorb, or take in, some of the light that hits them. Objects also reflect, or bounce back, some light. An opaque object (one that light cannot pass through) reflects whatever light it does not absorb. The color of the object is actually the color of the light it reflects. For example, a green shirt absorbs all the colors of the spectrum except green. Green is the color it reflects, and hence is the color we see. A white object reflects all colors.

Research Questions

1. What is the difference between an opaque object and a transparent object?
1. What makes white objects appear white and black objects appear black?
2. What makes laser light different from ordinary light?
3. What is color?
4. What are the colors of the spectrum?

Web Sites

http://library.advanced.org/28160/english/index.html
    This Web site describes various aspects of light, including lasers, diffraction, reflection, and the history of light. Each category can be clicked on for information, and each section includes a quiz. (S: 4–6)

Literature Resources

Anderson, L.W. (1988). *Read About Light and Color*. Milwaukee, WI: Raintree Children's Books.
    This book gives students a variety of information about light and color, including the spectrum, mirrors, and lenses, in language the students will easily understand.

Burnie, David. (1992). *Light*. New York: Dorling Kindersley.
   This book contains information about various aspects of light, including reflection, refraction, lenses, and the spectrum. Each page provides historical information about each topic.

Orii, Eyi & Orii, Masako. (1989). *Simple Science Experiments with Light*. Milwaukee, WI: Gareth Stevens.
   This book describes experiments that are easy for students to conduct about light and some of the "tricks" it can play on the eye.

Ward, Alan. (1991). *Experimenting with Lights and Illusions*. Philadelphia: Chelsea House.
   This book contains various projects and experiments for students to try pertaining to light and illusion.

Williams, John. (1992). *Projects with Color and Light*. Milwaukee, WI: Gareth Stevens.
   This book includes various easy and fun projects for students to do involving light and color.

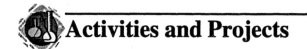Activities and Projects

1. Ask students to tape a piece of white paper to a desk near the windows. Provide them with a prism, and as the sunlight shines through the window, encourage students to "catch" the rays, making a rainbow on the paper. Provide opportunities for students to discuss the variety of colors created.

2. Set up three slide projectors in front of a white screen. Ask students to cut out circles from red, blue, and green cellophane wrap. Have students attach a different color to each projector using rubber bands. Turn off the lights and have students take turns forming various colors by combining different-colored lights.

3. Ask students to write about how their lives would be different if there was no light. What would they do to adapt to life without light? How would things be different?

4. Ask students to make a chart with the words "Transparent, " "Translucent," and "Opaque" listed across the top. (Transparent objects are those that light passes through readily, such as glass and clear plastic. Translucent objects are those that some light passes, but through which you cannot see clearly, such as waxed paper and shower doors. Opaque objects, such as wood or steel, permit no light to pass through.) Take students on a "field trip" through the school and have them make a list of the objects that could be placed in each of the three categories. Which category has the fewest items?

Magnetism

Introduction

A *magnet* is anything that pulls iron-bearing material to it. *Magnetism* is the force around a magnet. There are two types of magnets: natural and artificial. Natural magnets, or lodestones, are a type of iron ore known as magnetite. They occur in nature and have north and south poles, as do the magnets we use in our homes and schools. Artificial magnets are usually made of steel or alnico (an alloy of aluminum, nickel, copper, and cobalt). These magnets are commonly in the shape of a bar or horseshoe. Most of the magnets we use on our refrigerator doors and in our toys are alnico magnets.

Research Questions

1. What is magnetism?

2. What happens when a piece of iron is stroked with lodestone?

3. In an ordinary magnet, where are the strongest forces?

4. When a magnet is broken in half, what occurs?

5. What are some everyday objects that have magnets in them?

Web Sites

http://www.technicoil.com/magnetism.html

Although there is no clear definition of a magnetic field here, this site offers young learners a variety of theories on the subject. Students will be able to recognize that many of the magnetic forces come from the Earth itself. (S: 4–6)

http://www.science-tech.nmstc.ca/engine.cfm?function=link&idx=1367&museum=sat& language=english

Background Information for Magnets contains answers to some of the more commonly asked questions on this topic. Lots of great information! (S: All, T: All)

http://www.exploratorium.edu/snacks/iconmagnetism.html

Lots of activities, experiments, and information about magnets can be found on this site. (T: All)

Literature Resources

Branley, Franklyn M. (1996). *What Makes a Magnet?* New York: HarperCollins.

This book describes how magnets work and includes instructions for making a magnet and a compass. Students will find this simple-to-read book fascinating because it includes great projects for learning about magnetism. Students will also learn that the Earth itself is a magnet because the north-seeking pole of the compass points to the north and the south-seeking pole points to the south.

Catherall, Ed. (1982). *Magnets*. Morristown, NJ: Silver Burdett.

In this book magnets and the magnetic force are discussed, including making magnets, electromagnets, and the Earth as a magnet. This book offers different types of activities that can be performed with a magnet. Students will find out what the strongest part of the magnet is, how to make a magnetic compass, what magnetic attraction and repulsion are, and much more.

Challand, Helen J. (1986). *Experiments with Magnets*. Chicago: Children's Press.

This stimulating book offers several experiments on magnets and magnetism, demonstrating the magnetic field and the properties, strength, and uses of magnets. Students will find out what magnets are, about natural magnets and electromagnets, and what the uses of magnets are.

Kirkpatrick, Rena K. (1985). *Magnets.* Milwaukee, WI; Raintree Children's Books.

This is a very easy-to-read book about magnets. Readers will learn whether all magnets are the same, what the poles do, if both poles are the same, where the magnet has power, where the magnetic north pole is located, and much more. There is also a fact sheet that provides an overview of what was discussed in the book.

Parker, Steven. (1998). *Magnets*. Milwaukee, WI: Gareth Stevens.

This simple-to-understand book describes different kinds of magnets and how they are used and presents a variety of experiments and other activities invoking magnetism.

Vecchione, Glen. (1995). *Magnet Science*. New York: Sterling.

This book relates the discovery of magnetism, discusses the principles behind it, and suggests experiments that offer a "hands-on, mind-on" explanation of how it works. Students will understand that magnets are everywhere and find what does and does not attract.

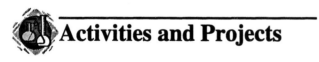

Activities and Projects

1. Obtain a sheet of thin cardboard and some iron filings (available at toy, hobby, or hardware stores). Draw a simple outline of a person's face on the cardboard (head, eyes, nose, mouth, ears, etc.). Place four water glasses on a table and place the cardboard so that the corners rest on the edges of the glasses. Sprinkle some iron filings in the middle of the illustration. Provide students with a strong bar magnet (available at most large toy stores) and invite them to move it underneath the cardboard so that the iron filings can be moved around the face. Encourage students to put a beard, mustache, eyebrows, and other "hair" on various parts of the face.

2. Put different things in a box: a penny, a paper clip, a nickel, a dime, a twig, bits of aluminum foil, rubber bands, and a piece of paper. Next, get a pencil; tie a piece of string to one end of the pencil and then tie a magnet to the other end of the string. Ask students to fish for selected objects. Students will discover which objects are attracted to and which are not attracted to the magnet. Ask the students to explain why some were attracted and others weren't.

3. Students can make their own magnets by stroking needles (remind them to handle these with care) along one end of a magnet. Tell the students to move the needles along the magnet in only one direction, twenty to thirty times. The pull of the permanent magnet will slowly line up the atoms in the needle. The students should then touch the ends of the needles to paper clips, which the needles should lift. If the clips aren't lifted, have the students stroke the needles across the magnet a few more times. Ask the students to write a short explanation of why the needles became magnetized.

4. Have students create their own magnetic compasses using the following instructions: Rub a bar magnet lengthwise on a sewing needle (in one direction only). Carefully stick the needle part way through the top of a small piece of sponge (about one inch square). Mix a few drops of liquid detergent into a small bowl of water. Place the sponge and needle assembly in the bowl, on edge. The needle should be parallel to the water, but not touching it. The sponge and needle should float in the center of the bowl. If they don't, add one or more drops of detergent until they do. After the needle stops moving, it is pointing to the Earth's magnetic north pole.

Simple Machines

Introduction

Today, almost all physical work is done by, or with the assistance of, machines. Simple machines are the basis for almost all machines used today. There are six simple machines: the lever, inclined plane, wedge, screw, pulley, and wheel and axle. Students will be surprised to learn that almost all of the machines used in their everyday lives involve some form of one or more of these machines. The following Web sites, books, and classroom activities will help students learn how these six simple machines work, and inform them of the many forms that they can take and purposes that they serve.

Research Questions

1. How do simple machines make work easier?

2. What kind of simple machine is used to pry things loose?

3. Which simple machines do you use for lifting heavy objects?

4. What is a compound machine?

5. How is a wedge like an inclined plane?

6. Which simple machine is a variation of the wheel and axle?

Web Sites

http://library.thinkquest.org/J002079F/sub3.htm

Lots of information about simple machines can be found on this all-inclusive site that's perfect for any unit. (S: 4–6, T: All)

http://sln.fi.edu/qa97/spotlight3/spotlight3.html

The Franklin Institute in Philadelphia provides classroom teachers with an all-inclusive guide to simple machines. (T: All)

http://www.looklearnanddo.com/documents/projects.html

At Look, Learn and Do students can discover instructions for building a variety of devises all of which use simple machines. (S: All, T: All)

# Literature Resources

Dahl, Michael. (1996). *Wheels and Axles*. Mankato, MN: Capstone Press.

The simple language used in this book makes it an easy read for beginning readers. It includes literature resources for teachers, directions for students to make their own wheels, and a "words" section filled with the new vocabulary introduced in the book.

Hodge, Debra. (1998). *Simple Machines*. Toronto: Kids Can Press.

This book provides a clear understanding of the function of a simple machine. Simple machine experiments are included that are easy to understand, and best of all, the materials can be collected at home.

Lampton, Christopher. (1991). *Seesaws, Nutcrackers, and Brooms: Simple Machines That Are Really Levers*. Brookfield, CT: Millbrook Press.

Levers are all around us: crowbars, wheelbarrows, and shovels. This book describes the many ways in which levers are used in everyday life.

Pine, Tillie S. & Levine, Joseph. (1965). *Simple Machines and How We Use Them*. New York: McGraw-Hill.

This book discusses the different types of simple machines and shows how and why they work. Children will be able to understand this book easily because there are several examples that the students are probably already familiar with for each machine.

Wells, Robert E. (1996). *How Do You Lift a Lion?* Morton Grove, IL: Albert Whitman.

Gravity makes lifting difficult, but this book shows how we can use levers, wheels, and pulleys to do some of our work. Kids will love the silly things that the author does, such as lift a lion, pull a panda, and deliver a basket of bananas to a baboon birthday party. This book is best for younger students.

Activities and Projects

1. Give each of the students a large piece of paper, a pencil, and something to color with. Encourage them to use their imagination to invent their own machines using one or more of the six simple machines as their basis. Have each student sketch the machine on paper and color and label the different parts. Ask the students to write about their "inventions" in their journals. They can include a physical description of the machine, explain how it works, and describe how it will make a job easier for someone. If the students are having trouble "inventing" machines, have them think about something that they have trouble doing, or something one of their family members usually needs help doing.

2. Conduct a survey in your class to determine how many students use some specific simple machines such as: scissors, ramps, can openers, or wheelbarrows. Have the students brainstorm as a class to determine what machines to cover in the survey. First conduct the survey orally in class, then have the students fill out a survey questionnaire containing the same items. Have the students take the survey home and give it to

their family members. When all the information has been collected, determine what simple machine(s) each item listed is made from and construct a bar or pie graph to show which machines are the most popular among students and their families.

3. Ask students to make up six file folders for permanent display on a bulletin board or in a file box. Have them label each of the folders with the name of a simple machine. Have students collect photographs and illustrations of simple machines from several old magazines (or keep an eye out for current magazines and newspapers), then file each example in the appropriate folder. Provide regular opportunities for students to discuss their collections and offer reasons for assigning selected photos to a particular folder.

4. If possible, arrange for students to visit a construction site. Ask them to list all the various ways in which inclined planes are used in and around the construction site. How are the inclined planes making the work easier for the construction workers? What would they be unable to do if they did not have a simple machine such as the inclined plane?

Sound

Introduction

No matter where we go or what we do, sound is all around us. From the time we wake up in the morning until we retire at night we are surrounded by all kinds of sounds: loud and soft sounds, pleasant and unpleasant sounds, and machine and human sounds.

Although we are constantly surrounded by sound, many people would find it difficult to describe what sound is. Sound is produced when matter vibrates. When a musician strums a guitar, the vibrating strings create sound. When people talk, their vocal cords vibrate and create sound. When phones ring, pieces of metal vibrate so that sound is produced. Sounds travel through the air in waves, much like the waves in the ocean.

Sound has several different qualities. *Volume* is the loudness or softness of sound. The loudness of a sound is measured in units known as decibels (the human ear can hear decibels of 0–85 without sustaining any damage). *Pitch* describes how high or low a sound is (a flute versus a bass drum, for example). *Frequency* is the speed at which an object vibrates to create sound.

Research Questions

1. What is a decibel?

2. What are sound waves?

3. What are the differences between a high pitch, a medium pitch, and a low pitch?

4. What is sound?

5. What is a spectrograph?

Web Sites

http://sea-css.ssd.k12.wa.us/woodland/WWBlowing.html

http://sea-css.ssd.k12.wa.us/woodland/WWRinging.html

http://sea-css.ssd.k12.wa.us/woodland/WWRulers.html

These sites invite students to construct their own blowing sounds, ringing sounds, and vibrations. Included are movie clips demonstrating the creation of various sounds. (S: 4–6)

http://library.advanced.org/19537/Main.html

This is an exciting and interactive site about sound. It covers the most basic concepts of what sound is as well as the specifics of how humans perceive it. (S: All)

Literature Resources

Ardley, Neil. (1990). *Sound Waves to Music*. New York: Gloucester Press.

This book focuses on the sounds of everyday life, from musical instruments to the sounds of aircraft. A great introduction to the science of sound.

Sabbeth, Alex. (1997). *Rubber-Band Banjos and a Java Jive Bass*. New York: John Wiley & Sons.

This book presents the science of sound and music. It includes how sound is made, how the ear hears sounds, and how different musical instruments are made. The book also explains sound and movement, sound and vibration, sound and air, sound and waves, and sound and hearing.

Activities and Projects

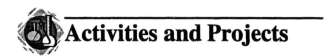

1. Ask students to blow up a balloon and stretch the neck sideways between their fingers. It makes a sound because escaping air causes the neck of the balloon to vibrate. Have the students pull hard to close the gap; a higher note will be produced. Then have them loosen the neck to open the gap and produce a lower sound. This shows that the vibration of an object makes sound. Ask students to compare and contrast the similarities between balloon and human vocal cords.

2. Have students hold a ruler over the edge of a table and twang it so it vibrates. The more effort is used, the more widely the ruler vibrates and the louder the sound is. Now have the students shorten the vibrating part. The vibration gets faster and the pitch rises as the vibrating part gets shorter. Ask the students to write down what they think would happen if they moved the ruler farther out than before and what would happen if they moved the ruler even closer to the table.

3. Stretch a piece of plastic wrap around the top of a bowl. Then have the students secure the plastic wrap around the bowl with a rubber band, making sure that the plastic is taut. Sprinkle some salt on the top of the plastic wrap. Have students make loud noises nearby, such as banging on a desk or a pan. The salt grains will jump as the waves of sound strike the plastic and make it vibrate. Have the students compare this project to the human eardrum. How is it the same?

4. If possible, borrow a tuning fork from a music teacher or from a music store. Tap the tuning fork and immediately place the fork tips barely into a bowl of water. Ask students to observe and comment on what happens to the water. Students should notice that the vibrating fork creates sound and that when the fork is placed in the water it creates waves similar to the sound waves that travel through the air.

5. Invite the school's music teacher to play several different musical instruments for your students. Ask students to classify the instruments on the basis of their pitch. Students should create a chart or graph of "Instruments with High Pitch" and "Instruments with Low Pitch."

Chapter 6

Earth Science

It's staggering to think that the planet we live on has been in existence for nearly 4.5 billion years. In many ways, that number is almost too large to comprehend. During that span of time the Earth has undergone some remarkable changes. Rocks have formed, primeval seas have ebbed and flowed across vast continents, and dramatic weather conditions have contributed to the geography and structure of our planet.

In this section students will learn about the geology of the Earth—its rocks, soil, and sand—and about how the forces of nature contribute to erosion, the Earth's temperature changes, and its never-ending cycle of rebirth and renewal. They'll discover some of the mysteries and marvels of various ecosystems around the world in addition to the climatic conditions that influence those areas.

This chapter provides innumerable opportunities for students to learn important concepts and dynamic principles that shape and govern the planet they live on. Students will not only gain an appreciation of the world around them but will be better prepared to preserve that world for their generation as well as future generations. In essence, we live on a most dynamic planet; knowing how that planet "works" will provide youngsters with significant opportunities to strike and maintain a harmonious relationship with that world.

Air Pressure

 ## Introduction

There is a strong, invisible force that pulls air down to the Earth, giving its molecules weight. The weight of the air molecules exerts a force on the Earth and everything on it. The amount of force exerted on a surface is called atmospheric pressure or air pressure. The air pressure at any level in the atmosphere can be expressed as the total weight of air, above a unit surface area, at that level in the atmosphere. Higher in the atmosphere, there are fewer air molecules pressing down from above. Consequently, air pressure always decreases with increasing height above the ground. Because air can be compressed, the density of the air (the mass of the air molecules in a given volume) normally is greatest at the ground and decreases at higher altitudes.

 ## Research Questions

1. What is air pressure?

2. How is air pressure measured?

3. How do changes in air pressure affect human activity?

4. How does altitude influence air pressure?

 ## Web Sites

http://seaboard.ndbc.noaa.gov/educate/pressure.shtml
This site provides a brief answer to the question: What is air pressure? (T: All)

http://ericir.syr.edu/Projects/Newton/10/lessons/AirPrss.html
From Newton's Apple comes this informative site on air pressure and some activities teachers can do with students. (T: All)

http://www.athena.ivv.nasa.gov/curric/weather/adptcty/pressure.html
This Web site provides the user with valuable information about air pressure. It discusses the causes of air pressure and how air pressure is measured. It also reviews how changes in air pressure affect human activity, what kinds of weather events are associated with high pressure and low pressure air masses, and how altitude influences air pressure. (S: 4–6)

Literature Resources

Dunn, Andrew. (1993). *The Power of Pressure*. New York: Thomson Learning.
This book explains how air and water pressure work and how they are used in machines.

Parramon, Jose Maria. (1985). *Air*. Hauppage, NY: Barron's.
This is a short scientific explanation of air, examining such phenomena as wind and atmospheric pressure.

Ruis, Maria. (1985). *Air: The Four Elements*. Hauppage, NY: Barron's.
This book provides a short, scientific explanation of air. It also examines such phenomena as wind and atmospheric pressure.

Activities and Projects

1. Divide the students into pairs and give each group a plastic cup. Ask students to fill the cups to the top with water. Instruct them to put an index card over the top of each cup and hold them firmly. Still holding the cards, the students should turn the cups upside down over the sink. Encourage students to write about what happened in their journals. Explain to the class that the card stays under the cup because of the air pressure. The air under the card pushes up so strongly that it keeps the card in place. That pressure is "stronger" than the weight of the water in the cup.

2. Set a small piece of paper on fire and drop it into a large glass bottle. Place one peeled, hard-boiled egg gently on the opening of the bottle, small end first. The egg may wobble on top of the opening and will then appear to be pulled into the bottle after the heated air from the fire has contracted. Explain to students that the egg was "pulled" into the bottle as a result of air pressure. The burning piece of paper used up the air in the bottle. As a result, the air pressure inside the bottle was considerably less than the air pressure outside the bottle, causing the egg to be pushed into the bottle by the increased pressure on its outer surface.

3. Place one end of a wooden ruler on a table with slightly less than half the ruler hanging off the edge. Lay a sheet of newspaper over the part of the ruler on the table. Allow students to predict what would happen if the protruding end was struck as hard as possible. Strike the protruding ruler as hard as you can. The newspaper will not move, but if you hit it hard enough, the ruler will break. This is due to the air pressure that is exerted downward. Because the paper is flat against the board and table, no air is beneath the paper to counteract the pressure from above. Ask students to calculate the surface area of the newspaper, length by width, and multiply the surface area by 14.7. This will yield the amount of air pressure exerted on the paper.

Climate

Introduction

Climate and weather are often confused. *Climate* is the "average" type of weather experienced in a particular region over an extended period of time. *Weather* refers to the atmospheric conditions that exist in a particular area at a particular time. For example, we can say that the climate in southern Florida is tropical, because over many years its weather "averages" out to tropical conditions. By the same token, we can say that the weather in Miami today is rainy, simply because that is the atmospheric condition at one specific point in time.

Research Questions

1. What is weather?

2. What is climate?

3. What part of the world has the most severe climate?

4. What part of the world has the hottest climate? Coldest climate?

Web Sites

http://www.panda.org/climate_event/report.htm
This Web site is a report about global warming and its effect on us. It's important because it talks about what causes global warming and what can be done to slow it down. A great Web site to lead off discussions and debates about this issue. (S: All, T: All)

Literature Resources

Arnold, Caroline. (1998). *El Nino: Stormy Weather for People and Wildlife*. New York: Clarion.
This is an informative and interesting book about this weather phenomenon and how it has disrupted the weather and climates around the world.

Craighead, Jean. (1997). *Arctic Son*. New York: Hyperion Books for Children.
This wonderful book takes a look at the Arctic, how people live there, and what they do there. It is an excellent book about Eskimo life.

Kroll, Virginia. (1994). *The Seasons and Someone*. San Diego: Harcourt Brace.
A wonderful book about the animals and people that live in the northernmost areas of the world.

Leslie, Clare. (1991). *Nature All Year Long*. New York: Greenwillow.
This book provides readers with a month-by-month seasonal guide to changes in plant and animal behavior.

McVey, Vicki. (1991). *The Sierra Club Book of Weatherwisdom*. San Francisco: Sierra Club.
Basic weather principles and experiments are presented in tandem with weather customs and traditions.

Stevenson, James. (1997). *Heat Wave at Mud Flat*. New York: Greenwillow.
This book is about a group of animals that can no longer take the heat where they live. They keep hoping for rain to come and relieve them. An enjoyable book that takes a funny approach to showing what happens when the climate becomes unbearable.

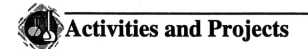 # Activities and Projects

1. Ask students to look at climates in other parts of the world. Divide the class into several small groups and ask each group to research a selected climate from around the world. They should examine the people who live in a particular climate, their habits, the clothes they wear, or the houses they live in. Have groups design an informational brochure for display in the classroom.

2. Ask students to gather newspaper and magazine articles about the weather from local and regional newspapers, then file the articles in shoe boxes that have been labeled with the names of selected climates. Over an extended period of time (several months), ask students to discuss any patterns or similarities in the weather reports.

3. Ask each child to select a different state and research the climate of that state. Students should construct an oversized map of the United States and identify specific climatic regions on the map using different colors of crayons or pencils. Ask students to discuss similarities and differences between various states as well as within a single state. (Hawaii, for example, has almost all of the 22 climatic zones found throughout the world.)

4. Invite a weather forecaster from the local television station to visit your classroom. Ask the forecaster to report on current weather conditions as well as weather predictions. The individual should explain to students how weather over an extended period of time determines the climate of an area. Ask the forecaster to discuss how the climate of your particular region of the country differs from other areas of the country.

5. Ask students to check an almanac for the yearly rainfall in your area, then locate several cities in the United States and find their normal annual precipitation. Ask them to compare the rainfall in several cities with that in your town or city. Plot this information on a large chart and ask students to note any similarities or differences.

Clouds

Introduction

Clouds are made up of countless numbers of tiny water droplets or ice crystals that have been formed from moist air being pushed upward and cooling. The three main types of clouds are cumulus, stratus, and cirrus. The cirrus clouds are at 20,000 feet or higher and are curly, white, and feathery. The stratus clouds appear from the surface up to 6,500 feet and are spread out as in sheets and layers. The cumulus clouds are at from 1,600 feet to 20,000 feet and are huge, puffy, and heaped up, looking like cotton balls.

Research Questions

1. What are clouds?

2. How were clouds named?

3. How do clouds determine the weather?

4. What causes clouds to have different shapes and sizes?

Web Sites

http://www.cloudyskies.net/form.html

This site describes the process of cloud formation from the ground up to the sky. Also included are the difference in the air pressure as the cloud rises from the ground to the sky, the air temperatures, and the atmospheric conditions relevant to the size and shape of a cloud. (S: All)

http://www-airs.jpl.nasa.gov/html/edu/clouds/What_are_clouds.html

Here students can learn what exactly clouds are and investigate how the clouds influence our source of energy, the Sun. The stability and instability of the atmospheric conditions and the formation of clouds in different regions due to elevation are discussed. (S: 4–6, T: 4–6)

http://vortex.plymouth.edu/clouds.html

At this site are pictures of actual cloud formations. The characteristics of clouds in regard to altitude, appearance, and origin are displayed. The names of the different cloud types and detailed descriptions of each are provided. (S: 4–6, T: 4–6)

http://www.cloudyskies.net/facts.html

Here students can learn the fascinating facts about clouds, from the colors they represent to the diameter of the average cloud droplet. (S: 4–6)

http://www.cloudyskies.net/clouds.html
Students will learn who discovered the differences in clouds, the names that were chosen for the different types of clouds, and why those names were chosen. (S: 4–6)

Literature Resources

Bendick, Jeanne. (1971). *How to Make a Cloud*. New York: Parents Magazine Press.
This informative book has easily readable text that includes information on how heat makes air rise, how to make a cloud, cloud shapes, cloud names, what can be told from clouds, and cloud poems.

Carle, Eric. (1996). *Little Cloud*. New York: Philomel Books.
This book tells the story of a little cloud that can't keep up with the others. The little cloud experiences many different shapes as it travels behind the other clouds; when it catches up to the others it helps form a large cloud and rain.

DePaola, Tomie. (1975). *The Cloud Book*. New York: Holiday House.
This book presents the ten most common types of clouds and the myths that are attached to their different shapes. Filled with great illustrations and simple text.

Hale, James Graham. (1997). *Down Comes the Rain*. New York: HarperCollins.
Young children can enjoy learning where the rain comes from. Using fun-loving characters, this book reveals the water cycle in action from invisible water droplets in clouds to hail.

Merk, Ann & Merk, Jim. (1994). *Weather Report, Clouds*. Vero Beach, FL: Rourke.
This short textbook pulls together information about how clouds form, different types of clouds, fog and smog, the color of clouds, and the clouds and sun. Realistic photos are used to enhance the short text.

Wegen, Ron. (1982). *Sky Dragon*. New York: Greenwillow.
This story shows young children outside watching clouds; as they stare into the sky they see different images of animals in the clouds.

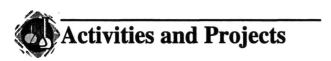

Activities and Projects

1. Designate a "Cloud Expert of the Day." Ask the selected individual to record the types of clouds that are visible on any single day, then make a brief presentation to the rest of the class on the clouds observed. Choose a new expert each day. Set up a chart or some other method for students to record their observations. Ask the students to identify what types of clouds were visible over the course of a week, a month, and three months.

2. Students may enjoy making their own rain. You will need a large glass jar, very hot tap water, 10 to 12 ice cubes, a foil pie pan, and a flashlight. Fill the jar with very hot tap water. Fill the pie pan with ice cubes. Put it on top of the jar. Turn out the lights. Shine a flashlight into the jar. Have students note what happens inside the jar. After the experiment, have students write down what happened and illustrate it step by step.

3. Ask each student to imagine that he or she is a particular type of cloud. Encourage students to write about their "life cycle" over the course of several days (how they were "born," where they traveled, what became of them in their "old age," etc.). Provide opportunities for students to share their "autobiographies."

4. If possible, ask selected students to take photographs of various cloud patterns. When the photos are developed, ask students to arrange them into an attractive display for the entire class. Students should include descriptions of each cloud type and what it means in terms of interpreting weather.

Deserts

Introduction

The desert is a magical and marvelous ecosystem. Full of life and adventures, it is also one of the world's most misunderstood environments. Many children believe deserts are dry, lifeless places, but in fact they are some of the most ecologically diverse regions on the surface of the Earth. The following Web sites, activities, and literature will help students learn about and appreciate these magnificent places.

Research Questions

1. What is the largest desert in the world?

2. What are some animals and some plants that live in the Sonoran Desert?

3. How are cacti able to maintain their water supplies?

4. What is most unusual about the kangaroo rat?

5. How do insects in the Namib Desert get water?

6. What is the driest desert in the world?

Web Sites

http://www.desertusa.com/index.html

This is the ultimate desert resource! Fabulous information about American deserts, their flora and fauna, their diversity, and their magnificent scenery make this a truly delightful site. It is updated daily. Students will garner loads of valuable data that will transform their perceptions of deserts. (S: All)

http://www.mobot.org/MBGnet/sets/desert/index.htm

This site offers young explorers a virtual biome. Here kids will learn all about deserts: what they are, where they're located, and what kinds of plants and animals can survive there. This is a great resource for learning about the mystery and magic of deserts. (S: 4–6)

http://www.pbs.org/edens/namib

Namib is a 2,000-kilometer strip of desert on the southwestern coast of Africa. It is one of Earth's most unforgiving environments and truly one of its harshest deserts. At this site students will learn about the flora and fauna of this remarkable place and how they have adapted to the harsh conditions. This site is an extension of PBS's *Living Edens* TV programs. (S: 4–6)

Literature Resources

Catchpole, Clive. (1984). *The Living World: Deserts*. New York: Dial Books for Young Readers.
Lots of illustrations and loads of information about the world's deserts highlight this book.

Siebert, Diane. (1988). *Mojave*. New York: HarperCollins.
This is a poetic examination of the Mojave Desert in California. This is a great read-aloud book for any age.

Silver, Donald. (1995). *One Small Square: Cactus Desert*. New York: W. H. Freeman.
This book is perfect book for older readers. It will expose them to the enormous diversity of life in a "typical" desert.

Wallace, Marianne. (1996). *America's Deserts*. Golden, CO: Fulcrum.
This is a good introduction to the four major desert areas of the Southwest. Lots of illustrations and information.

Yolen, Jane. (1996). *Welcome to the Sea of Sand*. New York: Putnam.
This is a lyrical journey into the desert with lots to discover and examine.

Activities and Projects

1. Have students create their own desert terrarium. The following directions will help them design a fully functioning terrarium:

    a. Fill the bottom of a large glass container with a layer of coarse sand or gravel. Combine one part fine sand with two parts of potting soil and spread this over the top of the first layer.

    b. Sprinkle this lightly with water.

    c. Place several varieties of cactus in the terrarium (wear gloves). Most nurseries carry cacti or they can be ordered through the mail-order nursery houses.

    d. When planting the cacti, be sure that the roots are covered completely by the sandy mixture.

    e. Desert animals such as lizards or horned toads may be placed in the terrarium. Be sure the animals have a sufficient quantity of food and water available.

    f. The desert terrarium can be left in the sun and does not need a glass cover. It should, however, be lightly sprinkled with water about once a week.

2. Have students create their own "Desert Dictionary." Ask them to form small groups, with each group responsible for gathering words and definitions for several letters of the alphabet. For example:

A	Atacama Desert
	Australian Thorny Devil
	Ananuca Lily
B	Beetles
	Blue Gilia
C	Camel
	California Poppy
D	Desertification
E	Endangered environment
F	Frilled Lizard
	Fennec Fox

Have students contribute their class dictionary to the school library.

3. Invite students to write to one or more of the following national parks and request information about the flora and fauna that inhabit those special regions. When the brochures, flyers, leaflets, and descriptive information arrive, ask students to assemble them into an attractive display in the classroom or a school display case.

Death Valley National Park
P. O. Box 579
Death Valley, CA 92328

Joshua Tree National Park
74485 National Park Drive
Twentynine Palms, CA 92277

Great Basin National Park
Baker, NV 89311

Big Bend National Park
Big Bend, TX 79834

4. If they can, students should visit a local gardening center or nursery and buy a cactus (these are typically very inexpensive). Ask them to carefully observe their respective cacti with the following questions in mind: What shape is it? Does the shape change as it grows? What do the needles look like? Students should observe cactus features with a magnifying lens and record their observations in a "Desert Journal."

Earthquakes

 ## Introduction

One very familiar and devastating natural disaster is an earthquake. Not all earthquakes cause damage or injury. Most happen without anyone knowing. Earthquakes are any sudden disturbance within the Earth that causes a shaking of the ground. Earthquakes are caused by the breaking of rocks that are under pressure. The pressure is caused by the slow movement of the Earth's plates. When the rocks can no longer handle the pressure they break, causing an earthquake. The seismic waves of an earthquake are measured on a seismograph.

A seismograph can measure even the smallest of earthquakes. The Richter Scale used to measure earthquakes was created by Charles F. Richter in 1935. He set up a magnitude scale for earthquakes. This scale is still used today in measuring earthquakes.

 ## Research Questions

1. What are seismic waves?

2. Where are faults located around the world?

3. What are foreshocks?

4. What should you do during an earthquake?

5. How does a seismograph work?

 ## Web Sites

http://tlc.ai.org/earthqua.htm
This guide to earthquakes is a teacher's treasure. Simple and complex facts about earthquakes are included, as well as complete lesson plans. (T: All)

http://users.netlink.com.au/~jhallett/earthquakes.htm
At this site students learn about what causes an earthquake as well as some famous earthquakes throughout history. (S: 4–6)

http://www.ngdc.noaa.gov/cgi-bin/seg/m2h?seg/haz_volume1.men
Lots of information, including a slide show of earthquakes, is provided for teachers on this site. (T: 4–6)

http://www.fema.gov/library/quakef.htm

A fact sheet from the Federal Emergency Management Agency offers up-to-the-minute information about this natural disaster. (T: 4–6)

http://www.crustal.ucsb.edu/ics/understanding/

This is a super site on "Understanding Earthquakes." Quizzes, facts, information, famous earthquakes and more are all on this complete site. (S: All, T: All)

http://www.germantown.k12.il.us/html/earthquakes.html

Lots of information on earthquakes for kids written by kids. A good resource tool. (S: 4–6)

http://wwwneic.cr.usgs.gov/neis/plate_tectonics/rift_man.html

The U.S. Geological Society presents the latest information on earthquakes and plate tectonics on this site. (T: All)

Literature Resources

Kehret, Peg. (1998). *Earthquake Terror*. New York: Viking Penguin.

This book tells of an earthquake on an island north of California. A family is left without food or other supplies after the earthquake. A twelve-year-old boy must find a way to keep himself and his family alive.

Moores, Eldridge. (1995). *Volcanoes and Earthquakes*. New York: Time-Life Books.

This incredible book overflows with fascinating information and eye-popping photos and illustrations. A complete reference work.

Sattler, Helen. (1995). *Our Patchwork Planet*. New York: Lothrop.

This book provides the reader with an interesting excursion through present-day tectonic theory.

Simon, Seymour. (1991). *Earthquakes*. New York: William Morrow.

Earthquakes shows illustrations of what causes earthquakes. Also described is what should be done during an earthquake.

Watt, Fiona. (1993). *Earthquakes and Volcanoes*. London: Usborne.

Lots of illustrations and a detailed text make this a fascinating book.

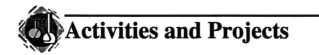

Activities and Projects

1. Show the film *The Great San Francisco Earthquake,* produced by PBS Video (1988) or the video *Our Dynamic Earth,* produced by the National Geographic Society (Catalog No. C51162). Ask students to discuss the similarities between the events portrayed in the film(s). Have students create a Venn diagram illustrating the similarities and differences.

2. Ask students to write their own newspaper articles about a recent earthquake. Afterwards, have students form small groups and discuss their articles and how those pieces compare with those presented in newspapers or newsmagazines.

3. Ask students to create a three-dimensional model of the different layers of the Earth by painting a huge circle using a piece of poster board. The inside of the circle can be painted in three colors according to the three layers of the Earth (the core, the mantle, and the crust). Students should then use a globe of the world to plot selected countries on their illustrations. They can also plot the locations of some of the major earthquakes that have occurred during the past 25 to 50 years.

4. Have students work in small groups to research books about earthquakes. Each group should prepare a brief summary of its findings and present the discoveries to the rest of the class. Ask each group to prepare a fact book about the collected data and present their finished products to the school library.

5. Appoint selected students as "Earthquake Monitors." Using one or more of the Web sites listed above, have a small group of students monitor an earthquake that has occurred somewhere in the world. The "team" should issue a daily report to the other members of the class. Daily "reports" should be written and posted on a selected bulletin board.

Erosion

Introduction

By definition, *erosion* is the process of taking away the products of weathering (weathering is the process of breaking down an object). Principally, erosion is carried on by water, ice, and wind.

Water is the greatest of all the forces that produce erosion. Water erosion takes place on the surface of the Earth as well as below the surface. Over long periods of time, water erosion can cause severe alterations in the landscape. Erosion by ice is the result of glaciers, large masses of ice formed where the climate and weather are very cold. Glaciers may be up to 14,000 feet thick (at the South Pole) and several miles long. Wind erosion is quite common in dry areas, where there are few plants or trees to cover the ground and protect it. Over a period of time wind can remove large quantities of soil, dust, and rock.

Research Questions

1. What are the main causes of erosion?

2. What can be done to reduce erosion?

3. What areas of the United States are most susceptible to wind erosion?

4. Where is the world's largest glacier?

5. Why is flooding considered a form of erosion?

Web Sites

http://www.abag.ca.gov/bayarea/enviro/erosion/erosion.html
This site offers tips and ideas that will prevent or seriously reduce the effects of erosion. Lots of information for teachers to use. (T: 4–6)

Literature Resources

Lauber, Patricia. (1996). *Flood: Wrestling with the Mississippi.* Washington, DC: National Geographic Society.
This photo essay depicts the devastation that resulted from the 1993 flooding of the Mississippi River. A thorough and compelling book.

Peters, Lisa Westberg. (1990). *The Sun, the Wind, and the Rain*. New York: Henry Holt.
This book describes how a mountain forms. Rock is eroded by wind and water and then rebuilt by sedimentary rocks.

Simon, Seymour (1999). *Icebergs and Glaciers*. New York: Mulberry.
Filled with incredible photography, in this book the well-respected science author presents the awe and majesty of glaciers and icebergs as few writers can.

Activities and Projects

1. Invite a soil conservationist to visit the class. Ask the individual to discuss ways of conserving land and ways in which land is being eroded. After the visit, have students create posters displaying what they learned about erosion.

2. Ask students to look through the daily newspaper for articles about any severe erosion taking place throughout the world (e.g., flooding, glacier movement, severe wind storms). Ask them to create a miniature bulletin board on which they can display the articles under the heading "Our Changing Earth." Be sure to provide opportunities for students to discuss with you some of the articles as well as the implications of these events for the surface of the Earth.

3. Mix three tablespoons of playground sand with three tablespoons of white glue. (You may need to adjust the mixture depending on the type of sand; the mixture should have the consistency of wet concrete.) Form the mixture into two or three "rocks" and allow them to dry in a low (250 degrees F) oven for several hours. Place the "rocks" in a tumbler or sturdy cup half-filled with water. Cover the cup with a tight-fitting lid. Ask students to shake the cup vigorously for several minutes and note the results. (The "rocks" will be worn down by the eroding power of the water.)

4. If possible, invite students from a local college or university to share specially prepared lessons on erosion. Additionally, students taking a geology course at the college can be invited to share their expertise with the class. Ask students to interview the college students.

5. Ask students to use one or more of the Web sites listed above to create an informational brochure on how community members and the general population can prevent erosion in your town or city. Do any laws have to be passed? What can the average person do? What can the average family do?

Fossils

 ## Introduction

Fossils are the remains of plants or animals in rock. The remains may be skeletons or the almost complete plants and animals themselves. Fossils are typically found in metamorphic or sedimentary rock, but rarely in igneous rock. Fossils are formed in several different ways, including dead animals being covered by sediment or animals falling into swamps or tar pits. Scientists who study fossils are known as paleontologists.

 ## Research Questions

1. What is a paleontologist?

2. How are fossils found?

3. Why are fossils important?

4. What happens to fossils after they are found?

 ## Web Sites

http://www.rom.on.ca/quiz/fossil/fosform.html

This is a good source for students to learn what fossils are, how an animal becomes a fossil, and who studies fossils. It gives a step-by-step example of an animal becoming a fossil. (S: All)

http://www.discovery.thorntons.co.uk/pages/fossils/content1.asp

This Web site is an interesting source for teachers and students to learn about the different fossils and how they are formed. It contains pictures of the different forms of fossils. (S: All, T: All)

http://skullduggery.com/fossils.htm

This Fossil Replicas Web site is an excellent source for older students and teachers to examine different fossil replicas, from a Tyrannosaurus rex tooth to a sloth claw. Teachers can also use this Web site to purchase these fossils for their classrooms. (S: 4–6, T: All)

http://www.rom.on.ca/quiz/fossil/fosgame.html

This fun Web site for students and even teachers includes an educational game to teach which types of sea life form which fossils. The answers are available for students to check their guesses. (S: All, T: All)

Literature Resources

Barton, Bryon. (1990). *Bones, Bones, Dinosaur Bones*. New York: Crowell.

In this book a group of characters go looking for dinosaur bones. The book provides an easy-to-understand explanation for younger children about how bones are found, what is done with them, and how they are reassembled.

Pallota, Jerry. (1993). *The Extinct Alphabet Book*. Watertown, MA: Charlesbridge.

This book is a good way to start a lesson about fossils. It goes through the alphabet, describing, for each letter, an animal that is extinct. Fossils have been found or would be helpful to find out more about these extinct animals.

Tanaka, Shelley. (1998). *Graveyards of the Dinosaurs*. New York: Hyperion.

This is an excellent book that looks at what it is like to discover the bones of prehistoric creatures. It contains actual photographs of fossils and places they were found. It also shows diagrams of the animals the fossils used to be and provides different theories about how some of these animals became extinct. The book provides a map that pinpoints locations of recent fossil finds.

Activities and Projects

1. Invite a paleontologist to come into the classroom to speak about how fossils are found and why it is important to find them. As a class, come up with an animal that everyone would like to know more about. Ask the paleontologist to talk about where fossils of that animal have been found and what fossils of that animal have been found. Have the class make a classroom map of the locations and have each student draw a part of the fossil that has been found. Display the drawings around the map.

2. Ask small groups of students to each construct a dictionary of fossil terms. What are some important words that scientists who study fossils need to know? Encourage students to use the Web site and literature resources above in putting together their dictionaries. What resource is most useful? Afterwards, ask each group to present their dictionary to the entire class.

3. Ask students to create their own fossils. Provide small groups of students with pie plates half filled with wet sand. Ask each group to place several chicken bones in the sand (soak the bones in vinegar to clean them, then apply a thin coating of petroleum jelly to them to facilitate removal later on). Have the students place circular strips of cardboard around the bones and pour a plaster of paris mixture into this makeshift mold. After the plaster of paris has dried, the students should remove the bones from each mold. Ask students to examine their "fossils" and discuss any similarities or differences.

Hurricanes

 Introduction

Hurricanes form over tropical waters. The surface of the ocean is heated and warm, moist air begins to rise rapidly. This warm air flows into a low-pressure area, picking up more moisture as it travels. As the air rises above the Earth, it cools, and this cooling causes moisture to condense into droplets of water that form clouds. The low-pressure area acts like a vacuum: Warm air is drawn in at the bottom, rises in a column, and spreads out. As the air inside rises and more air is drawn in, the storm grows.

Because the Earth's surface is rotating, the air within the storm travels in a spiral. In the Northern Hemisphere the spiraling winds travel counterclockwise; in the Southern Hemisphere they travel clockwise. Most of these storms die out within a few hours: in fact, only about one in ten of these storms develops into a full-blown hurricane. In the Caribbean Sea and North Atlantic, these storms are called *hurricanes*; west of the International Date Line they are known as *typhoons*; and in the Indian Ocean they are called *cyclones*.

 Research Questions

1. What causes a hurricane to form?

2. Why do hurricanes start over the eastern Atlantic Ocean?

3. What was the most powerful hurricane ever recorded?

4. How are hurricanes named?

5. What type of damage can a hurricane do?

 Web Sites

http://www.discovery.com/stories/science/hurricanes/hurricanes.html
At this site students can learn about hyper-hurricanes and the incredible damage that they would do to any populated areas. A super site that will stimulate lots of discussion. (S: 4–6, T: 4–6)

http://www.macontelegraph.com/special/hurr/hurr.htm
At this great site students will be able to learn about the power of hurricanes. (S: 4–6)

http://www.sun-sentinel.com/storm/history/
This site presents a time line of the "greatest" hurricanes from the time of Christopher Columbus to the present. Lots of opportunities for classroom projects are here. (S: 4–6)

http://www.worldbook.com/fun/bth/hurricane/html/hurricanes_.htm

This World Book site has tons of information about hurricanes. It explains how hurricanes move, how to protect buildings from storm damage, and much more. (S: 4–6, T: All)

http://kids.mtpe.hq.nasa.gov/archive/hurricane/index.html

This site provides a brief description of how hurricanes work and what they do. (S: 4–6)

http://www.hurricanehunters.com/askus.htm

At this site teachers and students can pose questions to the people known as "Hurricane Hunters," who fly over and into developing hurricanes. (S: 4–6, T: All)

http://members.aol.com/hotelq/index.html

At this site students can look at photographs taken from inside a hurricane. Cool! (S: All)

http://www.jannws.state.ms.us/hrcn.html

At this complete site kids can learn all about hurricanes and how to prepare themselves for one. Loads of other hurricane links, too. One of the best! (S: All, T: All)

Literature Resources

Cole, Joanne. (1995). *The Magic School Bus Inside a Hurricane.* New York: Scholastic.

Miss Frizzle and her class take another incredible journey, this time inside a hurricane to learn about its formation and destruction.

Lauber, Patricia. (1996) *Hurricanes: Earth's Mightiest Storms.* New York: Scholastic.

In this captivating book, Lauber presents young readers with the most up-to-date information on the power and might of hurricanes. Fantastic photos and a compelling text make this book an essential resource.

London, Jonathan. (1998). *Hurricane.* New York: Lothrop.

This is the story of a family in Puerto Rico and how they survive the onslaught of a devastating hurricane. A great read-aloud book.

Souza, D. M. (1996). *Hurricanes.* Minneapolis, MN: Carolrhoda.

This is a fascinating book jam-packed with loads of information and incredible facts about hurricanes. Lots to learn and lots to share in these pages.

Wiesner, David. (1990). *Hurricane.* New York: Clarion.

The author captures the magnificence of a hurricane from a child's perspective, with particular emphasis on the play and imagination of two boys after the storm.

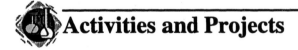# Activities and Projects

1. Ask students to imagine that they are in a hurricane-prone area. What types of precautions should they take as a hurricane approaches? What types of precautions are appropriate at other times of the year? How can families better prepare themselves for future hurricanes? Ask students to assemble a hurricane safety book that could be distributed through a local chapter of the American Red Cross or other disaster relief agency.

2. Ask students to log on to some appropriate Web sites. After students have looked at several sites, discuss how hurricanes begin, where they occur, and so forth. You may also wish to discuss how hurricane hunters track hurricanes across the open ocean. Ask students to maintain a weather report journal (on graph paper) throughout the months of September and October using a map of the eastern U.S. seaboard. Ask students to track hurricanes as they move across the ocean. With each new hurricane, students can initiate a new journal. Transfer the results to transparencies and layer the transparencies one on top of the other to compare the various paths hurricanes take across the Atlantic Ocean. As new hurricanes form, have students create new transparencies.

3. Have students contact hurricane survivors via various pen pal organizations (e.g., www.epals.com). Ask students to question their pen pals about their feelings and impressions of hurricanes before and after the identified events. Students should create imaginary stories about the sights and sounds of a hurricane based on the data shared with their pen pals.

4. Ask students to create a role-playing situation or simulation. Students can take on the role of local weather forecasters announcing the coming of a hurricane. Ask students to create a series of weather "broadcasts" over a period of several days. The inclusion of safety tips in these presentations would also be appropriate.

5. Ask students to create a chart similar to the one below. Over the course of the hurricane season they should record and graph various aspects of all the hurricanes for any respective year.

Name	Location	Highest	Wind Speed	Duration

6. Ask students to put together a timeline of this country's ten most disastrous hurricanes. When did they occur? Where did they occur? How much property was destroyed? How many people lost their lives? What were the long-term effects?

7. Divide the class into several groups. Assign each group a "famous" hurricane from the past. Encourage each group to locate as much information as possible about its assigned hurricane. Each group should post information about their respective hurricane on a specially designed "Hurricane Bulletin Board."

8. Ask students to bring in newspaper accounts of hurricanes during the course of a season. Encourage students to take on the roles of newspaper reporters and develop their own classroom newspaper ("Hurricane Watch"). The newspaper can be issued throughout the school on a daily basis during the hurricane season, keeping students and teachers up-to-date on the development and progress of selected hurricanes.

Oceans

Introduction

The five major oceans of the world contain more life than any other ecosystem of the world. They are home to the world's largest creature of all time—the blue whale—and have some of the planet's smallest creatures—diatoms, plankton, and other one-celled organisms. The oceans are worlds of extremes—the tallest mountains, deepest valleys, and most volcanoes are in the oceans, the heaviest and lightest fish can be found in the oceans; and the hottest and coldest waters anywhere on the planet are ocean waters. The longest worm (the bootlace worm grows more than 55 yards long), the fastest animal (the sailfish can swim at speeds of more than 68 mph, faster than a cheetah can run), the most poisonous animal (the box jellyfish's venom can kill a human in 30 seconds), the egg-laying champion (the ocean sunfish produces 300 million eggs), and the smallest fish (the Marshall Islands goby is less than one-half inch from nose to tail)—all inhabit the world's oceans.

The oceans of the world are where new discoveries are being made every day and where new and incredible adventures await those willing to make those discoveries. In fact, many biologists estimate that somewhere between 500,000 and 5,000,000 marine species have yet to be discovered and described. Sea treasures from sunken pirate ships to vast deposits of precious minerals to amazing new creatures are all part of the undiscovered riches of the world's oceans.

Research Questions

1. What is the name of the deepest ocean?

2. What effects does the ocean have on us?

3. Where is the saltiest water?

4. Where are the highest tides in the world?

5. What is the name of the fin on the dolphin's back?

6. What percent of the Earth's surface is water?

Web Sites

http://vpm.com/cordova/

This is a super Web site developed by teachers and students at an elementary school in California. Lessons on squids, sharks, fish, coastal ecosystems, and lots of other ocean items are included. (S: 4–6)

http://www.turtles.org/

This is a super Web site that focuses on marine turtles: their lives, where they live, why they are endangered, and what we can do to save them. (S: 4–6)

http://www.aboveall.com/bb/BBMAIN.html

Here's a great Web site that has dozens of photographs of ocean reefs and reef animals from around the world. (S: 4–6)

http://www.actwin.com/fish/species.cgi

At this site students can see more than 200 photographs of various marine organisms from around the world. (S: 4–6)

http://www.oceans.net/preserve.html

This site offers information on the preservation and protection of oceans as well as an index of resources. (T: All)

http://inspire.ospi.wednet.edu:8001/curric/oceans/

This site offers instruction units and projects on a variety of topics: tracking drifter buoys, investigating ocean currents, ocean color, and plant life in the ocean. (S: 4–6, T: 4–6)

http://www.nos.noaa.gov/

The National Ocean Service is the primary agency responsible for the health and safety of our nation's oceans. Students can find out about all their services and products on this Web site. (S: 4–6)

http://www.pbs.org/kratts/world/oceans/index.html

This Web site provides up-to-the-minute information about oceans and ocean creatures from around the world. (S: All)

http://seawifs.gsfc.nasa.gov/OCEAN_PLANET/HTML/resource_data_services.html

This Web site is a listing of oceanography-related resources that can be found on the Internet. Exploration of these resources will turn up a surprising variety of information. (T: All)

Literature Resources

Aliki. (1996). *My Visit to the Aquarium*. New York: HarperCollins.

A variety of marine habitats are explored in this well-done introduction to an aquarium.

Arnold, Caroline. (1990). *A Walk by the Seashore*. Englewood Cliffs, NJ: Silver Press.

A young child and an adult take a walk along the seashore and discover some marvelous treasures and surprises.

Baines, John. (1991). *Protecting the Oceans*. Austin, TX: Steck-Vaughn.

The author describes the importance of the oceans, threats to the ocean environment, and measures that may curb these threats.

Baker, Lucy. (1990). *Life in the Oceans*. New York: Watts.

This book presents readers with a thorough overview of ocean life and some of its most interesting elements.

Bendick, Jeanne. (1994). *Exploring an Ocean Tide Pool*. New York: Henry Holt.
Bendick examines the ecosystem of a tide pool. She discusses tides, tidal zones, and the plants and animals found in a tide pool.

Cole, Joanna. (1994). *The Magic School Bus on the Ocean Floor*. New York: Scholastic.
Miss Frizzles and her class take a marvelous journey through the ocean's depths to learn some important information.

Fredericks, Anthony D. (1998). *Exploring the Oceans: Science Activities for Kids*. Golden, CO: Fulcrum.
This all-inclusive resource book for kids is packed with loads of delightful investigations and fascinating activities. This is a "must-have" for any child or classroom teacher.

Ganeri, Anita. (1995). *I Wonder Why the Sea Is Salty and Other Questions About the Ocean*. New York: Kingfisher.
This book answers questions about the ocean, marine ecology, and marine life.

————. (1995). *The Oceans Atlas*. New York: Dorling Kindersley.
Packed full of information about major aspects of ocean life, this book is a "must-have" for any serious oceanographer.

Hirschi, Ron. (1990). *Ocean*. New York: Bantam.
Color drawings and high-quality photos complement this description of a variety of ocean creatures.

Hoff, Mary & Rodgers, Mary. (1991). *Our Endangered Planet: Oceans*. Minneapolis, MN: Lerner.
This book describes the threats posed by our use of the world's oceans.

Macquitty, Miranda. (1995). *Ocean*. New York: Knopf.
Incredible photographs and loads of fascinating information distinguish this book as one of the finest on ocean life.

McGovern, Ann. (1991). *The Desert Beneath the Waves*. New York: Scholastic.
This wonderful book describes some of the unusual sea creatures that live on the ocean bottom.

Pallotta, Jerry. (1991). *The Underwater Alphabet Book*. Watertown, MA: Charlesbridge.
This book is an alphabetical journey describing common and unusual creatures that inhabit the world's oceans.

Parker, Steve. (1990). *Fish*. New York: Knopf.
Lots of photos and an engaging text highlight some amazing sea creatures.

————. (1989). *Seashore*. New York: Knopf.
Parker introduces the various animals and plants of the seashore and discusses the importance of preservation.

Pratt, Kristen. (1994). *A Swim Through the Sea*. Nevada City, CA: Dawn Publications.
This richly illustrated book uses the letters of the alphabet to introduce a wide variety of ocean life.

Silver, Donald. (1993). *One Small Square: Seashore*. New York: Freeman.
This is a wonderful book for the budding oceanographer. Lots of projects and activities highlight this magnificently illustrated book. A definite "must-have."

Simon, Seymour. (1990). *Oceans*. New York: Morrow.
   This richly photographed book provides numerous insights into the major features of the world's oceans.

Wells, Susan. (1993). *The Illustrated World of Oceans*. New York: Simon & Schuster.
   This is an atlas of the Earth's oceans, with illustrations and information about their history, inhabitants, exploration, and uses.

Wu, Norbert. (1990). *Life in the Oceans*. New York: Bookwright Press.
   Spectacular photographs and lots of interesting information offer the reader a glimpse into selected aspects of ocean life.

Activities and Projects

1. Ask students to pour some water into a pie pan. Encourage them to blow hard at one end of the pan across the water. The water will ripple and form waves. The stronger students blow, the larger the waves will be. Discuss the formation of waves with students (wind blowing across the surface of the ocean).

2. Have students create a map of some of the world's major ocean currents, using the Web sites and literature resources above. Ask students to trace the movements of the currents for both hemispheres.

3. Provide students with a list of oceanic occupations similar to the one below. Ask them to conduct some research (via Web sites and literature) on one or more chosen occupations, with specific reference to job requirements, training and education, amount of time spent at sea, and occupational dangers. Provide opportunities for students to share their research with others.

   Commercial fishermen—catch ocean creatures to sell to markets.

   Marine geologists—study rocks and the formation of the ocean floor.

   Marine biologists—study the animals and plants of the ocean.

   Divers—assist in finding sunken treasures, repairing underwater equipment, gathering information for research, and so forth.

   Oceanographers—study and explore the ocean.

   Offshore drillers—explore beneath the ocean floor for deposits of petroleum and natural gas to be used for various forms of energy.

   Mariculturists—raise fish and other sea life for food and/or restocking the ocean.

   Marine ichthyologists—study fish, their habitats, the food they eat, and their relationship to their environment.

   Marine ecologists—study the relationships between sea creatures and their environment.

   Captain/crew of ship—work on a commercial boat or cruise ship.

   Navigators—use directions to determine a ship's course at sea.

   Have students report their findings to others or prepare a short report entitled "A Week in the Life of a _____."

4. Ask youngsters to keep a watch on the local television news or local newspaper for reports of ocean pollution from around the world. Although they may wish to focus on events related to grounded tankers, other types of pollution can be tracked as well. Ask students to hang up a large wall map of the world. For each incidence of ocean pollution, ask youngsters to write a brief summary (date, nature of occurrence, place, resolution, etc.) on a 3-by-5-inch index card. Post each card around the wall map and connect the card with the actual location on the map using a length of yarn (the yarn can be taped or pinned to the wall).

5. Ask students to visit a local grocery store and take along a list similar to the one below. This list represents several varieties of fish that are commonly found in most supermarkets throughout North America. Encourage students to check off each type of fish as it is located in the store. They may want to visit the fresh fish department, the frozen fish section, and the canned food section.

☐ herring
☐ salmon
☐ shrimp
☐ tuna
☐ orange roughy
☐ crab
☐ lobster
☐ scallops
☐ catfish
☐ cod
☐ haddock
☐ flounder
☐ perch
☐ clams
☐ whiting
☐ halibut
☐ monkfish
☐ grouper
☐ scrod
☐ oysters
☐ anchovies
☐ sardines
☐ whitefish
☐ mussels
☐ mackerel
☐ octopus
☐ pollock

6. The following activity will give students an opportunity to create a "homemade" ocean in a bottle.

Materials: an empty one-liter soda bottle (with a screw-on top), salad oil, water, blue food coloring

Directions: (1) Fill an empty one-liter soda bottle halfway up with salad oil. (2) Fill the rest of the bottle (all the way to the brim) with water dyed with a few drops of blue food coloring. (3) Put on the top securely and lay the bottle on its side. (4) Slowly and gently tip the bottle back and forth.

The oil in the bottle will begin to roll and move just like the waves in the ocean. Students will have created a miniature ocean in a bottle.

---

7. Invite students to contact several of the following groups and ask for information on the work they do and the types of printed materials they have available for students:

American Littoral Society
Sandy Hook
Highlands, NJ 07732
(201-291-0055)

American Oceans Campaign
725 Arizona Avenue, Suite 102
Santa Monica, CA 90401
(310-576-6162)

Center for Marine Conservation
1725 DeSales Street, NW, Suite 500
Washington, DC 20036
(202-429-5609)

Cetacean Society International
P.O. Box 953
Georgetown, CT 06829
(203-544-8617)

Coastal Conservation Association
4801 Woodway, Suite 220 West
Houston, TX 77056
(713-626-4222)

The Coral Reef Alliance
809 Delaware Street
Berkeley, CA 94710
(510-528-2492)

International Marine Mammal Project
Earth Island Institute
300 Broadway, Suite 28
San Francisco, CA 94133
(1-800-DOLPHIN)

International Oceanographic Foundation
4600 Rickenbacker Causeway
Virginia Key, Miami, FL 33149
(305-361-4888)

International Wildlife Coalition (IWC) and The Whale Adoption Project
70 East Falmouth Highway
East Falmouth, MA 02536
(508-548-8328)

Marine Environmental Research Institute
772 West End Avenue
New York, NY 10025
(212-864-6285)

Marine Technology Center
1828 L Street, NW, Suite 906
Washington, DC 20036-5104
(202-775-5966)

National Coalition for Marine Conservation
3 West Market Street
Leesburg, VA 20176
(703-777-0037)

National Wildlife Federation
8925 Leesburg Pike
Vienna, VA 22184-0001
(703-790-4000)

Ocean Voice International
P.O. Box 37026
3332 McCarthy Road
Ottawa, ON, Canada K1V 0W0
(613-990-8819).

8. Several organizations have brochures, leaflets, and guidebooks on ocean pollution and ways to prevent it. Encourage students to write to several of these groups requesting pertinent information. When the resources arrive, plan time to discuss with students ways in which they can participate to prevent or alleviate this global problem. Ask them to prepare an "Action Plan" for themselves and their friends in which they take a proactive stance against ocean pollution. The following organizations and publications will get them started:

a. The New York Sea Grant Extension Program (125 Nassau Hall, SUNY, Stony Brook, NY 11794-5002, 516-632-8730) has a 24-page booklet entitled "Earth Guide: 88 Action Tips for Cleaner Water." Copies are free.

b. Various informational brochures are available from the NOAA Marine Debris Information Office, Center for Marine Conservation, 1725 DeSales Street, NW, Washington, DC 20036.

c. If students are interested in "adopting" an endangered animal, specifically a whale, they can write for further information to the International Wildlife Coalition, Whale Adoption Project, 634 North Falmouth Highway, Box 388, North Falmouth, MA 02566.

d. To join a coalition of environmentally friendly youngsters from around the country, students can write to the Strathmore Legacy's Eco Amigos Club, 333 Park Street, West Springfield, MA 01089.

e. Invite students to contact Keep America Beautiful (99 Park Avenue, New York, NY 10016) and ask for "Pollution Pointers for Elementary Students," a list of environment improvement activities.

Pollution

Introduction

Pollution of our air, water, and land continues to be a serious environmental concern. In some parts of the country battles over these issues have been and will continue to be waged in courtrooms and by governmental bodies. It is vital that the next generation of children understands these problems, both the social aspects and the scientific ones. The following resources and activities can help develop that understanding.

Research Questions

1. What is the major source of pollution in this country?

2. What is the most dangerous form of pollution?

3. What efforts are being made to clean up polluted sites?

4. What are some national organizations involved in controlling pollution?

5. What can students do to reduce or eliminate pollution?

Web Sites

http://www.discovery.com/news/earthalert/earthalert.html
At this site kids can get daily updates about the state of the planet. A super site packed with tons of information. (S: 4–6)

http://oceanlink.island.net/
Here's a great site where kids can stay up to date on the latest information related to ocean pollution. Tons of ocean related data, too. (S: 4–6)

http://www.epa.gov/oar/
From the U.S. Office of Air and Radiation, this site will help students keep track of the latest information on air pollution. (S: 4–6)

Literature Resources

Bright, Michael. (1987). *Pollution and Wildlife*. New York: Gloucester Press.
The effects of pollution on animal wildlife are convincingly portrayed in this book.

Cherry, Lynne. (1992). *A River Ran Wild.* San Diego: Gulliver.

The life of a New England river and the people who work together to save it are detailed in this "must-have" book for any elementary classroom.

Earthworks Group. (1990). *50 Simple Things Kids Can Do to Save the Earth.* Kansas City, MO: Andrews and McMeel.

This classic book contains an abundance of environmentally friendly activities. A super resource for any teacher.

Hadingham, Evan & Hadingham, Janet. (1990). *Garbage!: Where It Comes From, Where It Goes.* New York: Simon & Schuster.

What garbage is, what we do with it, and what happens when we have too much of it are all answered in this delightful book.

Spurgeon, Richard. (1988). *Ecology.* London: Usborne.

Filled with lots of illustrations, this book is a great introduction to the science of ecology.

Van Allsburg, Chris. (1990). *Just a Dream.* Boston: Houghton Mifflin.

What happens when there's too much pollution? Noted author and illustrator Chris Van Allsburg weaves a tale that will impress every young reader.

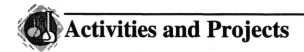# Activities and Projects

1. Following is a list of organizations to which you and your students can write for information, brochures, leaflets, and pertinent data on pollution problems. Post the list on the bulletin board or send it home to parents in the form of a newsletter.

   Adopt-A-Stream Foundation
   P.O. Box 55589
   Everett, WA 98201

   National Audubon Society
   15 Third Avenue
   New York, NY 10022

   Alliance for Environmental Education
   Educational Services
   211 Wilson Boulevard
   Arlington, VA 22201

   National Geographic Society
   17th and M Streets, NW
   Washington, DC 20036

   American Forestry Association
   P.O. Box 20001
   Washington, DC 20010

National Recycling Coalition
101 Thirtieth Street, NW
Washington, DC 20007

Center for Marine Conservation
1725 Desalles Street, NW
Washington, DC 20036

National Wildlife Federation
1412 Sixteenth Street, NW
Washington, DC 20036

Environmental Defense Fund
257 Park Avenue, South
New York, NY 10010

Renew America
1400 Sixteenth Street, NW
Washington, DC 20036

Friends of the Earth
218 D Street, SE
Washington, DC 20003

Sierra Club
730 Polk Street
San Francisco, CA 94109

World Wildlife Fund
P.O. Box 96220
Washington, DC 20077

Greenpeace
1436 U Street, NW
Washington, DC 20009

2. Arrange for a trip to a nearby garbage dump. Have the students generate questions that they may have for the speaker at the dump. Have students ask questions, record answers and then write a story about what it would be like to live in a world where everything is garbage.

3. Ask students to write a letter to the governor's office asking for information on the state's recycling program, including which counties and towns also have recycling programs. Compare and contrast counties and towns that do have programs with those that do not. Have students put a letter/pamphlet together about starting a recycling program. Send these out to the mayor or officials of those towns.

4. Using fresh cut celery, blue or red food coloring, and a glass of water, show your students what polluting the water can do to plants and other living things. Carefully cut off the bottom of the celery stalk. Put a few drops of food coloring into the glass of water. Ask the class to pretend the food coloring is pollution. Then put the celery into the glass. Let it sit for a few hours. Then have students write down their observations about how the "pollution" contaminated the plant.

5. Provide student groups with several index cards and a jar of petroleum jelly. Direct students to smear the jelly over the face of five separate cards. Have students place the cards in various locations around the school (cafeteria, office, basement, etc.). Cards should be placed inside and outside the building as well as at different heights (ground level, head level, etc.). Periodically over the course of several days have students check their cards to note the amount of air pollutants covering the petroleum jelly. Have students speculate about the effects of these pollutants over a span of several weeks, months, or years.

6. **Demonstration by adult only**: Place a clean white sock over the tailpipe of a car (be sure the tailpipe is cool). Secure the sock with a rubber band. Turn on the car and allow it to run for one minute. Turn off the car and allow it to cool for several minutes. Remove the sock and ask students to note the amount of pollution on the sock. Ask them to calculate the amount of pollution pumped into the air on your daily drive to school. How much pollution do all the teachers' cars contribute each day? Each week? During the school year?

Rainforests

Introduction

Rainforests are luxuriant forests, generally composed of tall, broad-leaved trees and usually found in wet tropical uplands and lowlands around the equator. Rainforests usually occur in regions where there is a high annual rainfall of generally more than seventy inches and a hot and steamy climate.

Tropical rainforests are found primarily in South and Central America, West and Central Africa, Indonesia, parts of Southeast Asia, and tropical Australia. Other kinds of rainforests include the monsoon forests, mangrove forests, and temperate rainforests.

Research Questions

1. Where are rainforests typically found?

2. Why are the rainforests so important to us?

3. What is the primary cause of the endangerment of animals in the rainforests?

4. What are some of the effects of the destruction of the rainforests?

5. Who are some of the people who inhabit the rainforests?

6. What are some things we can do to prevent the future destruction of our rainforests?

Web Sites

http://www.davesite.com/rainforests/review1.shtml
This site contains a lot of valuable information about rainforests. It teaches us what exactly rainforests are and where they are found. Students can also learn the importance of the rainforests and what they can provide for our nation, as well as about the unfortunate destruction of the rainforests and what they can do to help prevent it. (S: 4–6, T: All)

http://forests.org/ric/whatsnew.htm
This Web site provides up-to-date information on the different rainforests around the world and how global warming is affecting our rainforests. Students can learn about what is left of the world's forests and some background information to help them understand what constitutes a rainforest. They can also read the top ten stories about rainforests; these are updated occasionally to remain current. (T: All)

http://forests.org/ric/deep-eco/biblio.html

On this site students can research many different topics related to rainforests. They can get periodicals, learn about environmental issues and ecology, and be taught some applications of ecological principles. They can also get the titles of many different types of literature based on rainforests and other topics related to the environment. (S: 4–6, T: All)

http://www.enviroWeb.org/rainrelief/

This site is centered on rainforest relief. It gives students some tips on getting involved and also information about some internships or volunteer research they can do. They also can read updated news notes on the latest rainforest reports. Students also are taught what the authors think they should know. (S: All, T: All)

http://www.ran.org/ran/kids_action/index.html

Developed by the Rainforest Action Network, this site offers an excellent overview of rainforest life, ideas on how kids can become involved in preservation efforts, and a question-and-answer section. (S: All, T: All)

http://kids.osd.wednet.edu/Marshall/rainforest_home_page.html

This magnificent site was developed by students in Olympia, Washington. Here you and your students will discover tons of information along with lesson plans and resource materials. A super site! (S: 4–6, T: 4–6)

Literature Resources

Fredericks, Anthony D. (1997). *Clever Camouflagers*. Minnetonka, MN: NorthWord Press.

The world's most amazing lizard, an insect that looks like a leaf, and a rainforest frog that looks like a plant are a few of the incredible animals populating this delightful book.

Fredericks, Anthony D. (1996). *Exploring the Rainforest: Science Activities for Kids*. Golden, CO: Fulcrum.

Through a variety of practical science activities and experiments, students can investigate the layers of the rainforest, how it touches their lives, and how they can help preserve it. A super resource!

Landau, Elaine. (1991). *Tropical Rainforests Around the World*. New York: Watts.

The various chapters of this book acquaint readers with the variety of animal life, the diversity of plant life, and the significance of rainforests in all our lives.

Llewellyn, Claire. (1998). *Some Plants Grow in Midair and Other Amazing Facts About Rainforests*. Brookfield, CT: Copper Beech.

This book explains why rainforests are shrinking, how their wildlife is endangered, and why they and their wildlife are important.

Petty, Kate. (1993). *Rainforests: Around and About*. Hauppage, NY: Barron's Juveniles.

Harry and Ralph visit and explore the rainforests of South America and Southeast Asia and discuss the effects of their destruction.

Ross, Kathy. (1977). *Crafts for Kids Who Are Wild About Rainforests*. Brookfield, CT: Mill-brook Press.

This book features 20 different projects designed to appeal to crafters as well as to rainforest fans.

Silver, Donald. (1993). *Why Save the Rain Forest?* New York: Messner.

This book tells of the many dangers facing the rainforest and the ways we can all work together to preserve this valuable environment.

Activities and Projects

1. Ask students to create a terrarium—a miniature controlled environment containing plants and animals in an artificial situation that closely imitates the natural living conditions of rainforest organisms. Following are directions for making a terrarium:

Materials:

A glass container, preferably an old aquarium (purchased at a pet store or garage sale), but a large pickle jar or even a two-liter soda bottle can be used

Small pebbles or rocks

Bits of charcoal (wood charcoal from a fire or aquarium charcoal from a local pet store work equally well)

soil or potting soil

plants, rocks, pieces of wood

small land animals (see below)

---

   a. Be sure the container is thoroughly cleansed (there is no soap or detergent residue left behind).

   b. Sprinkle the bottom of the container with a layer of small pebbles mixed with bits of charcoal. Follow with a layer of soil about twice as deep as the pebble/charcoal mixture. Soil from outside or potting soil (obtained from any garden center) will suffice.

   c. Sprinkle the ground with just enough water to make it moist (too much will stimulate the growth of molds).

   d. Place several plants such as mosses, ferns, lichens, small tree seedlings, and liverworts in the soil. Grass seed may be sprinkled in one section of the terrarium.

   e. Place several large rocks and decaying pieces of wood or tree branches in the terrarium, too.

   f. You may wish to introduce small land animals such as snails, earthworms, turtles, frogs, or salamanders to the terrarium. Be sure there is sufficient food and water for the animals living there.

g. Place a loosely fitting sheet of glass over the top of the terrarium (to permit the humidity level to build up). Make sure that some air can enter the terrarium and be certain it is kept out of direct sunlight.

2. The following activity illustrates how rapidly nutrients are depleted from rainforest soil. Add one-quarter teaspoon of blue tempera paint (dry) to one-half cup of dry dirt and mix thoroughly.

Place a coffee filter in a funnel and set the funnel in a large jar. Pour water into the funnel and note the color running into the jar. Keep adding water and note how quickly the color fades.

3. Look in the local phone book for the nearest recycling center (paper, aluminum, or glass). Make arrangements to take students to the center and observe the operation. Ask students to generate a list of questions before the visit. Students should be aware that recycling helps preserve the environment as well as plant and animal life. (Kids may be interested in learning that 60,000 trees are needed for just one run of the Sunday *New York Times.*) After the visit ask students to discuss the need for additional recycling efforts in their community or city. Is a letter-writing campaign necessary to have city officials mandate recycling? How can local citizens get involved in recycling efforts? What can kids do to promote recycling in the local area?

4. The Rainforest Action Network (450 Sansome Street, Suite 700, San Francisco, CA 94111, 415-398-4404) produces a series of "Fact Sheets" offering updated information on the destruction and preservation of the world's rainforests. These sheets are free for the asking. Ask students to write for one or more. Following are just a few of the dozens available:

   Native Peoples of Tropical Rainforests (#13C)—This sheet provides valuable information about the indigenous peoples of the rainforest.

   Tropical Rainforest Animals (#13D)—Using a question and answer format, this sheet offers a variety of interesting facts about the different animals of the rainforests.

   Seven Things You Can Do (#1C)—This sheet describes seven worthwhile activities for families to do right now to help preserve the rainforests of the world.

   Species Extinction and the Rainforests (#3B)—This sheet offers up-to-date information on several animal species in danger of extinction.

   Rates of Rainforest Loss (#4B)—This sheet contains amazing information on the escalation of rainforest destruction currently taking place.

   The Clean-Up Kids (#13E)—This sheet provides a listing of environmental groups around the country involving or started by kids. This would be a wonderful way to "connect" with students in all parts of the United States.

5. Help the students keep their families up to date on rainforest products and encourage them not to buy those products that come from endangered plants or animals. For current information on those products families shouldn't purchase, students can contact TRAFFIC at the World Wildlife Fund (1250 Twenty-fourth Street NW, Washington, DC 20037, 202-293-4800). They should ask for a free copy of the "Buyer Beware" booklet.

6.   Ask students to adopt a nearby stream or pond. They can work to clean up a section of the water, plant new trees along the shore, or report any pollution in the area. This long-term project can help them appreciate some of the efforts being expended in preserving large sections of the rainforest. They may want to write to The Izaak Walton League of America (1401 Wilson Boulevard, Level B, Arlington, VA 22209) and ask for a copy of the free booklet, "Save Our Streams."

7.   Encourage students to plant some trees. By planting trees students are helping contribute to the world's oxygen supply. Inform them that approximately 50 percent of the world's oxygen comes from the rainforest. By planting and caring for trees in the local community they are helping reduce the carbon dioxide in the air while adding beauty to the environment. Following are organizations that can help with tree-planting efforts:

National Arbor Day Foundation (Arbor Lodge 100, Nebraska City, NE 68410)

American Forestry Association (Global ReLeaf Program, P.O. Box 2000, Washington, DC 20013)

Tree People (12601 Mulholland Drive, Beverly Hills, CA 90210)

Rocks and Soil

Introduction

There are three different kinds of rocks. *Igneous* rocks are those that form from melted minerals and can often be found near volcanoes. Granite is one type of igneous rock. *Sedimentary* rocks are those that are usually formed under water as a result of layers of sediment pressing down on other layers of sediment. Sandstone and limestone are examples of sedimentary rocks. *Metamorphic* rocks are those that result from great heat and pressure inside the Earth's surface. Marble is an example of a metamorphic rock.

Soil is actually rocks that have been broken up into very fine pieces. Soil is usually created over hundreds or thousands of years and is the result of weathering, erosion, and freezing. Soil also contains air, water, and decayed matter (known as *humus*). Basically, there are three types of soil: clay, sandy, and loam (a rich mixture of clay, sand, and humus).

Research Questions

1. What are the different types of rocks?

2. What are the two main types of soil?

3. What causes erosion of soil?

4. What is the first eight inches of soil called?

Web Sites

http://sln.fi.edu/fellows/payton/rocks/create/index.html

At this site kids can discover how rocks are formed in the earth. Lots of colorful illustrations are included. (S: All, T: All)

http://www.fi.edu/fellows/payton/rocks/index2.html

There's just about everything a teacher would want for a rock unit on this site. A fabulous resource. (T: All)

http://pelican.gmpo.gov/edresources/soil.html

This site provides a brief overview about the major components of soil. (S: 4–6, T: All)

http://ltpwww.gsfc.nasa.gov/globe/index.htm

The Soil Science Education Home Page is another all-inclusive site that is filled with information and activities for any classroom. (S: All, T: All)

Literature Resources

Catherall, Ed. (1991). *Exploring Soil and Rocks*. Austin, TX: Steck-Vaughn.

This book is great for facts about soil and rocks. It deals with many aspects of rocks and soil such as history, movement, volcanoes, mountains, earthquakes, erosion, weathering, and fuels. There are also sections on the types of rocks and soil.

Cole, Joanna. (1987). *The Magic School Bus Inside the Earth*. New York: Scholastic.

Ms. Frizzle's class goes on another field trip, this time into the Earth. They discover different kinds of rocks and get stuck in a volcano. They learn about what rocks are found in the Earth. When they go back to school, they know what each type of stone is at the school.

Horenstein, Sidney. (1993). *Rocks Tell Stories*. Millbrook, CT: Millbrook Press.

This book describes the three groups of rocks and discusses where to find them and how they form. The book also has a rock cycle showing how the three groups of rock are interrelated. Students can learn about rocks and landscapes, fossils that are found inside rocks, and rock collecting.

Lye, Keith. (1993). *Rocks and Minerals*. Austin, TX: Steck-Vaughn.

In this book students can learn about what rocks are and how they are formed. Here students can learn about the many different types of rocks, as well as about crystals, minerals, valuable metals, and precious stones.

Activities and Projects

1. Provide students with several sealable plastic sandwich bags. Take a "field trip" through your town or neighborhood and ask students to collect as many different soil samples as possible. Upon your return to the classroom, ask students to gently pour each sample onto a white sheet of paper. Provide students with some toothpicks and hand lenses (available at most toy or hobby stores). Ask students to carefully sift through each sample to determine its components. What "ingredients" are found in each sample? Are the samples distinctively different or about the same? How big or small are the particles in each sample? Which sample would be best for growing plants?

2. Invite a local gardener or employee of a local gardening center to visit your classroom to talk about soil conditions in your area. What recommendations would that person make for turning the native soil into the best possible growing medium? What special nutrients or additives should be added to the soil to begin a garden? What is distinctive about the native soil that makes it appropriate or inappropriate for growing vegetables, for example?

3. Obtain some organic clay and some modeling clay from a local arts and crafts store. Ask students to note the difference in the composition of the two clays. Encourage students to make a simple piece of pottery from each sample. Place each piece of pottery in the sun. After a few days, ask students to note the difference between the two pottery pieces. What has changed? What has remained the same? Share with students the fact that pottery pieces more than 5,000 years old have been found at various archeological sites around the world.

4. **Demonstration by adult only:** Bring a small piece of brick to the classroom, soak it in water, and place it in a bowl. In a separate large container, mix together 1/2 cup of water, 1/2 cup of bluing (from the laundry section of the grocery store), and 1/2 cup of ammonia. (Open a window for ventilation.) Use a measuring cup to pour some of this mixture over the brick. Sprinkle the brick with salt and let it stand for 24 hours. The next day students will be able to see crystals forming on the surface of the brick. Continue to add some more of the mixture to keep the crystals growing. Explain to students that this is similar to a process in nature known as *crystallization,* in which crystals are formed over long periods of time (hundreds of years).

Seasons

Introduction

As Earth revolves around the sun, we experience a change in the duration of sunlight, changes in temperature, and other modifications. These changes occur primarily because Earth is tilted 23.5 degrees from a line perpendicular to the plane of its orbit. This tilt causes individuals living in the Northern Hemisphere to experience less sunlight during a certain time each year and experience winter. While the Northern Hemisphere is experiencing winter, the Southern Hemisphere is having summer. This situation is reversed six months later.

As Earth orbits the sun, the sun appears at different positions in the sky at a designated time of the day. At noon, for example, the sun is much higher in the sky on June 21 in the Northern Hemisphere than it is on December 21. The direct rays of the sun are striking the Northern Hemisphere and for a longer time because that part of Earth is exposed to direct sunlight for more hours on June 21 than on December 21; hence it warms the Earth and there are fewer hours for it to cool. When the sun is directly overhead, at its zenith, at the equator, equal degrees of latitude north and south of the equator are receiving the same amount of sunlight. This is the beginning of spring in one of the hemispheres and of fall in the other. The determining factor is the direction of Earth's rotation. The four seasons are labeled winter, spring, summer, and fall. The beginning of each season is determined not by weather in a particular location but by where the sun will be directly overhead at noon at a particular location on Earth.

Research Questions

1. What causes winter, summer, spring, and fall?

2. What is the longest day of the year? The shortest?

3. Are there parts of the world that have no seasons?

4. How does each season have an effect on your life?

Web Sites

http://www.worldbook.com/fun/seasons/html/seasons.htm

This is a great site. There is a seasons quiz that students can take before a season unit and re-take at the end of that unit. It explains why we have four seasons. There are diagrams to help students understand what they are reading. (S: 4–6, T: All)

http://www.4seasons.org.uk/mainmenu.htm

This Web site provides students with project ideas relating to the weather and the four seasons. It has a database of various weather parameters from a site in New England to use for comparison. (S: 4–6)

Literature Resources

Fowler, Allan. (1991). *How Do You Know It's Summer?* Chicago: Children's Press.
   This simple description of summer describes pronounced characteristics of this season. The photographs depict children participating in a plethora of summer activities.

Gibbons, Gail. (1994). *The Reasons for Seasons*. New York: Holiday House.
   This excellent book describes in simple terminology how the tilt of the Earth's axis and the relationship of the sun determine why we have seasons.

Lerner, Carol. (1980). *Seasons of the Tallgrass Prairie*. New York: Morrow.
   This book describes the plant life of the American prairie. The plants are described and written about through the seasons. The reader can see how the plants change from season to season.

Livingston, Myra Cohn. (1982). *A Circle of Seasons*. New York: Holiday House.
   This poetry book of the seasons is beautifully illustrated. It paints vivid descriptions of the four seasons. The book can easily be integrated into a poetry and/or senses thematic unit. It is suitable for students of all ages.

Maestro, Betsy. (1994). *Why Do Leaves Change Color?* New York: HarperCollins.
   The life process of trees is described along with the reasons why their leaves change color. This book discusses how trees prepare for winter.

Turner, Ann Warren. (1993). *Apple Valley Year*. New York: Macmillan.
   The Clark family keeps busy throughout all four seasons caring for their apple orchard. They are pruning the dead branches at the end of winter, carrying bee hives among the trees in May, propping up branches heavy with summer fruit, and harvesting apples in the fall.

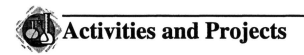

Activities and Projects

1. Ask students to construct a bulletin board. Create a tree out of construction paper or felt. Ask students to create objects (snowflakes, birds, ornaments, brown leaves, etc.) from pieces of construction paper, each of which can be placed on the tree to designate a particular season. Encourage students to write the names of the corresponding seasons on the backs of the pieces.

2. Ask students to construct a bar graph. Encourage them to interview students in other classes to determine what their favorite season is. The results can be tabulated on the graph (for example, snowballs cut from construction paper can designate a certain number of people who like winter; robins can designate a certain number of people who enjoy spring most). If each object represents five people, students will be able to construct a most interesting and revealing chart.

3. Ask students to research one or more of the Web sites or literature resources listed above. Ask them to work in small groups to put together a mini-lesson on the seasons that could be presented to another class at their grade level or to a class at a grade lower than theirs. Provide opportunities for students to present their lessons. Discuss those presentations.

4. Divide the class into four groups. Assign each group one wall of the classroom. Ask each group to research the resources above and to create a large, oversized mural of facts, pictures, collages, illustrations, and so forth, for one designated season of the year. Each group can be responsible for adding to its mural for a designated period of time. Provide opportunities for students to share their murals and reasons why certain objects were placed on the wall.

Storms

 Introduction

Thunderstorms are formed whenever warm, moist air is pushed upward rapidly, accompanied by equally rapid downdrafts of cool air. Lightning, thunder, heavy rain, and strong gusts of wind usually accompany thunderstorms. Most thunderstorms are short, rarely lasting more than two hours, but it is possible to have many thunderstorms in a day. Each year there are more than 16 million thunderstorms around the world.

Thunderstorms are the most powerful electrical storms in the atmosphere. In 20 minutes, a single thunderstorm can drop 125 million gallons of rain and give off more electrical energy than is used by a large city in a week. Basically, there are two types of thunderstorms: air-mass thunderstorms and frontal thunderstorms. An air-mass thunderstorm, often called a summer thunderstorm, is formed within an air mass during hot summer afternoons. It happens when hot, moist air above the Earth's surface rises, forming cumulus, then cumulonimbus, clouds. Most summer thunderstorms are localized. A frontal thunderstorm is formed when a cold front arrives, pushing warmer air ahead of it. This air movement forms a series or long line of thunderstorms, which may be hundreds of miles long and up to 50 miles wide.

 Research Questions

1. What can you do to protect yourself during a storm?

2. Why does lightning strike? How often does lightning strike?

3. How fast does a lightning bolt travel?

4. What are the different types of lightning?

5. What is a thunderstorm?

6. What is thunder?

 Web Sites

http://www.azstarnet.com/anubis/zaphome.htm

This site was made by a kid for kids. The pictures are all hand-drawn and there is easy-to-understand information on lightning. The site was created by a girl who had been struck by lightning, and she has included other stories about children and adults who have been struck. She also mentions safety precautions and stresses the dangers of lightning. (S: All)

http://library.advanced.org/15325

In this Weather Wizardry site, one can find out about all types of weather. Thunderstorms, blizzards, hurricanes, flooding, drought, tornadoes, and monsoons are explained along with some fun facts and safety tips. (S: 4–6)

http://www.whnt19.com/kidwx/index.html

This Wild, Wild Weather page contains information on the causes and effects of wind, tornadoes, hurricanes, and more. There is a section on lightning with statistics and safety tips, along with a section that would be great for teachers. (S: All, T: All)

http://tqjunior.advanced.org/6298/

This site includes facts on lightning and hurricanes and how they occur. The large type and illustrations that are all drawn by children make this site great for kids. Some fun activities are a lightning flash quiz and a hurricane word search. (S: All)

http://www.co.honolulu.hi.us/ocda/thunder.htm

At this site students can learn about thunderstorms and how to protect themselves during a lightning strike. Lots of good information! (S: 4–6)

http://www.srh.noaa.gov/oun/skywarn/spotterguide.html

This is an illustrated guide to spotting severe storms. Filled with detailed photographs and clear explanations, this is a superior reference tool. (S: 4–6, T: 4–6)

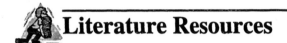 **Literature Resources**

Branley, Franklyn M. (1985). *Hurricane Watch*. New York: Crowell.

The beginnings of a hurricane are covered in this book. Dark colors used in the illustrations set the mood for the horror these storms can produce. The author mentions several tips people should follow to safeguard their lives and belongings.

Broekel, Ray. (1982). *A New True Book: Storms*. Chicago: Children's Press.

In this brief introduction students learn about the various storms that occur. Along with life-like pictures of storms, hurricanes, tornadoes, and lightning, the author includes a glossary of terms.

Hiscock, Bruce. (1993). *The Big Storm*. New York: Macmillan.

Using a description of a storm that crossed the United States in 1982, Hiscock explains basic facts about storms. He does an excellent job helping his readers understand how one storm can produce different types of storms.

Lesser, Carolyn. (1997). *Storm on the Desert*. San Diego: Harcourt Brace.

A beautifully illustrated and captivating text about a sudden thunderstorm on the desert make this book an ideal read-along for any unit on storms. This is a book you will share over and over again.

Simon, Seymour. (1997). *Lightning*. New York: Morrow Junior Books.

Seymour includes amazing photos that attract readers to this topic. He describes the dangers of lightning and safety precautions for people to follow. One suggestion is for people to avoid open fields. Teachers and students alike will love reading this book again and again.

———. (1989). *Storms*. New York: Mulberry Books.

Atmospheric conditions that turn violent produce storms. With full-color pictures and easy-to-read text, this book provides basic information about how storms are formed. The pictures in this book are incredible.

Smith, Howard E., Jr. (1972). *Play with the Wind*. New York: McGraw-Hill.

This book discusses wind storms in a way that children can easily understand. Meaningful learning occurs when using this book as an introduction to the different types of storms.

Activities and Projects

1. Invite students to log on to the Web site http://www.nssl.noaa.gov/edu/ to learn about various types of storms. Encourage students to print and complete Billy and Maria's storm safety coloring book, available from the Web site. When students finish, ask them to bind it into a book they can keep for reference.

2. Divide students into groups and ask them to create a storm safety bulletin. Ask them to make use of the literature and Web sites offered to get safety tips to use for the bulletin. Students should include precautions to take when preparing for a storm and include tips for staying safe during a storm. Each group should distribute their bulletin to a different classroom in the school to use as a reference for storm safety.

3. Ask students to create a "Question Box" to be placed in the school lobby where any student may submit a question about storms. The students should answer these questions in writing and deliver them back to the questioners' classrooms. From the questions received, students should compile a list of frequently asked questions and distribute it to the other classes in the school.

4. Provide students with copies of *USA Today* and ask them to cut out the weather maps on the back of the front section for a period of two weeks. Encourage students to examine the weather maps closely. Ask them to note the presence and movement of cold and warm fronts across the country. Ask students to list the kinds of weather changes the appearance of each front might bring and compare those with the actual weather conditions in succeeding days. Encourage students to compare weather found in various parts of the country.

Tornadoes

Introduction

Tornadoes are the smallest, most violent, and most short-lived of all storms. They occur almost exclusively in the United States, chiefly in the Mississippi Valley and the eastern half of the Great Plains (Iowa, Kansas, Texas, Oklahoma, Arkansas, Mississippi, Illinois, Indiana, and Missouri).

Tornadoes most frequently occur during the spring and early summer and usually in the afternoon. Tornadoes are formed when a layer of cold, dry air is pushed over a layer of warm, moist air (typically cold, heavy air moves under warm, light air). The warm, moist air then quickly forces its way in a spiral movement through the layer of cold air. Strong whirling winds are formed around a center of low pressure, producing a tornado.

Tornadoes vary in size, but can be as much as one mile wide. Although the tornado moves in a wandering path of about 25 to 40 mph, the winds spin around like a top and can reach speeds of up to 500 mph. Most tornadoes last for approximately eight minutes and will travel approximately 15 miles.

Research Questions

1. How are tornadoes formed?

2. Where are most tornadoes found? Why?

3. Why do most tornadoes occur in the United States? Where are they most likely to occur?

4. How are tornadoes measured? Why are they measured?

Web Sites

http://www.chaseday.com/

Students can see the many different shapes tornadoes make, types of tornadoes, damage caused, and even follow the tornado storm season. There are archives of pictures depicting damage and tornadoes in action. (S: 4–6, T: 4–6)

http://www.nssl.noaa.gov/edu/tornado/

This site of the National Severe Storm Laboratory provides the teacher and student with a solid background about the origin, location, and detection of tornadoes. It also provides information about what you can do to protect yourself in the event that you are in a tornado's path. The site has good information in a relatively easy-to-follow format. (S: 4–6, T: All)

http://www.howstuffworks.com/tornado.htm

This is an excellent site that explains how tornadoes work. There are diagrams depicting the development of a tornado, which is useful for students to see how a tornado actually occurs. (S: 4–6, T: All)

http://www.tornadoproject.com/

Tornado Project Online discusses the myths, oddities, and safety issues related to tornadoes. There is a section on the page devoted to facts and questions. Also included are real-life stories about tornadoes. (S: 4–6, T: 4–6)

 # Literature Resources

Adoff, Arnold. (1977). *Tornado!: Poems*. New York: Delcorte Press.

This book contains poetic descriptions of a tornado and its aftermath. It provides great examples of poetry being used to describe a natural disaster.

Beard, Darleen. (1999). *Twister*. New York: Farrar.

Wonderfully written, this story tells how two children are able to survive an oncoming tornado. This is a very reassuring tale.

Branley, Franklyn M. (1988). *Tornado Alert*. New York: HarperCollins.

In a simple format, this book describes how tornadoes are created. The book discusses safety precautions necessary to survive a tornado.

Byars, Betsy. (1996). *Tornado*. New York: HarperCollins.

As they wait out a tornado in their storm cellar, a family listens to their farmhand tell about a dog that was blown into his life by another tornado when he was a boy.

Harshman, Marc. (1995). *The Storm*. New York: Cobblehill Books/Dutton.

Confined to a wheelchair, Jonathan faces the terror of a tornado by himself. He saves the lives of horses on his family's farm.

Kramer, Stephen. (1992). *Tornado*. Minneapolis, MN: Carolrhoda Books.

This book describes how tornadoes form, how they are studied, and the various types of tornadoes.

Morris, Neil. (1999). *Hurricanes and Tornadoes*. Hauppage, NY: Barron's.

This book describes why tornadoes happen and where they happen. There are stories from victims who survived hurricanes and tornadoes as well.

 # Activities and Projects

1. Ask students to research safety precautions they would have to take during a tornado, at home, school, and after the storm is over. Then have students, in groups of two, create a tornado safety book to share with their reading buddies (in another grade).

2. Ask students to use the listed literature and Web sites to come up with what it is like to be involved in a tornado crisis. Students can interview people who have been involved with tornadoes, read stories, watch videos, do research via the Internet, or correspond with a pen pal who may have experienced a tornado. Students should compile a classroom book or videorecord a weather program or talk show on what it is like to be involved with a tornado, safety precautions that should be taken, and the impact these natural disasters have on our communities.

3. Ask the students to bring in the Sunday comics. Have them read the comics over the weekend. Model the creation of a comic strip for the class. Divide the students up into groups of three or four. Brainstorm some of the facts that they know about tornadoes that they might wish to include in their informative and amusing comic. Ask the students to create their own comic strip (pictures and sentences) depicting the development of a tornado and the destruction it can cause. Students can access http://www.chaseday.com. and literature resources to complete this project.

4. Have students be tornado trackers, pretending they are die-hard tornado hunters. How would they go about predicting where and when the tornadoes are most likely to roam? What would they pack? What kind of things would be important to measure while tracking tornadoes? What would they be measuring and why? Following are some Web sites for additional information: http://www.wx-fx.com/chase.html. Have students go into the introduction to stormchasing. This site will provide information about the equipment that students may wish to take along. http://www.sunnysuffolk. edu/-mandias/honors/student/tornado/intensity.htm. This site provides concise details about the grading of tornadoes. Have students go to the section on measuring tornado intensity. They can write this information up in a story format if desired.

5. How are tornadoes graded? Have students go to http://www.nssl.noaa.gov/edu/tornado/ as well as http://www.sunnysuffolk.edu/-mandias/honors/student/tornado/intensity.htm and try to answer the following questions: How many of each grade of tornado occurred in the United States in the past three years? Do you notice any patterns? How do you account for these patterns. Have students look at the year 1896 and answer this question: Do you have any theories about why 1896 may have been one of the deadliest years for tornadoes in American history? Students may find the Web site http://php.iupui.edu/-eabeaver/toroccur.html extremely helpful.

6. Have students write an acrostic poem about tornadoes and illustrate it. Display the poems and pictures on a clothesline in the classroom. A sample poem is:

> Thundering clouds loom
> Over our heads.
> Rumbling with an eerie sound,
> Never have I trembled so
> Alas,
> Deadly silence.
> Oh no, we're in the middle of the eye!

Volcanoes

Introduction

A volcano is a mountain or a hill formed around a crack in the Earth's crust, through which molten rock and other hot materials are thrown out. The rock inside the Earth's mantle is very hot, but it is solid because of the great pressures on it. When the pressure on some of this solid rock is reduced, such as when a crack or fault forms in the Earth's crust, the rock becomes a liquid known as magma. This magma flows upward to the Earth's surface through the crack that was formed or through a weak spot in the Earth's surface. This is known as a volcanic eruption.

Not all volcanic eruptions are violent; many, such as those in Hawaii, are quiet. Others, however, are quite explosive, such as those in the East Indies and Mediterranean. Some alternate between being quiet and explosive.

Volcanoes are classified as active (currently erupting or have recently erupted, such as Kilauea in Hawaii), dormant (have not erupted for some time but still show signs of some activity, such as Mt. Rainier in Washington), or extinct (have not erupted for some time, with no signs of activity).

Research Questions

1. What are the different parts of a volcano?

2. What are some different ways a volcano can form?

3. What are some of the different types of eruptions?

4. What are the main types of volcanoes?

5. What was the greatest volcanic explosion of all time?

Web Sites

http://volcano.und.nodak.edu
   This site is simply the best! It offers opportunities for students to e-mail volcanologists, keep up to date on the latest volcanic eruptions, and discover how volcanoes work. Teachers can get complete lesson plans on volcanoes. This site is outstanding in every way! (S: All, T: All)

http://windows.ivv.nasa.gov/cgi-bin/tour_def/earth/interior/volcanos_general.html
   At this site students can learn several ways in which a volcano can form and about several different kinds of volcanoes, as well as about the process of eruption. (S: All, T: All)

http://www.geo.mtu.edu/volcanoes
   This site provides information about volcanoes, current global volcanic activity, research in remote sensing of volcanoes and their eruptive products, and hazard mitigation, as well as links to government agencies and research institutions, and even some volcano humor. (T: All)

http://library.advanced.org/17457/english/volcanoes/index.php3?action=legend

This site goes over certain legends of volcanoes, mostly Italian legends, types of volcanoes, and types of volcanic eruptions. Students can also learn about the types of eruptions, volcanic features, and the effects of volcanoes. (S: All, T: All)

http://library.advanced.org/17457/

This site has loads of information about volcanoes and plate tectonics. It was created by kids especially for kids. (S: 4–6, T: 4–6)

http://www.nps.gov/havo/

Learn all about Hawaii Volcanoes National Park, one of the most fascinating and incredible national parks in the country, at this site. Take a virtual journey and a most informative trip. (S: 4–6, T: All)

http://www.learner.org/exhibits/volcanoes/

At this site students can learn about what causes volcanoes and find case studies of famous volcanoes from around the world. Loaded with information! (S: 4–6, T: 4–6)

http://www.germantown.k12.il.us/html/volcanoes1.html

This site contains facts, photos, and tons of information about volcanoes created by students for students. Lots of valuable information for teachers as well. (S: 4–6, T: All)

Literature Resources

Lasky, Kathryn. (1992). *Surtsey: The Newest Place on Earth*. New York: Hyperion.

Lyrical prose and spectacular photographs recount the story of this newest volcanic island, created off the coast of Iceland in 1963.

Lauber, Patricia. (1986). *Volcano: The Eruption and Healing of Mount St. Helens*. New York: Bradbury.

The events leading up to and following the eruption of Mt. St. Helens in Washington are described in rich detail in this book.

Lewis, Thomas P. (1985). *Hill of Fire*. New York: Harper.

This is the exciting story of the eruption of Paricutin, the volcano in Mexico that burst from a farmer's field and changed the lives of the people who lived nearby.

Simon, Seymour. (1988). *Volcanoes*. New York: Morrow.

Using clear and concise language, the author explains how volcanoes are formed, how they erupt, different types of lava, and how volcanoes affect the earth.

Taylor, Barbara. (1993). *Mountains and Volcanoes*. New York: Kingfisher.

This wondrously illustrated text is highlighted by informative details and stories about mountains and volcanoes.

Vancleave, Janice Pratt. (1994). *Janice Vancleave's Volcanoes*. New York: John Wiley & Sons.

Student researchers can choose from 20 experiments, including one that tests how pressure affects rock in the asthenosphere and another that explores how the viscosity of lava affects flow rate. Kids can make the classic erupting volcano and create their own molten lava rock.

Watt, Fiona. (1993). *Earthquakes and Volcanoes*. London: Usborne.
   Lots of illustrations and a detailed text make this a fascinating book.

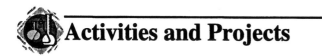 # Activities and Projects

1. Bring in samples of volcanic ash and/or lava and show them to students. (These can be obtained through science supply companies such as Hubbard Scientific, P.O. Box 104, Northbrook, IL 60065, 800-323-8368; The Institute for Earth Education, P.O. Box 288, Warrenville, IL 60555, 509-395-2299; or Scott Resources, P.O. Box 2121F, Fort Collins, CO 80522, 800-289-9299). Ask students to discuss the feel of these substances in comparison with the descriptions in the literature resources above.

2. Ask students to record the titles of each of the four different kinds of volcanoes on four separate sheets of oaktag. Encourage them to draw illustrations of selected volcanoes (from around the world) on each sheet of oaktag. Students should consult other references (e.g., Web sites and/or literature resources).

3. Ask students to construct comparative charts of volcanoes according to different climatic regions of the world (e.g., how many active volcanoes are located in tropical regions versus how many active volcanoes are located in polar regions). Is there a relationship between climate and the location of active and/or inactive volcanoes?

4. Ask students to make charts of the dormancy periods of selected volcanoes. For example, which volcanoes have remained dormant the longest? Which volcanoes have had the most recent eruptions? Where are the most dormant volcanoes located? Where are the most active volcanoes located?

5. Ask students to compare the photographs and videos in the Web sites listed above with the photos in selected books. What similarities are there? What kinds of differences are noted? How can students account for the differences in photos of the same volcanoes? Have students record their conclusions in their journals.

6. Ask students to speculate on what happens when a bottle of soda pop is vigorously shaken. How is that action similar to the action of a volcano? Are there other "actions" similar to those that take place inside a volcano?

7. Ask students to watch a video of a volcano erupting (e.g., *The Violent Earth*, National Geographic Society, Washington, DC 20036; Catalog No. 51234). Afterwards, ask students to pretend that they are at the site of one of the eruptions. Ask them to put together an "on-the-spot" newscast (videotape) recording their reactions during the "eruption."

8. Ask students to conduct some library research on famous volcanoes in history (e.g., Krakatoa, Mt. Fuji, Vesuvius). Have them assemble collected information in a large class book or present it via a specially prepared videotape.

9. Some students may be interested in investigating the myths and legends of volcanoes throughout history. Ask them to investigate how those stories and tales compare with what modern science knows about volcanoes today.

Weather

Introduction

   Simply stated, weather is the conditions that exist in the air around us at any given time: the temperature and pressure of the atmosphere, the amount of moisture it holds, and the presence or absence of wind and clouds. When predicting weather, meteorologists look at the kinds of air masses that are moving across the Earth. These air masses are responsible for changes in the weather.

   An air mass is a huge body of air that may cover a vast portion of the Earth's surface and may be very wide and quite high. In any air mass the temperature and the humidity are about the same throughout. However, air masses differ greatly from each other, and the weather that an air mass will bring depends mostly on the particular temperature and humidity that it has. An air mass is formed when the atmosphere stays quietly over a certain part of the Earth's surface until it picks up the temperature and humidity of that part of the Earth's surface. Air masses may be tropical (warm), polar (cold), continental (come from continents), or maritime (come from oceans). Once an air mass is formed, it is usually carried to another place by the general movements of the atmosphere.

Research Questions

   1.   What is the difference between weather and climate?

   2.   What does a meteorologist do?

   3.   What are the differences between high pressure and low pressure air masses?

   4.   How does weather affect the things we do?

   5.   What are some instruments used to measure the weather?

Web Sites

http://athena.wednet.edu/curric/weather
   Lots and lots of instructional materials, links, resources, lesson plans, multimedia programs, and education programs on every aspect of the weather can be found on this site. A magnificent research tool. (T: All)

http://www.weatheronline.com
   This incredible Web site has just about every type of resource and information that teachers would need for weather studies. Scores of links and tons of data highlight this powerful site. (T: All)

http://www.learner.org/exhibits/weather/

This is a great resource for students. Here they will be able to discover loads of fascinating information about many aspects of the weather cycle. (S: 4–6)

http://tqjunior.advanced.org/3805/

This site has tons and tons of materials about the weather created for kids by kids. It is a superior site that will keep students occupied and informed for hours on end. (S: All)

http://www.niceweather.com/ww/

This delightful site comes from the Jersey Weather Service. Here teachers and students can pose any type of weather-related question to a meteorologist and get an accurate and speedy response. Perfect for any kind of research project! (S: All, T: All)

http://www.srh.noaa.gov/oun/severewx/glossary.html

A comprehensive glossary of weather terms by the National Weather Service is located on this site. (T: All)

Literature Resources

Ardley, Neil. (1992). *The Science Book of Weather.* New York: Gulliver Books.

This book contains several great low-budget weather experiments you and your class can conduct.

DeWitt, Linda. (1991). *What Will the Weather Be?* New York: HarperCollins.

This brief book is a wonderful introduction to meteorologists, the instruments they use and what they measure, and weather patterns and changes.

Gibbons, Gail. (1990). *Weather Words and What They Mean.* New York: Holiday House.

This terrific book introduces young readers to common meteorological terms and their definitions.

Leslie, Clare. (1991). *Nature All Year Long.* New York: Greenwillow Books.

This book provides readers with a month-by-month seasonal guide to changes in plant and animal behavior.

Markle, Sandra. (1993). *A Rainy Day.* New York: Orchard.

This is an illustrated explanation of why it rains, what happens when it does, and where the rain goes.

Martin, Bill & Archambault, John. (1988). *Listen to the Rain.* New York: Henry Holt.

This is a playful and creative introduction to the sounds of rain.

McMillan, Bruce. (1991). *The Weather Sky.* New York: Farrar.

This book presents a year's worth of sky changes along with color photographs and descriptive illustrations.

McVey, Vicki. (1991). *The Sierra Club Book of Weatherwisdom.* San Francisco: Sierra Club.

Basic weather principles and experiments in tandem with weather customs and traditions highlight this book.

Otto, Carol. (1990). *That Sky, That Rain.* New York: Crowell.
This is an introduction to the water cycle with emphasis on the creation of rain.

Polacco, Patricia. (1990). *Thunder Cake.* New York: Philomel.
An approaching storm frightens a young girl until her grandmother shows her how to bake a thunder cake.

Serfozo, Mary, (1990). *Rain Talk.* New York: McElderry Books.
During a summer rainstorm, a small girl notices the way the rain affects her senses.

Steele, Philip. (1991). *Rain: Causes and Effects.* New York: Watts.
This excellent introduction to rain and its effects on humans includes several simple experiments.

Wyatt, Valerie. (1990). *Weatherwatch.* Reading, MA: Addison-Wesley.
This book is packed with weather lore, weather facts, weather data, and loads of experiments.

 # Activities and Projects

1. Temperature experiment: Have your students, working in pairs, do the following experiment:

   a. Get two clear cups and two thermometers.

   b. Put a thermometer in each cup.

   c. Fill one cup halfway with water. Fill the other cup halfway with dirt.

   d. Keep the cups in a cool spot in the classroom for 30 minutes. Read each temperature and record and label it.

   e. Move the cups to a sunny spot outside. Wait one hour.

   f. Read each temperature and record it.

   g. Subtract the inside temperature from the outside temperature to find each change in temperature. Record this also.

2. Invite a local weather forecaster to visit your classroom to talk about her or his job. Brief your students beforehand so they can generate questions for the guest. Follow up the visit by inviting students to share their thoughts about being a weather forecaster.

3. Ask students to gather newspaper and/or magazine articles about weather or bring in information from daily weather forecasts from local newspapers or television news shows. Have the students file the articles in shoeboxes and share them in a "Weather News" area. Ask students to examine the clippings and compile a list comparing and contrasting the different types of forecasts.

4. Discuss why weather is different in different places. How can we find out about the weather in the United States? What symbols could we use to record and report the weather on a map? For homework, have students find out about the weather patterns in the United States using the map in the local newspaper. Make weather symbols from pieces of construction paper and position them on a map of the United States to denote the weather forecast for that particular day. Change these as the conditions in selected areas change.

5. Designate a "Weatherperson of the Day" each day to predict the next day's weather. Ask each student chosen to write her or his prediction on a card and put it on the bulletin board to be uncovered the next morning. Be sure to talk about the current weather conditions and how they might affect the weather the following day.

6. Ask students to complete a temperature chart, working in groups of two or three, as follows:

   a. Place a thermometer outside in a shady area.

   b. Note the temperature in the morning, at noon, and in the afternoon on each of several days.

   c. Put three dots on a graph to indicate the temperatures measured for that day. Connect the dots to illustrate the rise and fall in daily temperature.

   d. Keep an ongoing record of daily temperatures over a span of several weeks. (Post the temperature charts on a bulletin board or collect them in a scrapbook.)

7. Ask students to make weather word cutouts. They should begin by cutting out shapes of clouds, the sun, raindrops, and snowflakes. On each shape they should write one or more appropriate weather-related words. Display the weather words on a bulletin board and add new cutout words as they are learned.

8. Divide the class into various groups. Ask each group to assemble a collection of amazing weather data or weather facts. For example:

   a. Lightning strikes the Earth as frequently as 100 times every second.

   b. In 1953, hailstones as big as golf balls fell in Alberta, Canada.

   c. In a blizzard, winds often reach speeds of 186 mph.

   d. The wettest place in the world is a spot on the island of Kauai in the state of Hawaii. It rains more than 450 inches every year (that's more than 37 feet) on one mountaintop.

   e. The fastest tornado had a recorded speed of 280 mph.

9. Many local television weather forecasters make visits to elementary classrooms as a regular part of their jobs. Contact your local television station and inquire about scheduling a visit from the local weatherperson. Be sure students have an opportunity to generate questions prior to the visit.

Weather Forecasting

Introduction

Weather forecasting entails predicting how the present state of the atmosphere will change. Present weather conditions are obtained from ground observations, observations from ships and aircraft, Doppler radar, and satellites. This information is sent to meteorological centers, where the data are collected, analyzed, and made into a variety of charts, maps, and graphs. These charts, maps, and graphs are then sent electronically to forecast offices, where local and regional weather forecasts are made. In addition, these offices prepare weather advisories and warnings of impending severe weather.

Research Questions

1. What is a weather forecast?

2. Who is responsible for forecasting weather?

3. What are the major guidelines in forecasting weather?

4. Name and define five basic meteorology terms.

5. What is today's local weather forecast?

Web Sites

http://www.weather.com/twc/homepage.twc
Up-to-date weather information is available for all U.S. states and major cities, as well as most countries and major cities around the world. Weather maps and satellite images help students visualize the weather. (T: All)

http://www.atmos.uiuc.edu
Information available at this site includes current weather data, pointers to climate data, hypermedia instructional modules, and links to other resources. Some of the teaching modules include a thematic unit on weather for grades 2–4 and a unit on forces and winds. Of interest is a slide series, *A Look at Thunderstorms and Their Severe Weather Potential.* (T: All)

http://www.ncsa.uiuc.edu/Edu/RSE/RSEred/WeatherHome.html
Weather Here and There is an integrated weather unit, incorporating interaction with the Internet along with hands-on, collaborative problem-solving activities for students in grades 4–6. The unit is divided into six lessons. Math, science, geography, and language arts are integrated into the process of learning about weather phenomena. (S: 4–6, T: 4–6)

Literature Resources

DeWitt, Lynda. (1991). *What Will the Weather Be?* New York: HarperCollins

This story explains the basic characteristics of weather—temperature, humidity, wind speed and direction, and air pressure—and how meteorologists gather data for their forecasts. The author discusses cold and warm fronts, various weather instruments, including thermometers, wind vanes, anemometers, hygrometers, and barometers, and shows how forecasters use these to find fronts and predict the weather.

Gibbons, Gail. (1993). *Weather Forecasting*. New York: Aladdin Paperbacks.

This is a look at all four seasons, as observed, recorded, and predicted by experts at a weather station. It describes forecasters at work as they use sophisticated equipment to track and gauge the constant changes in the weather.

Palazzo, Janet. (1989). *What Makes Weather (Now I Know)*. Mahweh, NJ: Troll Communications.

The text and pictures in this book present different kinds of weather and suggest how to tell from the sky what the day's weather might be like.

Weigelt, Udo. (1992). *All-Weather Friends*. New York: South-North Books.

His animal friends are convinced that frogs can predict the weather, but Moss the frog frequently disappoints them with his inaccurate predictions.

Activities and Projects

1. Bring in a videotape containing clips of a few different weather broadcasts. Ask the class to discuss the format and information that was shared. Divide the class into groups of three or four students. Each group is responsible for assembling costumes, creating charts, writing scripts, and incorporating weather terms. Encourage them to practice several times before broadcast day arrives. Students will perform their broadcasts in front of the class.

2. Talk to the students about how thermometers are used to measure temperature and how the warmer the weather, the higher the liquid in a thermometer rises. Temperature is measured in degrees Fahrenheit. Many thermometers go up and down by two-degree steps, starting from zero degrees. Thirty-two degrees Fahrenheit is freezing. Give groups of students thermometers to examine. Provide the groups with cups of both ice and hot tap water. Ask students to try testing the temperatures by inserting the thermometers into each of the cups. Demonstrate to the students how you would take a reading of the temperature. Give students a handout with pictures of thermometers; Ask students to review different temperatures with a partner. Students will read each thermometer, record the temperature, and decide which type of clothing is appropriate for that particular temperature. Students should also draw a picture representing the types of weather that may occur at those particular temperatures.

3. Have students design their own weather maps. Give each child and a partner a portion of a U.S. map. Provide the students with a list of requirements to be labeled on the maps. For example, students could be given a map of the northeast region of the United States. They may be asked to label items such as a cold front coming toward New Jersey and snow in New York City. Temperatures can also be added, such as 32 degrees in Newark, New Jersey, and 29 degrees in Hartford, Connecticut.

4. Have students observe and record the weather patterns that occur in your area of the country. Be sure they have an opportunity to record weather conditions over a long period of time (two to three months, if possible). Have them create their own "Weather Notebooks" to keep track of rainfall, cloud conditions, temperature, humidity, barometric pressure, and the like. A Weather Watching Kit is available from Delta Education (P.O. Box 950, Hudson, NH 03051, Catalog No. 5J-738-2253). Also available from the same company are two classroom weather charts, Chalkboard Weather Station (Catalog No. 57-230-1639) and Weather Chart (Catalog No. 57-230-1640).

Weathering

Introduction

The process of breaking down rocks is called weathering. Weathering is caused by the action of the sun, air, and water. There are two basic types of weathering: mechanical weathering and chemical weathering. *Mechanical weathering* is the breaking down of rock into small pieces without any chemical changes in the rock itself. In *chemical weathering* chemical changes take place in the rock, forming new products that can be carried away more easily than the original rock.

The process of taking away the products of weathering is called erosion, and it is carried on by water, ice, and wind. It's important for students to know that the forces of weathering and erosion are constantly at work on the Earth's surface.

Research Questions

1. What is weathering? What are the major types of weathering?

2. How do temperature, humidity, wind, and rain affect rock over periods of time?

3. What different factors will affect the weathering process? How?

4. Do you feel that weathering is a beneficial or a harmful process?

5. What is erosion? How is erosion different from weathering? How are they related?

Web Sites

http://schoolsite.edex.net.uk/192/envhome.htm
This site provides an excellent starting point outlining the basic concept of weathering and the various types of weathering. There are concise definitions, examples, and illustrations of weathering. Erosion is also discussed, and both the teacher and student will gain a greater appreciation of the similarities and differences between erosion and weathering. A self-quiz will enable teachers to better assess their understanding of the concepts. (S: 4–6, T: All)

http://www.encyclopedia.com/articles/13706.html
This site includes short, concise, dictionary type definitions that a teacher might want to use on a bulletin board about weathering. (T: 4–6)

http://members.tripod.com/CMSMIG/weathering.htm
This Web site provides short definitions of the various types of weathering. It also cites examples of these types. Most notable, however, are several graphs that chart the relationship of weathering with independent variables (temperature, humidity, surface area, etc.). This will help to further facilitate a teacher's understanding of weathering. (T: 4–6)

http://members.tripod.com/Geography_homework/weather.htm

This site discusses biological and chemical weathering. It concentrates on the weathering process of the riverbed rock surfaces. Granite and other rocks are specifically mentioned. The various types of erosion are also explained. This site will further enhance the teacher's knowledge of the weathering process. (T: 4–6)

Literature Resources

Ettlinger, Doris. (1995). *Rocks and Minerals: Mind Boggling Experiments You Can Turn into Science Fair Projects*. New York: John Wiley & Sons.

This is a great book to help students understand how rocks break apart, how fossils are created, and so forth. This text entices students to experiment with these hands-on activities to find out how these things happen.

Hooper, Meredith. (1996). *The Pebble in My Pocket: A History of Our Earth*. New York: Viking Children's Books.

This is an awesome look at the history of our Earth, how mountains were created, how animals evolved, and much more. The history of our planet is looked at in a unique fashion. Students will develop an understanding of where our Earth came from and where it is today.

Winner, Cherie. (1999). *Erosion (Earth Watch)*. Minneapolis, MN: Carolrhoda Books.

This is a good book for students looking at erosion and a great way to incorporate weathering as well. The text looks at how our Earth erodes.

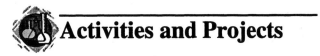

Activities and Projects

1. Ask students to collect several examples of different types of rocks or stones from around their homes or from the school grounds. Encourage students to examine the rocks and note any effects of weathering. What indicators are there? Why are some rocks more weathered than others? What types of weathering might have been at work on selected rocks? Students should construct a graph or chart of their results.

2. Ask students to explore in their community for things that have weathered (for example, statues, plaques). Ask students to discuss the various forces that may have contributed to that weathering process. Why are some items more weathered than others?

3. Ask students to investigate one or more of the Web sites listed above. If they were to construct a unit on "Weathering" which of the sites would provide them with the most useful information? Which site has information appropriate for primary students? Which one has information appropriate for intermediate students? What makes one site more informative than another?

4. Soak pieces of sandstone in water overnight. Place a piece of saturated sandstone in a plastic bag and seal it tightly. Put the bag in the freezer overnight. Ask students to observe the results. (Water expands as it freezes, causing the rock to split. The same type of weathering occurs in nature, breaking large rocks into smaller ones.)

Wetlands

Introduction

Wetlands are magnificent and diverse environments. They are home to an incredible variety of plant and animal life, some of it found nowhere else on the planet. Scientists have estimated that more than 5,000 different kinds of plants and trees can be found in wetlands.

Wetlands are defined as a mingling of water and land. The water may be standing (as in a pond or marsh) or it may be slowly moving (e.g., the Everglades). The water may be only a few inches or up to several feet deep. Most of the wetlands in the United States are located in the Southeast, the Gulf Coast, the Northeastern coastal states, and selected areas in the upper Midwest. It is estimated that there are currently 95 million acres of wetlands in this country.

Research Questions

1. Why are wetlands endangered?

2. What is a wetland?

3. Where are some of this country's largest wetland areas?

4. What can we do to protect wetlands?

Web Sites

http://www.mobot.org/MBGnet/fresh/wetlands/index.htm

This site offers students a great resource for learning about freshwater and saltwater wetlands. Students will find a ton of information regarding shores and beaches, estuaries, salt marshes, mangroves, and mudflats, as well as freshwater swamps, marshes, bogs, flood plains, and fens. (S: 4–6)

http://www.epa.gov/OWOW/wetlands/vital/wetlands.html

This is an excellent educational site about America's wetlands. Students can learn what wetlands are, what kinds of animals and plants they support, why they are very valuable habitats, current statistics, how they are being endangered, and how they are being protected. (S: 4–6, T: All)

http://nwf.org/nwf/wetlands/

This is a really neat site full of information on current wetland issues and news pieces. (S: 4–6, T: All)

Literature Resources

Asch, Frank (1996). *Sawgrass Poems*. San Diego: Harcourt Brace.
   This delightful collection of poems investigates the wondrous array of plants and animals that live in wetlands.

Hirschi, Ron. (1994). *Save Our Wetlands*. New York: Delacorte Press.
   This is an exploration of wetlands and includes endangered wildlife in threatened wetland habitats.

McLeish, Ewan. (1996). *Habitats: Wetlands*. New York: Thomson Learning.
   This is a great introduction to wetlands and is filled with information about and pictures of wetland habitats all over the world. Children can also learn about the great impact people have on wetlands.

National Wildlife Federation. (1998). *Ranger Rick's Nature Scope: Wading into Wetlands*. New York: Learning Triangle Press.
   Geared to the instructor, this book is filled with a plethora of wetland information and related activities and learning projects.

Staub, Frank (1995). *America's Wetlands*. Minneapolis, MN: Carolrhoda Books.
   This is a thorough and convincing description of America's wetlands and how and why they should be preserved.

Activities and Projects

   1.   Students can learn a lot about the growth and development of frogs when they raise a group of tadpoles in the classroom. Depending on the species, they will be able to observe the changes a tadpole undergoes (metamorphosis) over a period of several weeks.

Materials:

frog's eggs (Students can visit a pond in the spring and look for clumps of jelly-covered eggs. Encourage them to scoop up one to two dozen eggs and place them in a large plastic sandwich bag along with some pond water.)

a long-handled net (available at any pet store)

a large glass jar (an oversized mayonnaise jar works well)

magnifying lens

pond plants

Directions:

a. Take students to a pond to obtain frog eggs, pond water, and pond plants.

b. Upon returning to the classroom, ask them to fill the clean jar about three-quarters full with pond water.

c. Ask students to put the eggs in the jar and place the jar in a location away from direct sunlight (the jar should be kept at room temperature).

d. Ask students to observe the eggs twice a day for a week using the magnifying lens. Have them record what the eggs look like and how they are developing using a journal or an inexpensive scrapbook.

e. The eggs will hatch in about a week. When an egg hatches, place a pond plant in the water (the tadpoles attach themselves to the leaves of the plant).

f. Students will be able to keep the tadpoles (and watch their development) for several weeks.

If students are not able to obtain frog eggs in your local area, you can order the *Grow A Frog* kit (Catalog No. 54-110-0296) from Delta Education (P.O. Box 3000, Nashua, NH 03061-3000, 800-282-9560). At this writing, the kit costs about $15.00 and includes a frog house, food, instructions, and a coupon for tadpoles.

2. Provide students with a set of index cards. Have them record on each card a name of a wetlands plant or animal, such as the following:

   algae
   mosquito
   fish larva
   insects
   leopard frog
   osprey
   bacteria
   nutrients

The cards represent the line of succession in a food chain. Ask students to arrange the cards in a line indicating each organism and the other organisms that are dependent on it for their survival. Students should attach lengths of yarn to the card to denote the relationships. Later, ask students to add additional cards to the deck and create additional relationships in the food chain or food Web. Additional library resources may be necessary (see above).

3. The following experiment will help students learn about various forms of pollution and their effects on an environment, such as a wetlands ecosystem. This activity requires adult supervision and guidance.

Provide students with four empty, clean baby food jars. Label the jars "A," "B," "C," and "D." Prepare each jar as follows: Fill each jar halfway with aged tap water (regular tap water that has been left to stand in an open container for 72 hours). Put a half-inch layer of pond soil into each jar, add one teaspoon of plant fertilizer, then fill each jar the rest of the way with pond water and algae. Allow the jars to sit in a sunny location or on a windowsill for two weeks.

Next, work with students to treat each separate jar as follows:

Jar "A":   Add two tablespoons of liquid detergent.
Jar "B":   Add enough used motor oil to cover the surface.
Jar "C":   Add 1/2 cup of vinegar.
Jar "D":   Do not add anything.

Allow the jars to sit for four more weeks.

Students will notice that the addition of the motor oil, vinegar, and detergent prevents the healthy growth of organisms that took place during the first two weeks of the activity. In fact, those jars now show little or no growth taking place, but the organisms in jar "D" continue to grow. Detergent, motor oil, and vinegar are pollutants that prevent wetlands organisms from obtaining the nutrients they need to continue growing:

The detergent illustrates what happens when large quantities of soap are released into a wetlands area.

The motor oil demonstrates what happens to organisms after an oil spill.

The vinegar shows what can happen to organisms when high levels of acids are added to a wetlands area.

Chapter 7

Space Science

Look at the sky. Look at the stars and constellations scattered across the heavens. Observe the planets and artificial satellites that crisscross the emptiness of space on their regular, and often irregular, journeys. What an incredible array of bodies, both large and small. As we stand on this planet, it's amazing to realize that this world is only a microcosm in the vastness of the universe. It is but one particle in a galaxy of stars, satellites, meteorites, and other celestial bodies. Perhaps even more amazing is the fact that most of the universe is nothing . . . that's right, 99 percent of the entire universe is composed of nothing at all. So when we see a star or planet, it's incredible to think that it is simply an infinitesimal speck in the sweeping panorama of emptiness.

As have humans since the dawn of time, students have always been fascinated with space. In these lessons they will have multiple opportunities to examine and explore each of the planets in our solar system, be able to travel to distant stars and faraway comets, be able to soar into the deepest reaches of the universe, and learn about the contributions and discoveries of the women and men who have reached out beyond the stars.

Students will be able to grapple with the limitless dimensions of outer space. The study of space is surrounded by a myriad of questions and a thousand different ways of answering those questions. Indeed, the more we learn about the heavens around us, the more we realize how little we know and how much we still need to explore. Here students will journey toward brave new worlds and examine dynamic new possibilities.

Asteroids

Introduction

Asteroids are a belt of about 25,000 celestial bodies that circle the Sun between Mars and Jupiter. They all revolve around the Sun in the same direction as the larger planets. Most asteroids are irregular chunks of rock, often mixed with various metals that differ in both size and brightness.

Asteroids come in many sizes. The largest is Ceres, which is about 600 miles across (that's a little less than one-third the size of our moon). Most asteroids, however, are less than a mile across. Astronomers estimate that there may be more than a million asteroids in the asteroid belt, with dozens of new ones being discovered every year.

Sometimes asteroids fall out of their orbits as a result of a collision with another asteroid, a loss of orbital speed, or the gravitational pulls of the planets Mars and Jupiter. When that happens, these asteroids sometimes head on a collision course with Earth. These bodies, which have not yet entered Earth's atmosphere, are known as *meteoroids*. Meteoroids are rocky fragments that frequently range in size from several inches across to as small as a grain of rice. A few, however, may be quite large.

Sometimes these meteoroids come close enough to the Earth to be affected by its gravitational pull. As a result, they are pulled into the Earth's atmosphere. Because they are traveling at high rates of speed, friction makes them and the air molecules around them heat up tremendously. As a result, these meteoroids burn up and disintegrate.

On clear nights, these meteoroids produce brilliant flashes of light. These flashes of light are called *meteors*. This is what we see when we say that there is a "shooting star." On most nights, you can see about three meteors each hour in the early evening and about six each hour between midnight and dawn. Remember that a meteor is *not* a solid object; but rather a flash of light.

Research Questions

1. What is the largest asteroid?

2. Where are asteroids found?

3. What is the difference between an asteroid and a comet?

4. Have asteroids ever struck the Earth?

Web Sites

http://www.hawastsoc.org/solar/eng/homepage.htm
    View of the Solar System provides information on asteroids. There is a list of good information as well as interesting pictures at this site. (S: 4–6)

http://www.star.le.ac.uk/edu/comets/index.html
    This Web site teaches students how to distinguish between asteroids and meteoroids. From the main page, one can easily find more information on either asteroids or meteoroids by clicking on links. The main Asteroid Belt and the origins of meteor showers are both shown. (S: K–3)

http://neo.jpl.nasa.gov/
    Asteroid and Comet Impact Hazards contains a lot of valuable information for students. News reports, pictures, and radar images are included on this site. (S: 4–6)

http://www.s-d-g.freeserve.co.uk/intro.html
    This site deals with the theory that a comet or meteoroid caused the dinosaurs' extinction. Testimonies and news coverage from more recent impacts are given. (S: 4–6)

Literature Resources

Simon, Seymour. (1998). *Comets, Meteors, and Asteroids*. New York, NY: William Morrow.
    This book explains how asteroids and meteors are formed. Examples of meteors hitting the Earth are shown. Actual meteorites have been found in Antarctica and are showcased.

Vogt, Gregory L. (1997). *Asteroids, Comets, and Meteors*. Brookfield, CT: Millbrook Press.
    The distinction between asteroids and meteoroids is discussed in this book. Exquisite illustrations and photographs are an excellent touch.

Activities and Projects

1. Pour flour into several deep cake pans. Divide the students into groups, allowing each group to have a pan. Make the flour surface relatively smooth. Give each student a marble. Allow each student to toss a marble into the pan. This shows how craters are formed and what happens to the surface of a planet when it is hit by a large asteroid.

2. Meteor showers are predictable events, occurring at regular intervals throughout the year. Table 7.1 lists some of the major meteor showers, when they normally occur, and the maximum number of meteors that can be seen in an hour.

    Seeing a meteor shower doesn't require a lot of preparation or expensive equipment. In fact, students will enjoy the "show" more if they don't use a telescope. Encourage them to go outside at night when there is very little light coming from the moon (the darker the sky, the easier it is to see the meteors, simply because many of them are very faint). Students will be able to see more meteors after midnight than they will in the early hours of the evening.

Students may find it easier to lie down on a blanket looking up at the sky. This helps keep the head still, and they'll be able to focus on a larger part of the night sky. They will probably notice that the meteors tend to originate from the same area of the sky. A meteor shower gets it name from the constellation nearest that part of the sky.

Table 7.1
Annual Meteor Showers

Shower	Dates	Maximum Number per Hour
Quadranids	January 1–4	50
Lyrids	April 2–22	10
Eta Aquarids	May 3–5	10
Delta Aquarids	July 26–30	25
Perseids	August 9–15	50
Orionids	October 20–24	20
Leonids	November 14–20	10
Geminids	December 10–13	50

Tell students to keep in mind that the number of meteors in a meteor shower may vary from year to year. In some years there may be lots of meteors in a shower, but in other years there may be few.

3. If possible, invite students to visit a beach, lakefront, or other sandy area. Ask them to tie a piece of string to the middle of a horseshoe magnet and drag it through the sand. Have students place the items that are found in a sealable sandwich bag. Upon returning to the classroom, invite them to use a hand lens or microscope to observe the tiny items they have collected.

    Students will notice that they collect many different items with their magnets. Most of the items are quite small and may be dust-like in their appearance. It is estimated that up to 10 percent of those magnetic particles may be micrometeorites, or very tiny meteorites. That's because tons and tons of meteorites rain down on the surface of the Earth every day. Also, because one of the principle elements in meteorites is iron, they are attracted to the magnet.

    Another place to search for micrometeorites is the dry lakebeds and desert areas of the American Southwest. Iron-bearing rocks are less prevalent in those regions and the particles that are attracted to the magnet have a higher likelihood of being micrometeorites.

    If you live in an area of the country that receives substantial amounts of snow in the winter, gather a bucket of snow and allow it to melt. Invite students to dip their magnets into the melted snow and see if any potential celestial objects are attracted to them.

Comets

Introduction

A comet is a celestial body that revolves around the sun in a long, oval-shaped orbit. Comets have a head and a tail. The comet's head is made up of small rocks and dust, mixed with frozen gases. It is only when the comet approaches the sun that it has a tail. As the comet nears the sun, the frozen gases in the comet's head melt and are changed into vapor. The comet's tail is actually this very thin stream of melted gases. The tail may be millions of miles long. When the comet travels away from the sun, the gases freeze again and the tail disappears.

The pressure of the light from the sun makes the tail point away from the sun when the comet both approaches and leaves it. Comets gain speed as they near the sun and the sun's pull of gravity on them becomes stronger. Comets slow down again as they travel away from the sun and the sun's pull of gravity becomes weaker. The orbital path of most comets is often predictable. Some comets return very quickly and others take much longer to return. (Halley's comet returns every 76 years.)

Research Questions

1. What is a comet?

2. How are comets formed?

3. What is the difference between comets, asteroids, and meteors?

4. Why do comets have tails?

Web Sites

http://smallcomets.physics.uiowa.edu/
Here students can discover the latest information on comets and their destinations. (S: 4–6, T: 4–6)

http://encke.jpl.nasa.gov/whats_visible.html
This page provides a quick summary of comets that can be observed visually. Positions for the comets are given as well as images. Here students can obtain current information and summaries and observe these comets in action. (S: 4–6)

http://comets.amsmeteors.org
At this site students can learn why it is important for us to know about comets and their impact. They can also learn the difference between a comet and a meteor, which a lot of people confuse. There are many outstanding links available through this Web site, containing visuals, animation, and 3-D images. The student will be able to learn about what a comet is, what it looks like, and other information dealing with comets. (S: All)

Literature Resources

Bonar, Samantha. (1998). *Comets*. New York: Franklin Watts.

This book describes the composition, orbits, and existence of several well-known comets. Readers will learn what comets are and where they come from. They will also learn how comets affect us.

Carpenter, Mary-Chapin & Andreasen, Dan. (1998). *Halley Came to Jackson*. New York: Harper-Collins Juvenile Books.

A father shows his baby daughter Halley's comet as it soars across the Jackson sky in 1910. In 1986, that baby, now an adult, comes back to Jackson to see the return of Halley's comet. The illustrations in this book are very colorful and true to life. A wonderful book to capture a historical event.

Moore, Patrick. (1994). *Comets and Shooting Stars*. Brookfield, CT: Copper Beech.

This book explores the history of comets and shooting stars. It is readable and nicely illustrated book and should capture young readers' attention in discovering comets and shooting stars.

Nicolson, Cynthia Pratt. (1999). *Comets, Asteroids, and Meteorites*. Toronto: Kids Can Press.

This book features the latest NASA photos of comets, asteroids, and meteorites. It includes close-up glimpses from the space probe *Galileo*.

Rosen, Sidney & Lindberg, Dean. (1993). *Can You Hitch a Ride on a Comet? (A Question of Science Book)*. Minneapolis, MN: Carolrhoda Books.

This book answers a variety of questions about comets. It covers what they are, where they come from, and where they go. Definitions of words that are in boldfaced type are included in the back of the book.

Simon Seymour. (1994). *Comets, Meteors, and Asteroids*. New York: William Morrow.

This book contains information on comets, meteors, and asteroids: their composition and behavior, where they fit into the greater galactic scene, and how they have been interpreted. It is easily read and contains colorful illustrations to keep the reader interested.

Sipiera, Paul B. (1997). *Comets and Meteors Showers*. Chicago: Children's Press.

This book provides an introduction to comets. It covers where they come from, how they travel, and what their importance is, as well as their relationship to meteor showers. The book contains extra factual information for young readers to pique their creative juices. There is also a glossary of words to expand and challenge their vocabulary.

Vogt, Gregory. (1996). *Asteroids, Comets, and Meteors*. Millbrook, CT: Millbrook Press.

This book presents information on the different types of celestial m matter known as asteroids, comets, and meteors. One can discover what scientists learned from the impact of a comet on the surface of Jupiter.

Activities and Projects

1. Invite the students to read *Halley Came to Jackson*. Ask the students to write down their thoughts about the story. Invite the students to visit the Web site http://starchild. gsfc.nasa.gov/docs/StarChild/StarChild.html. Encourage them to find factual information about Halley's comet. Have the students share this information with the class. Divide the class into groups and invite them to brainstorm what it would be like to see a comet. What feelings might they have? Encourage each group to create a play using this information. Invite them to share their plays with other classes.

2. Invite the students to create their own comet and watch what happens as it melts. This activity must be done with adult supervision. The ingredients are two cups of water, two cups of dry ice, two spoonfuls of sand or dirt, a dash of ammonia, and a dash of dark corn syrup. You will need an ice chest, a large plastic mixing bowl, four medium plastic bags, work gloves, a hammer, a large mixing spoon, and paper towels. Keep the dry ice in an ice chest when transporting it.

    Line your mixing bowl with the plastic bag and place the water in the mixing bowl. Add the sand or dirt and stir well. Add the dash of ammonia and the corn syrup, stirring well after each ingredient. Place the dry ice in the remaining three garbage bags, which have been placed one inside the other. Make sure you wear gloves! Crush the dry ice by pounding it with a hammer. Add the dry ice to the rest of the ingredients in the bowl, stirring vigorously until the whole mixture is almost frozen. Lift the comet out of the bowl, using the plastic liner as a wrap, and mold the mixture into a ball. You should still be wearing your gloves! Unwrap the comet as soon as it can hold its shape. Place the comet on the paper towels on an old cookie pan or cardboard box. The comet is reasonably safe to touch, but use the spoon as a safety precaution.

3. Read *Comets* to the students. Encourage them to discuss what they learned about a comet. Invite the students to visit the Web site http://stardust.ipl.nasa.gov/ kids.html. Once logged onto the Web site they should click on Captain Comet. This will take them to a site devoted to comets. Encourage the students to investigate the various topics they find there.

4. Read *Can You Hitch a Ride on a Comet* to the students. Ask them to share their reactions to the story. How did the characters in the book bring the story alive? Encourage the students to brainstorm what type of characters they would include if they were to write stories about the life of a comet. Then have them write a fictional stories about the life of a comet.

5. Invite students to visit the Web site http://comets.amsmeteors.org. Encourage the students to investigate the facts about comets. What makes them different from a meteor? What exactly are they? Where do they come from and where do they go? What do they look like? Have the students record their answers to these and any other questions that they might have. Invite the students to participate in a class discussion about comets. Based on the information discussed, encourage students to brainstorm further information that they would like to know. Encourage the students to revisit the above Web site and explore the other Web links that will lead them to more visuals and information about comets and specific comets. Ask them to prepare a journal with facts and

figures about comets. Encourage them to add the various information that they have discovered. Ask them to write a story about comets. This story should be nonfiction and should contain the various information that they have gathered. Invite the students to share their stories with the class.

6. Read *Comets, Meteors, and Asteroids* to the students. Encourage them to discuss what they have learned by creating a Venn Diagram. After they have discussed what they know about comets, invite the students to visit the Web site http://stardust.ipl.nasa.gov/ comets.html. Here they can discover what a comet's orbit looks like and the latest pictures of the Comet Wild-2 path. This site is updated every 10 minutes. The images are sharp and the detail is wonderful! Encourage students to write down their discoveries. When all the students have had the chance to view the site, hold a discussion about what they saw.

Constellations

Introduction

The stars above us have always fascinated humans. When observing the heavens, human beings often would imagine patterns or drawings within groups or clusters of stars. Many cultures around the world have invented their own unique and distinctive constellations. But it is those invented and described by ancient Babylonians and Greeks more than 2,500 years ago that we use and know today.

A constellation can be described as a pattern of stars in the night sky. It is important to remember that the stars that make up a particular constellation are not really close to each other. Often stars that look close to each other are millions of miles apart; they just happen to form a two-dimensional pattern when seen from the Earth.

Research Questions

1. What is a constellation?

2. Who named the constellations?

3. How many constellations are there?

4. What are some stories or myths behind the constellations?

Web Sites

http://library.advanced.org/25763/

This site contains information on the universe, including stars and how to watch them, black holes, and our solar system. It includes interactive movies on different subjects relating to stars. There are also interactive sections, resources, and a glossary section. An interactive Planetarium is also on this site to look at the night sky. It is a great site for students to learn all about the constellations and what they look like in the night sky. (S: 4–6, T: 4–6)

http://www.siennasoft.com/sienna/

This site will help students discover a fast sky simulator that provides an easy-to-use and beautiful rendition of the night sky. The students will be able to simulate the constellations. (S: 4–6)

http://www.hawastsoc.org/deepsky/

This is a great site. Here students can see a good online atlas of the heavens. This site provides large, detailed maps of the constellations and then takes the user even closer with a quartered detail map. The site also provides the myth or story behind each constellation. (S: 4–6)

http://www.astro.wisc.edu/~dolan/constellations/constellations.html
Tons and tons of information about the constellations can be found on this site—one of the most popular on the Web (during a two-year period it was accessed over 2 million times)—so you know it's good! (S: 4–6, T: All)

Literature Resources

Branley, Franklyn M. (1987). *Star Guide.* New York: Crowell.
This book answers questions about stars and constellations in a clear and clever way. It contains easy-to-follow guides for studying the constellations.

———. (1991). *The Big Dipper (A Let's Read and Find out Book).* New York: HarperCollins.
This book is an excellent introduction to the night sky and the Big Dipper. It explains the facts about the Big Dipper, where it's located, what stars make up the constellation, and how it points to the North Star.

———. (1981). *The Sky Is Full of Stars.* New York: HarperCollins.
This book describes how to view the stars that make up a constellation. It shows what to look for and when and explains why some stars are brighter than others and why some have colors.

Mitton, Jacqueline & Balit, Christina. (1998). *Zoo in the Sky: A Book of Animal Constellations.* Washington: National Geographical Society.
The animal constellations are highlighted in this book. Star maps are included to help the reader understand their location. Silver foil stars help the reader visualize the constellations. This book is great for the young reader.

Silver, Donald M. (1998). *The Night Sky (One Small Square).* New York: McGraw-Hill.
Using this book, children can locate Orion and other constellations, stars, and planets in one small square of night sky. They can use their eyes, binoculars, the position of the moon, and even their fingers as guides when they learn the amazing facts about the night sky. Activities are included for northern and southern hemispheres.

Sipiera, Paul P. (1997). *Constellations.* Chicago: Children's Press.
This book identifies the groups of stars known as constellations. It discusses their origins, uses, and observations. The reader can investigate the constellations through an interactive page format and large, full-color photographs.

Taylor, Harriet Peck. (1997). *Coyote Places the Stars.* New York: Aladdin Paperbacks.
In this book a coyote shoots arrows at the stars in the night sky, rearranging them to make pictures of his friends. His friends include Bear, Lion, Goat, Eagle, and Owl. Coyote does this so that his friends can be remembered forever.

Vancleave, Janice Pratt. (1997). *Janice Vancleave's Constellations for Every Kid: Easy Activities That Make Learning Science Fun.* New York: John Wiley & Sons.
This book contains step-by-step activities to teach children how to locate the most prominent constellations and explore the galaxies in their own backyards. The constellations included are the Big Dipper, Orion, Cancer, Cassiopeia, and 16 more.

Activities and Projects

1. Invite the students to read Janice Vancleave's *Constellations for Every Kid: Easy Activities That Make Learning Science Fun.* Ask them to participate in the step-by-step activities that teach them how to locate various constellations. Encourage students to go out once a month and draw a constellation that they see in the sky. When they are finished with their drawings, have them write a story for their constellation drawings. At the end of the project, have the students assemble their drawings and stories into a book to share with the class.

2. Invite the students to read *The Night Sky (One Small Square).* Encourage them to participate in the activities in the book that make it easier to locate the constellations. Ask the students to graph the constellations on graph paper. Invite the students to visit the Web site http://www.hawastsoc.org/deepsky to find information and locations of different constellations. Students will be able to research the coordinates for at least five different constellations and graph them on the paper through this site. Once they have finished this, encourage students to create their own constellation book and write a story about the origin of this constellation, based on the information that they learned.

3. Encourage the students to read the myths that go along with different constellations by visiting the Web site http://einstein.stcloudstate.edu/Dome or http://www.hawastsoc. org/deepsky. Ask them to make nightly observations of the stars, the same time each night. Encourage the students to keep a journal of their observations including the color, brightness, and patterns the stars form. Then ask the students to create their own star maps using the material that they have collected in their journals. To create a star map, the students will need graph paper and the coordinates of the constellations. These coordinates can be found on the Web sites listed. Once the students have successfully graphed the constellations, have them transfer them onto drawing paper. Encourage the students to choose their favorite constellations and write short essays explaining why. Aspects of the constellations that might help them choose a favorite include the constellation's myth, the shape of the constellation, the way it looked in the sky, and the brightness of the constellation's stars.

4. To spark interest in the constellations, put up a few drawings or pictures of constellations on the bulletin board. Invite the students to guess the names of the constellations. Read *Zoo in the Sky* to them and invite them to name the constellation and its myth. Ask the students to participate in a glow-in-the-dark constellation activity. Give each student a sheet of black construction paper and some glow-in-the-dark self-stick stars. Encourage the students to create their own constellation with the stars. Have students put their constellations near a light or flashlight for a minute. Turn off the lights in the classroom and close the shades on the windows. Invite the students to share their constellations with the rest of the class and explain why they chose to create theirs and what they chose to name them. Shine a flashlight on each student's constellation in turn to ensure that all will be lit effectively.

5. One of the most well-known constellations is the Big Dipper. Why is it called the Big Dipper? Simply because it looks like a giant dipper or ladle of water. Here's how you can help your students locate this constellation: On a cloudless, moonless night away from the bright lights of the city, face true north (use a compass) and look up. You'll see a pattern of seven stars, four of which form the "bowl" of the Big Dipper and three of which form the "handle." Once you've sighted the Big Dipper, draw an imaginary line along the two stars on the outer end of its bowl. That line will take you to a star on the handle end of the Little Dipper constellation, which is one of the most famous in the sky: the North Star, or Polaris.

Earth: The Planet

 ## Introduction

Four and a half billion. It's a number almost too large to comprehend. Yet that's how many years the Earth has been in existence. During that time it has undergone some remarkable changes. Rocks have been formed, primeval seas have ebbed and flowed across vast continents, and dramatic weather conditions have contributed to the geography and structure of our planet. Still, it's amazing to realize that this planet is but one particle in a universe of stars, satellites, and other celestial bodies. The beauty of our world and its place in the universe are areas ripe for exploration.

 ## Web Sites

http://earth.jsc.nasa.gov

Wow! Earth From Space: An Astronaut's Views of the Home Planet provides young scientists with more than 250,000 images of the earth, all of which can be downloaded. Included are landscapes, distinctive features, weather patterns, water habitats, and numerous geographical regions. Loads of information and eye-popping photos will keep kids coming back again and again. (S: 4–6)

http://www.hawastsoc.org/solar/eng/earth.htm

Loads of information about our planet can be found on this all-inclusive site. Included are data on the Earth's interior and plate tectonics, Earth from space, craters, volcanoes, scale maps, and numerous Earth images. The information is sophisticated and, at times, technical, but it's well worth the visit. (T: 4–6)

http://eis.jpl.nasa.gov/origins/index.html

On this site students can begin to discover and discuss some of the origins of the planets, including the planet Earth. Maintained by NASA, this site poses one of the most intriguing questions of our time: What is the origin of the universe? Lots of information and incredible photos make this a delightful Web site. (S: 4–6)

 ## Literature Resources

Brown, Julie. (1990). *Exploring the World*. Milwaukee, WI: Gareth Stevens.

This is a wonderful introduction to the world we live on: how it developed, what it's made of, and how it endures.

Brown, Robert. (1990). *The Changing Face of Earth*. Milwaukee, WI: Gareth Stevens.
The earth is constantly changing and this book offers young readers some explorations into that process.

Ford, Adam. (1981). *Spaceship Earth*. New York: Lothrop.
Why is our planet often referred to as a spaceship? Here, young readers will discover some interesting reasons why.

Hirst, Robin & Ride, Sally. (1990). *My Place in Space*. New York: Watts.
How does an astronaut view the planet Earth? This is a wonderful examination of Earth by someone who has seen it from above.

Stacy, Tom. (1990). *Earth, Sea and Sky*. New York: Random House.
Everything young readers would want to know about the planet they live on is in this all-inclusive book.

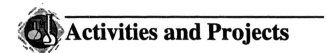

Activities and Projects

1. Students may enjoy receiving some aerial photographs of the planet Earth taken from satellites, space shuttles, and other spacecraft. Encourage them to write to the Earth Resources Observation Systems Data Center (U.S. Geological Survey, Sioux Falls, SD 57198) and request information on the availability of specific photos.

2. If students are interested in maps and mapping, have them write to the American Association for the Advancement of Science (1776 Massachusetts Avenue, NW, Washington, DC 20036) and ask for the "Maps and Mapping" pamphlet that is part of the Association's Opportunities in Space series.

3. Obtain a medium-sized Styrofoam ball from a local hobby or art store. Poke a pencil through the ball. Have a selected student trace a large circle on paper with the pencil. Explain that the ball is moving like the Earth revolving around the sun. Then have the student spin the ball on the pencil. This represents the Earth rotating. Ask the student to retrace the original circle while spinning the ball. This demonstrates the revolution (the Earth spinning around on its axis, once every 24 hours) and rotation (the Earth spinning around the sun, once every year) of the Earth.

4. Invite students to assemble a collection of "Amazing Facts About the Earth." This book can be made part of the classroom library or donated to the school library. Following are a few facts to get students started:

   a. The average orbital speed of the Earth around the sun is 66,641 mph.

   b. The Earth receives only one-half of one-billionth of the sun's radiant energy.

   c. Due to the rotational velocity of the Earth, a person standing on the equator is moving at a speed of 1,040 mph.

Solar System

Introduction

Our solar system, which is located in the Milky Way galaxy, is believed to have originated approximately 5 billion years ago as a large nebulous cloud, part of the matter and energy expended after the Big Bang. The particles of the clouds were drawn to one another because of gravity; as a result, the cloud began to contract toward its center. During this process the entire cloud rotated in a whirlpool manner, drawing material together toward the center and building up small concentrations at various distances from the center. These collections of matter eventually became the planets and their moons. You could say that a planet is a big round ball of gas or rock that travels around (orbits) a star (for example, the sun). Some planets are also made of ice and frozen gases.

One of the most fascinating aspects of our solar system is that everything is moving. Planets move around the sun (they orbit the sun). Several planets have moons that revolve around them. There are lots of celestial bodies such as comets, meteoroids, and asteroids whizzing through space. The solar system itself moves along on one of the enormous spiral arms of our galaxy.

Two terms that are frequently used when talking about the solar system and frequently confused are revolution and rotation:

- **Revolution** is when one object travels around another object. For example, the Earth travels around (revolves around) the sun. It takes the Earth about 365 days to make one complete revolution (or orbit) around the sun. We call this a year.

- **Rotation** is when an object spins around on its own axis. Imagine a basketball player holding a basketball on the tip of his or her finger and spinning it around and around. That ball is rotating around its axis (an imaginary line through the center of the ball). The Earth, for example, rotates on its axis. It does this once every 24 hours. We call this a day.

Research Questions

1. What does the solar system consist of?

2. How old is our solar system?

3. How many planets are in our solar system?

4. What else is in our solar system besides planets?

5. What is the hottest planet? The coldest?

# Web Sites

http://www.germantown.k12.il.us/html/solsus.htm
 The Solar System Web site features animated pictures, the theme song from *Star Wars,* and lots of information on all nine planets, comets, and asteroids. It explains the way planets move and has diagrams that are easy to comprehend. (S: 4–6, T: All)

http://www.brainpop.com/solarsys/
 On this site students can answer questions about the solar system. The questions range in difficulty. Students can also view a short movie about the solar system. (S: 4–6)

http://www.germantown.k12.il.us/html/solsys.htm
 A journey through the solar system written by kids for kids is presented on this colorful site. (S: 4-6)

http://www.smplanet.com/planets/planetintro.html
 This is a great site that provides kids of all ages with refreshing and fascinating information about the solar system. (S: All)

http://amazing-space.stsci.edu/trading/directions.html
 A unique way for kids to learn about the solar system – Solar System Trading Cards. Quizzes and lots of information. (S: All)

http://www.nationalgeographic.com/solarsystem/splash.html
 Here, teachers and students can explore the solar system in a 3-D environment. (S: All, T: All)

http://www.solarviews.com/cap/index.htm
 Teachers and students can obtain dozens of views of various aspect of the solar system on this site. (S: All, T: All)

Literature Resources

Beasant, Pam. (1992). *1000 Facts About Space.* New York: Kingfisher.
 Fun and informative, this book is crammed with facts and exciting data about every aspect of space. An ideal reference source.

Branley, Franklyn M. (1981). *The Planets in Our Solar System.* New York: Crowell.
 Branley uses real-life pictures and fun illustrations to teach students about every aspect of the planets in our solar system. He includes statistics such as distance and temperature. He also includes fun activities for students to do so they may get a "hands-on" feel for the unit.

Cole, Joanna. (1990). *The Magic School Bus Lost in the Solar System.* New York: Scholastic.
 Ms. Frizzle and her class take a wild and crazy ride through the solar system, discovering lots of information along the way.

Fredericks, Anthony D. (2000). *Exploring the Universe: Science Activities for Kids*. Golden, CO: Fulcrum.

This is a thorough and complete introduction to the mysteries and marvels of the universe. Jam-packed with incredible information and lots of hands-on activities, this book is the ideal companion to any study of the solar system.

Gibbons, Gail. (1993). *Planets*. New York: Holiday House.

This brief but thorough introduction to the planets is particularly suited to young readers.

Gustafson, John. (1992). *Planets, Moons and Meteors*. New York: Messner.

A wonderfully detailed text, filled with photographs and engaging activities, highlights this valuable resource.

Kelch, Joseph. (1990). *Small Worlds: Exploring the 60 Moons of Our Solar System*. New York: Messner.

This is an inviting look at the 60 moons spread throughout our solar system.

Lampton, Christopher. (1988). *Stars and Planets*. New York: Doubleday.

Everything a young reader would want to know about the solar system is in this complete book.

Leedy, Loreen. (1993). *Postcards from Pluto*. New York: Holiday House.

"Dr. Quasar" takes readers on a tour of the solar system, pointing out interesting facts along the way. Each page contains a postcard from a student to her or his parents about the different elements of the solar system.

Mitton, Jacqueline. (1991). *Discovering the Planets*. Mahweh, NJ: Troll.

Good explanations and lots of information about the planets are included here.

Moore, Patrick. (1995). *The Starry Sky*. Brookfield, CT: Copper Beech.

This book covers *everything* about the solar system. Moore provides an in-depth look at each planet and stars. His writing on constellations, the star cycle, our galaxy, and theories about other galaxies is very insightful.

Simon, Seymour. (1992). *Our Solar System*. New York: Morrow.

This wonderful book contains up-to-date information about the sun and the planets, moons, asteroids, meteoroids, and comets that travel around our sun.

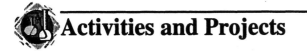 # Activities and Projects

1. Ask youngsters to assemble a "Book of Facts" about the solar system, based on information obtained from their readings. Students may decide to organize the book by assigning one planet or celestial body to each chapter. Following are some facts that could be included in the book:

   • The surface temperature on Mercury can reach 425^0 Celsius.

   • Two other planets besides Saturn have rings.

   • The original name for the planet Uranus was "Herschel."

   • Thousands of meteorites bombard the Earth every year.

- It takes Pluto nearly 250 Earth years to orbit the sun.

- The tail of a comet can extend for about 90 million miles, or the distance between the sun and Earth.

2. Students may enjoy conducting some library research to determine the origin of the names of the planets. Questions they should address are: For whom were the planets named? Who is responsible for naming the planets? Are there any similarities in the names of the planets? If a new planet were to be discovered, how would it be named?

3. Students may be interested in obtaining some information or printed materials on the travels and discoveries of spacecraft such as *Voyager* and *Viking*. Invite students to write to the NASA Jet Propulsion Laboratory (California Institute of Technology, Pasadena, CA, 91109). Provide opportunities for students to discuss the materials they receive with the entire class.

4. The first trip from the Earth to the moon took approximately four days. Ask students to calculate the time it would take for a rocket ship to travel from the Earth to each of the nine planets. Use an average rocket speed of 40,000 miles per hour for the calculations. After students have computed the approximate times, encourage them to discuss some of the preparations and provisions that would have to be considered prior to some of the longer manned voyages. What difficulties might be encountered?

5. Ask students to gather a collection of related books on the solar system (see "Related Literature") or specific Web sites (see "Web Sites"). Encourage them to assemble a collection of "Incredible Facts" about the planets in our solar system. These facts can be prepared as a large wall chart to be added to over a long period of time.

    Ask youngsters to include one or more incredible facts for each planet. If possible, obtain or prepare beforehand a large illustrated wall chart of the major celestial bodies. The factual data can be printed on small strips of paper and attached to the chart with pins or tape. Encourage the addition of new facts as more information is learned about the planets. The following facts will help the students get started:

    Sun......................The sun is so big that 110 Earths would fit across its face.
    Mercury..A year on Mercury lasts only 88 days.
    Venus........................Venus is one of only two planets that have no moons.
    Earth ....Earth is the only planet with water and life (that we know of).
    Mars ....A volcano on Mars is three times the height of Mt. Everest.
    Jupiter...A day on Jupiter lasts only 10 hours.
    Saturn......................Winds up to 1,120 mph have been recorded on Saturn.
    Uranus ....This planet is the only one that spins on its side.
    Neptune...............Neptune has a moon that orbits the planet every 17 hours.
    Pluto ....Pluto is the farthest planet from the sun.

6. You can help youngsters appreciate the relative distances between the planets with this activity. Take a group of children to the local high school football field. Have one youngster (who will represent the "sun") stand on the end zone line at one end of the field. Ask nine other individuals to take on the roles of the nine planets and to place themselves at the following distances from the "sun":

Planet Distance from "Sun"

Mercury	2.5 feet
Venus	4.5 feet
Earth	6.5 feet
Mars	10 feet
Jupiter	11.5 yards
Saturn	20.5 yards
Uranus	41.5 yards
Neptune	65 yards
Pluto	86 yards

Take time to discuss with youngsters the fact that the sun is the center of our solar system. The planets are not strung out in a straight line as in this re-creation. If there is a very large open field available, you can set up this demonstration with the "planets" arranged in many different directions.

7. Students may wish to obtain some astronomical charts and posters of the solar system and other celestial objects. They can contact the following companies about the availability and cost of selected items. Invite students to write to them, obtain catalogs, and inquire about their various offerings.

Celestial Arts
231 Adrian Road
Millbrae, CA 94030

Nature Company
P.O. Box 7137
Berkeley, CA 94707

Sky Publishing Co.
49 Bay State Road
Cambridge, MA 02238

Edmund Scientific
101 East Gloucester Pike
Barrington, NJ 08007

Astronomical Society of the Pacific
1290 Twenty-fourth Avenue
San Francisco, CA 94122

Mercury

Introduction

Mercury is named after the Roman god Mercury, who was the swift messenger of the gods. The planet Mercury is swift, too, taking only 88 days to complete one revolution around the sun. It's also our solar system's second smallest planet (after Pluto).

Mercury is only 36 million miles away from the sun. Although that may seem like an enormous distance, it's close enough that the temperature on the surface of this planet gets as high as 800°F. Because Mercury is small and so close to the sun, it has almost no atmosphere.

Web Sites

http://www.kidsnspace.org/mercury.htm

This site is very well organized, with categories of information that make everything easily accessible. The "What can I see?" page is really exciting; it tells children what to look for in the sky if they want to see Mercury. In addition, the site gives some general information about the planet Mercury, including what is on the surface and what is inside the planet. (S: All, T: All)

http://seds.lpl.arizona.edu/billa/tnp/mercury.html

This site provides users with detailed information in many different categories about the planet Mercury. Students can click on words and pictures to lead them to a more in-depth study of certain aspects of the planet. There are also a series of great pictures and information on *Mariner 10*, the first and only spacecraft to ever visit Mercury. (S: 4–6)

Literature Resources

Brimner, Larry. (1998). *Mercury*. New York: Children's Press.
    This is an easy-to-read introduction to the planet closest to the sun.

Simon, Seymour. (1992). *Mercury*. New York: Morrow.
    This book uses extensive descriptions and beautiful pictures to inform readers about the planet Mercury; everything from what is on the surface to what lies deep within the core is mentioned.

Vogt, Gregory. (1996). *Mercury*. Brookfield, CT: Millbrook Press.
    This book includes current information on Mercury as it was photographed by the spacecraft *Mariner 10*.

Venus

Introduction

Venus is the second planet in our solar system. It was named for the Roman goddess of love. Interestingly, all the physical features on the surface of this planet have been named for real or imaginary women.

Venus has often been referred to as our sister planet because it shares some of the characteristics of the planet Earth. Venus is often seen as a bright object in the night sky, second in brilliance to the moon. It does differ from the Earth in one significant way: It rotates from east to west, whereas most planets, including Earth, rotate from west to east. This means that on Venus the sun rises in the west and sets in the east.

Web Sites

http://pds.jpl.nasa.gov/planets/welcome/venus.htm
This great site, simply entitled Venus, provides students with a profile of that planet. The information in the profile is great. In addition, there are more than 20 enhanced images included in this profile, which makes it incredibly interesting. These surface images range from impact craters to the Lavinia region. (S: 4–6)

http://seds.lpl.arizona.edu/billa/tnp/venus.html
This site is jam-packed with detailed information about the planet Venus. There are areas where students can click to receive more information on topics that they find of particular interest. One section is made up of open issues that children can comment on; each question in this part leads to more questions. This provides the kids with specific facts about their chosen topic. (S: 4–6)

http://www.hawatsoc.org/solar/eng/venus.htm
This site, Venus Information, comes complete with a great movie, awesome images, exciting topography animation, and several different views of the planet Venus. It is a must for any older students studying this interesting planet. They will learn about everything on Venus. (S: 4–6)

http://www.kidsnspace.org/venus.htm
This Venus site is great for young students who want to discover the planet. It includes information about what is on the surface of the planet and the dimensions of it. It also tells how to look for Venus in the night sky. A great section includes fun facts on the planet. (S: K–3)

Literature Resources

Asimov, Isaac. (1996). *Earth's Twin? The Planet Venus*. Milwaukee, WI: Gareth Stevens.

This book discusses the many interesting characteristics of the planet Venus. With its beautiful photographs and computer images, it is a great book for young children wanting to see what this planet looks like.

————. (1990). *Venus: A Shrouded Mystery*. Milwaukee, WI: Gareth Stevens.

In this book Asimov explains what has been discovered beneath the thick layer of clouds surrounding the mysterious planet of Venus.

Schloss, Muriel. (1996). *Venus*. New York: Watts.

Photographs and other recent findings describe the atmosphere and geographic features of Venus.

Simon, Seymour. (1992). *Venus*. New York: Morrow.

Clear, concise text and spectacular photographs highlight another one of Simon's books about the planets.

Mars

Introduction

Mars is named after the Roman god of war. In the night sky there is a reddish hue to its surface and the atmosphere surrounding it. For centuries, it has been one of the most intriguing planets in out solar system. It is frequently referred to as the "Red Planet."

Mars has a very thin atmosphere made up primarily of carbon dioxide. It's also a very dry planet, with no liquid water. However, many scientists now believe that Mars may have had water at one time. This theory is supported by recent evidence gathered by the *Pathfinder* mission to the surface of Mars in 1997. This mission placed a small robot rover known as "Sojourner" on the planet's surface, where it traveled for several weeks gathering important data and information.

Web Sites

http://tqjunior.advanced.org/5579/

This interactive site allows students to create their own passport to journey to Mars. There are quizzes to take to get stamps for the passport. The site provides interesting information about Mars in an easy-to-understand fashion. Students can even send a postcard from Mars. Definitely a lot of fun! (S: All, T: All)

http://mars.jpl.nasa.gov/

Tons of information is included on this site by NASA. Missions, history, and architecture are explained in detail. There are also other science topics covered such as weather, atmosphere conditions, and terrain. This site would be excellent for teachers to visit for quality information when planning lessons. (S: All, T: All)

Literature Resources

Asimov, Isaac. (1988). *Mars: Our Mysterious Neighbor*. Milwaukee: Gareth Stevens Publishing.
Comparisons between Earth and Mars are made regarding seasons and climate. The author asserts that Mars is an interesting place to explore and that hopefully one day humans can live there. Detailed pictures enhance the author's text. Along with a glossary, the author includes places to write and visit for more information.

Fradin, Dennis. (1999). *Is There Life on Mars?* New York: Simon & Schuster.
This book for older readers speculates about the possibility of life on the "Red Planet."

Simon, Seymour. (1987). *Mars*. New York: Morrow.

Large print makes this book easy for younger students to read. The vivid pictures amaze readers as they learn factual information about Mars, such as the weather conditions. Additionally, the author explains the reason for the nickname "Red Planet."

Vogt, Gregory. (1994). *Mars*. Brookfield, CT: Millbrook Press.

This book is great for elementary students because it has a lot of interesting facts about Mars. Despite its fluctuating temperatures, Vogt believes that Mars is livable with proper protection.

Wunsch, Susi. (1998). *The Adventures of Sojourner: The Mission to Mars That Thrilled the World*. New York: Mikaya Press.

This book tells the story of the mission that placed the "Sojourner" remote-control rover on Mars on July 4, 1997.

Jupiter

Introduction

Jupiter is the largest planet in the solar system. It is 300 times heavier than the Earth and more than twice as heavy as all the other planets *combined*. Jupiter is made up primarily of the gases hydrogen and helium. Its atmosphere, on the other hand, is composed of gases such as methane and ammonia. This combination of gases often changes color, frequently making the planet look different (through a telescope) over a period of several nights.

One of the most distinctive features of this planet is the "Great Red Spot" that has been observed on the surface of the planet for at least 300 years. This swirling whirlpool of gases is an enormous storm cloud that seems to rage constantly on the planet. It has been estimated that this storm is about 25,000 miles long and 7,000 miles wide and that its winds may be blowing at up to 900 mph.

Web Sites

http://kidsnspace.org/jupiter.htm

This site contains excellent information on Jupiter, such as weather, size, terrain, gases, and information on the "Great Red Spot." Different missions to Jupiter are covered, along with the fact that there are over 16 moons. (S: All, T: All)

Literature Resources

Asimov, Isaac. (1995). *Planet of the Extremes: Jupiter*. Milwaukee, WI: Gareth Stevens.

This book explains that the "Great Red Spot" that has been associated with Jupiter is like a giant tornado that never stops. Colorful pictures make this book appealing to students. Teachers will enjoy the reference to other educational materials such as books and videos.

Branley, Franklyn M. (1981). *Jupiter: King of Gods, Giant of the Planets*. New York: E. P. Dutton.

This easy-to-read book presents the history of Jupiter. The detailed index allows students to easily locate information about the many missions to Jupiter. The author compares Jupiter to Earth in many examples throughout the book.

Brimner, Larry. (1999). *Jupiter*. New York: Children's Press.

This source provides solid, up-to-date information about our current knowledge concerning Jupiter. Perfect for young readers.

Simon, Seymour. (1998). *Destination: Jupiter*. New York: Morrow.

This award-winning author does an outstanding job describing Jupiter. His use of understandable text and wonderful pictures makes this book great for elementary students. It is a must for anyone wanting to explore Jupiter.

Saturn

Introduction

Saturn is the second largest planet in the solar system and, arguably, the one that has been observed most frequently by generations of astronomers. This planet is noted for its rings (although it is not the only planet with rings). Its rings are distinctive and can be seen clearly from Earth with powerful telescopes. Each of the rings is a band of ice and rocks formed long ago, perhaps when an asteroid came too close to Saturn and was torn apart by the strong gravity of the planet. The rings, made of billions of chunks of material, may be up to 170,000 miles wide and only one mile thick. Most of the chunks of material in each ring are about the size of a baseball, although there are a few the size of a small house. Although we can see three rings from Earth, Saturn is actually comprised of tens of thousands of rings.

Web Sites

http://www.kidsnspace.org/saturn.htm
Basic information and lots of fun facts highlight this site, which is perfect for young astronomers. (S: All)

http://www.solarviews.com/eng/saturn.htm
Loads of information highlights this site, which has just about all the information a young scientists would want to know about Saturn. (S: 4–6, T: 4–6).

http://seds.lpl.arizona.edu/billa/tnp/saturn.html
There's more than enough information on this site to create a complete and thorough unit on the planet Saturn. It is sometimes technical. You'll find everything you need to know here. (T: 4–6)

Literature Resources

Asimov, Isaac. (1989). *The Ringed Beauty*. Milwaukee, WI: Gareth Stevens.
This is a delightful and complete introduction to Saturn, with information on its discovery as well as current knowledge about this mysterious planet.

Brimner, Larry. (1999). *Saturn*. New York: Children's Press.
Filled with captioned color photos, this book for young readers contains fascinating and detailed information.

Simon, Seymour. (1987). *Saturn*. New York: Morrow.
This book describes the sixth planet from the sun, its rings, and its moons, and includes photographs taken in outer space.

Uranus

Introduction

Like Jupiter and Saturn, Uranus has no solid surface. Its outer layers are made up of hydrogen, helium, and methane. It is this methane that gives Uranus a slightly blue color when viewed through a telescope.

The most distinctive characteristic of this planet is that it is lying on its side. That's right, Uranus does not rotate side to side like the Earth, but actually rotates top to bottom. For example, the planet Earth is tilted about 23.5 degrees from its axis. It is this tilt that causes the seasons. Uranus, on the other hand, is tilted at an angle of 98 degrees, which means it spins on its side

Uranus has 15 known moons, most of which are quite small—less than 90 miles in diameter. Its largest moon *Ariel* is 720 miles in diameter. Much of what we know about this planet was relayed back from the spacecraft *Voyager 2*, which flew by Uranus in 1986 after a journey of nearly eight and one-half years. It was this spacecraft that identified four new rings encircling the planet (Uranus has 13 rings in all).

Web Sites

http://www.hawastsoc.org/solar/eng/uranus.htm
Filled with basic facts and insightful information about Uranus, this site is complete and thorough. (T: All)

http://www.solarviews.com/eng/uranus.htm
This site includes information on the planet and its rings, including data collected by the *Voyager II* spacecraft. (T: 4–6)

http://seds.lpl.arizona.edu/billa/tnp/uranus.html
Tons and tons of technical and fascinating information about Uranus is included at this site. There's lots to use here. (T: 4–6)

Literature Resources

Brimner, Larry. (1999). *Uranus*. New York: Children's Press.
Designed for younger readers, this book offers a panorama of information and colorful photographs.

Shephard, Donna. (1996). *Uranus*. New York: Watts.

   For older readers, this book is packed with data and information about the seventh planet in our solar system.

Simon, Seymour. (1987). *Uranus*. New York: Morrow.

   This book is an introduction to Uranus. It provides information about how it was discovered and other facts. The book also contains a lot of information about the moons that surround the planet.

Neptune

Introduction

Neptune was discovered in 1846 as a result of complicated mathematical calculations in France, England, and Germany. Slightly smaller than Uranus, it has eight moons. The two largest moons are Triton and Nereid. Triton is the coldest object in the solar system, with temperatures plunging to an icy –455°F. The surface of this satellite has melted and refrozen repeatedly since its creation, forming a network of huge cracks over its surface. It also does something very unusual for a moon: It orbits the planet in the opposite direction from the planet's own spin.

Neptune, like Uranus, has an atmosphere of hydrogen, helium, and methane. Often a large dark spot will appear on the surface of this planet, but unlike Jupiter, this spot will come and go at irregular times. The surface of the planet is violent, with winds of over 600 mph—much greater than any hurricane on Earth.

Web Sites

http://www.hawastsoc.org/solar/eng/neptune.htm
Loads of data, information, and current understandings about the planet Neptune can be found at this site. Great information for intermediate teachers. (T: 4–6)

http://www.kidsnspace.org/neptune.htm
Basic but fun information about the planet Neptune highlights this comprehensive site. (S: K–3)

http://www.solarviews.com/eng/neptune.htm
Thorough and complete, this detailed site has loads of data about the planet Neptune. (T: 4–6)

Literature Resources

Brimner, Larry. (1999). *Neptune*. New York: Children's Press.
This book presents facts about the large gaseous planet, from its discovery to the latest findings from the *Voyager II* space probe.

Landau, Elaine. (1996). *Neptune*. New York: Watts.
This book uses photographs and other recent findings to describe the atmosphere and geographic features of Neptune.

Simon, Seymour. (1991). *Neptune*. New York: Morrow.
The sparse text in this book is carefully matched to the uncaptioned photographs and drawings, providing lots of information about this planet.

Pluto

Introduction

Pluto was named for the Greek god of the underworld. It is the smallest known planet in our solar system, and not a great deal is known about this mysterious frozen rock. Many people mistakenly say that Pluto is the farthest planet from the sun. That is partially correct. Pluto has a strangely elongated orbit around the sun. It spends 20 years of the 248 years it takes to revolve around the sun inside the orbit of Neptune (which, most recently, occurred between the years 1979 and 1999). For those 20 years Neptune then becomes the most distant planet in our solar system.

For most of its very long year the materials that make up Pluto's surface are frozen. But when Pluto moves closer to the sun (within about 3 million miles) the solid materials turn into gases and the planet has a thin atmosphere of methane, nitrogen, and carbon dioxide. As it moves to its farthest point from the sun (5 million miles) these materials freeze once again and the planet is completely frozen.

Web Sites

http://www.hawastsoc.org/solar/eng/pluto.htm
Filled with the most up-to-date information on the planet Pluto, this site contains an abundance of data. (T: 4–6)

http://www.solarviews.com/eng/pluto.htm
This site contains a fascinating array of information about Pluto and its moon Charon, including some speculations about the mission that will fly by them in 2013. (T: 4–6)

http://seds.lpl.arizona.edu/billa/tnp/pluto.html
This is another complete and incredible site overflowing with information. (T: 4–6)

http://nssdc.gsfc.nasa.gov/planetary/planets/plutopage.html
This site has lots of links to other sites about Pluto, its moon, and some of the planned explorations of this most distant planet. (T: 4–6)

Literature Resources

Brimner, Larry. (1999). *Pluto*. New York: Children's Press.
This is another fascinating book on one of our solar system's most mysterious planets. Ideal for young scientists.

Vogt, Gregory. (1996). *Pluto*. Brookfield, CT: Millbrook Press.

This book presents information on Pluto and its moon Charon. Includes a glossary and "Pluto Quick Facts."

Wetterer, Margaret. (1996). *Clyde Tombaugh and the Search for Planet X*. Minneapolis, MN: Carolrhoda Books.

This is the amazing and fascinating story of the man who discovered Pluto. It provides a wonderful insight into the life of an astronomer and the painstaking work he did.

Space Exploration

Introduction

Space has always been fascinating to humans, ever since the first humans looked up into the sky and saw all its wonders. We have often imagined what was above us, what celestial bodies, what amazing information, and what new discoveries! The exploration of outer space has been popularized in books and magazines for centuries and still remains one of the most intriguing aspects of scientific discovery.

Helping students become aware of the various types of space exploration taking place as well as that which is planned to take place will help them appreciate the wonders of the sky. It will also help them appreciate all the unanswered questions scientists have and the various ways in which they are seeking answers to those questions.

Research Questions

1. What can we learn from space exploration?

2. What type of training do astronauts go through?

3. What are some important historical events in space exploration?

4. Why is it so important to travel to other planets?

5. Who are the important people involved in space exploration?

Web Sites

http://ginan.gstc.nasa.gov/k12/StarChild.html

The Star Child project connects NASA and the K–12 classroom. Students can click on images to find pointers about stars, the universe, moons, planets, the sun, Earth, astronomy, galaxies, and space. This is a great resource to find out about space and space exploration. (S: 4–6)

http://athena.wednet.edu/curric/space/index.html

This site features space and astronomy. It also is a good site for educational material related to the solar system and a great resource for information for students about space. Here students can find information on what makes up a galaxy, universe, or solar system. (S: 4–6)

http://www.stsci.edu/

This is the site for the Space Telescope Science Institute. Included on this site are classroom activities, teacher tips, and evaluations. This would be a great site for students to use when studying galaxies. (S: All, T: All)

http://antwrp.gsfc.nasa.gov/apod/astropix.html

This is a great site to discover the cosmos. Students can check this site on a daily basis and view a different image or photograph of the universe along with a brief explanation written by a professional astronomer. (S: 4–6)

http://www.nss.org/askastro/

This is a great site for students. There are photos, sounds, and movies from an astronaut's mission. There are over 250 questions that have been answered about space. It is the only Web site offering direct access to men and women who have flown in space. It also gives students the opportunity to have their space-related questions answered. (S: 4–6)

http://www.nasa.gov/index.html

This site will give students the latest information that comes from NASA's aeronautics and space research departments. It would be useful for students doing research on space exploration. Here students can find out why it is important to explore space and what we have learned from space exploration. (S: 4–6)

http://seds.lpl.arizona.edu/nineplanets/nineplanets/nineplanets.html

This site contains a multimedia tour of the solar system. It also shows the history, mythology, and current scientific knowledge of each of the planets and moons in our solar system. The graphics are outstanding. This is a great resource on the planets for students and teachers alike. Students will be able to find out where the planets are located and what importance they have to space exploration. (S: 4–6, T: 4–6)

http://spaceart.com/solar/eng/homepage.htm

This is a great site with vivid pictures. It is a multimedia adventure for discovering the universe, the latest scientific information, the history of space exploration, rocketry, astronauts, missions, and spacecraft. Students and teachers will enjoy traveling through this site and discovering the solar system. They will be able to find out all sorts of information on the individual planets, the sun, comets, meteorites, and the many people involved in space exploration. (S: 4–6, T: 4–6)

http://spacelink.msfc.nasa.gov/html/resources.html

This is the site for the NASA Spacelink, which is an aeronautics and space resource for educators. It includes great resources for teaching ideas dealing with space, the planets, and the universe. (T: All)

 # Literature Resources

Berliner, Don. (1991). *Our Future in Space*. Minneapolis, MN: Lerner.

This book examines current space research and proposed space projects. The book weighs the costs of the projects against the risk. It covers possible space projects such as a permanent space station, an observatory and research base on the moon, and the search for extraterrestrial life.

Branley, Franklyn. (1999). *Is There Life in Outer Space?* New York: Harper Trophy.

This book examines the search for extraterrestrial life using fabrications. This book stretches the imagination and discusses some of the ideas and misconceptions about life in space.

Cole, Joanna. (1993). *The Magic School Bus: Lost in the Solar System*. New York: Scholastic.

The magic school bus visits each planet in the solar system. The book is packed with information and sparks the imagination and excitement of the reader.

Kirkwood, Jon. (1999). *Exploring Space (Look into Space)*. Millbrook, CT: Millbrook Press.

This book describes the sun, the moon, the stars, and our solar system. It also includes space exploration, the equipment being used, and the spacecraft used. The reader learns about the discoveries made in space and the men and women who them possible.

Petty, Kate. (1997). *You Can Jump Higher on the Moon (I Didn't Know That)*. Millbrook, CT: Millbrook Press.

This book focuses on exploration of space by citing notable facts that were discovered while visiting and investigating the moon and planets.

Stott, Carole. (1997). *Space Exploration (Eyewitness Book)*. New York: Knopf.

This book blasts off to the excitement and discoveries of space exploration. The reader will learn about the history of space exploration, starting with the first rocket launch, through the present day, and on into the future.

Troutman, Felicity. (1998). *Exploration of Space (Great Explorers Series)*. New York: Barrons Juvenile.

This book demonstrates that cosmonauts and astronauts are the leading explorers when it comes to space exploration. It illustrates the first years of space travel with pictures, facts, and discoveries.

Vogt, Gregory. (1991). *Missions in Space—Viking and the Mars Landing*. Millbrook, CT: Millbrook Press.

This book discusses the United States Space Program and *Viking* and its mission to Mars. It discusses what we have learned about Mars and what we hope to learn about it.

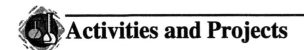# Activities and Projects

1. Ask the students to use a dictionary to find as many words as possible that begin with "astro." Help them interpret what the words mean. Read *Exploring Space (Look into Space)* to them. Encourage the students to look at space exploration as an adventure. Ask them to think about a space adventure that they know about and/or want to know about. Have the students brainstorm their ideas in small groups. Encourage each group to write a story based on their ideas. Will their story be fact or fiction? Who are the characters in the story? Ask the students to identify the characters by using descriptions. Remind them that all stories have a beginning, a middle, and an end. Invite the students to share their stories with the class.

2. Invite the students to visit the Web site http://spaceart.com/solar/eng/homepage.htm and explore the different icons on the Web page. Have students break into small groups, enough groups so that each planet and the Sun are covered. Each group should construct an informational brochure on selected facts about their designated body. Provide opportunities for students to share their brochures.

3. Invite the students to visit the Web site http://www.nss.org.askastro/ and submit a question there. This site highlights one or two of the astronauts who will be answering the questions. Students might have some specific questions for the astronaut that have not been asked before. Encourage them to participate in a discussion of what questions that they would like answered and as a group decide on two or three that will be submitted. This discussion will take place after the initial visit on the site but before any questions are submitted. When the answers are received, encourage the students to share their thoughts on the answers. Could there be a follow-up question? The following are questions that they might ask: How long did it take you to be an astronaut? How intense is the training? What is it like to be in space?

4. Read *Is There Life in Outer Space?* to the students. Encourage them to share their opinions about extraterrestrial life. Do they believe that there is any? Could the book be wrong? What evidence do they know that could back this up? Invite the students to imagine that an extraterrestrial life form comes down in their backyard. What would they do? Encourage the students to write a story about what it would be like to meet someone from outer space. What would be the first thing that they would show them about life on Earth? Ask the students to create a drawing of their newfound friends and have them share their stories and pictures with the rest of the class.

5. Ask the students to depict the life of an astronaut. What are the pros and cons of being an astronaut? Would they like to be astronauts? Have the students write a short story describing their lives as astronauts. Have them share their stories with the rest of the class. Ask the students to combine their stories to create a play. Encourage them to brainstorm as a class. How would they script it? How would they tie the events together? Ask the students to combine their individual acts and perform the play.

6. Read *The Magic School Bus Lost in the Solar System* to the students. Invite them to participate in a group discussion on what they learned from the book. What place that the Magic School bus visited did they like the best, and why? Invite the students to write a fictional story of what would happen if they went on a field trip to one of the planets in the solar system. Encourage the students to make a drawing of the planet that they visited and what they saw.

7. Invite the students to visit the Web site http://athena.wednet.edu/curric/space/index.html. Encourage them to find information about the solar system, planets, stars, and constellations. Invite them to display their collected information in a series of posters to be displayed in the school library. Students may also wish to visit the Web site http://seds.lpl.arizona.edu/nineplanets/nineplanets/nineplanets.html and research one of the nine planets.

Stars

Introduction

Stars are formed when clouds of gas and dust (called a nebula) in space get squeezed together by gravity. This squeezing motion causes the gas and dust molecules to rub against each other, thereby producing a lot of heat. This ball of gas (usually hydrogen) acts just like an enormous nuclear power plant, producing tremendous amounts of heat and energy (the star is now called a protostar). In fact, the temperature in the center of this new star may reach $18,000,000°F$.

The enormous heat inside the star changes the hydrogen atoms into helium atoms. When this happens there is an "atomic reaction" and a flash of energy is given off. Billions of these flashes of energy are what make a star visible, particularly at night when they can be seen against the backdrop of a darkened sky. It's important to remember that this "birth" took place over many millions of years.

Hydrogen is the "fuel" for every star. The rate at which a star burns hydrogen determines how long it will "live." Stars that burn their hydrogen very quickly are the hottest stars and are blue-white in color. Stars that burn their hydrogen steadily, like our sun, are yellow in color. Stars that burn hydrogen very slowly are the coolest stars and are red in color.

Research Questions

1. How are stars formed?

2. Why is the sun the only star that can be seen during the day?

3. Why do stars seem to move in the sky?

4. Why do stars have different colors?

5. What is the closest star to the Earth?

Web Sites

http://starchild.gsfc.nasa.gov/docs/StarChild/universe.level1.stars.html
This Web site explains where stars come from and discusses sizes of stars. There are two different levels of information, for younger and older students. (S: All)

http://www.eia.brad.ac.uk/btl/sg.html
This site has a lot of information on the life cycle of stars. Pictures and diagrams can be downloaded, and there are even audio sections to download. (S: 4–6)

http://www.geocities.com/CapeCanaveral/Launchpad/1364/Stars.html

This site describes what stars are made of, how they die, and various classifications and categories of stars. (T: 4–6)

http://hyperion.advanced.org/23830/

This site is a complete and thorough astronomy site that has loads of valuable information on stars (as well as other celestial bodies). There's lots to discover on this site! (T: All)

http://www.dustbunny.com/afk/

This is one of the most "kid friendly" sites on the Web. Loads of interesting and valuable information can be found here, all in "kid-talk." (S: All)

 # Literature Resources

Apfel, Necia. (1982). *Stars and Galaxies*. New York: Watts.

This book explores topics such as constellations, galaxies, stars that are close to Earth, and bright stars. There is a helpful glossary in the back of the book, as well as a map of the constellations' positions in December.

Bailey, Donna. (1991). *Facts About Looking at Stars*. Austin, TX: Steck-Vaughn.

This book includes various information about stars, including constellations, the history of astronomy, telescopes, the sun, and the life of a star.

Berger, Melvin. (1999). *Do Stars Have Points? Questions and Answers About Stars and Planets*. New York: Scholastic.

Questions and answers explore various aspects of stars and our solar system, including the sun, planets, moons, comets, and asteroids.

Gibbons, Gail. (1992). *Stargazers*. New York: Holiday House.

This book contains information about stars in a simplified manner. Topics discussed include colors, movement, constellations, and telescopes.

Hatchett, Clint. (1988). *The Glow-in-the-Dark Night Sky Book*. New York: Random House.

This book has glow-in-the-dark pictures of various constellations and their positions throughout the four seasons. The back also gives a brief description of the constellations.

Moore, Patrick. (1995). *The Stars*. Brookfield, CT: Copper Beech.

This book uses simple language to describe aspects of stars, such as constellations, color of stars, how stars are born and die, and the Milky Way and other galaxies.

Petty, Kate. (1997). *I Didn't Know That the Sun Is a Star and Other Amazing Facts About the Universe*. Brookfield, CT: Copper Beech.

This book provides facts about space that students may not have been aware of. A true or false statement is present on almost every page, along with the answer and an explanation.

Rockwell, Anne. (1999). *Our Stars*. New York: Silver Whistle.

The author describes stars and other celestial bodies using short sentences and very simple illustrations. A good book for very young readers.

Simon, Seymour. (1989). *Stars*. New York: Morrow.
    The author provides readers with the most up-to-date information about the many varieties of stars. The book includes loads of outstanding photographs.

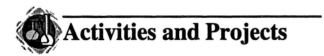

Activities and Projects

1. **Adult demonstration only:** Heat a wire in an open flame until it glows. It will glow orange at first; as it becomes hotter, it will glow yellow. Turn on a lamp with the shade removed. Ask students to observe the light bulb filament. The extremely hot wire will glow a yellowish-white. Point out to students that the hottest stars are blue-white and white and, as they become cooler, they turn yellow, orange, and then red.

2. Invite students to assemble a bulletin board display of different types of stars. Encourage them to download illustrations and photographs of various stars from selected Web sites (see above). Have them arrange their collected stars in various groups (e.g., stars closest to the Earth, stars arranged by heat, stars in selected constellations).

3. Obtain a variety of flashlights and give one to each of several different students. Darken the classroom and ask a student to stand near the front. Invite other students to place themselves at different distances away from that child and shine their flashlights at her or him. Point out to students that when stars are close to Earth they appear large (as do the flashlights); when stars are far away they appear small. Inform students that scientists can often measure the distance stars are from the Earth by the intensity (or brightness) of their light.

4. Using the resources listed above, invite students to assemble an informational brochure or newsletter that focuses on amazing facts about stars. Following is some information to get them started:

    The closest star to Earth, not counting the sun, is Alpha Centari, which is 25 trillion miles away.

    Every second, on each square yard of its surface, the sun produces enough energy to light 100,000 homes.

    Every star would explode if gravity did not hold its material together.

    The sun is 5 billion years old and is expected to last another 5 billion years.

    Stars are "born" over a period of millions of years.

Sun and Moon

Introduction

The Sun

The sun is at the center of our solar system. It is also the largest body in our solar system. In fact, if it were possible to gather all the planets together, the sun would be 600 times larger than all those planets. Even more amazing is the fact that if the sun were hollow it would be able to hold 1,300,000 Earths.

Many scientists consider the sun to be an ordinary star, with an average size and an average temperature. It has existed for about 5 billion years and is expected to last for another 5 billion years.

All of the sun's energy is generated at its center, where the temperature reaches $27,000,000^0F$. Here, in a process known as *nuclear fusion* (in which hydrogen atoms are combined, or "fused," into helium atoms), the sun changes 600 million tons of hydrogen into helium every second. As it does this, it loses 4 million tons of its mass (every second), which escapes as light and heat energy. This is the same process that takes place in a hydrogen bomb, but the sun doesn't explode like a bomb because its gravity holds it together.

The Moon

Many people are surprised to learn that even though we can easily see the moon in the night sky, it does not produce any light of its own. The light we see is actually reflected sunlight. As the moon orbits the Earth, its position in the sky changes, so the direction of the sun's light on it also changes. This creates the different "shapes" on the sunlit part of the moon during the course of a month. These changes are known as phases of the moon.

If you've ever looked at the moon through a telescope, you probably noticed that the surface looked rough and uneven. What you saw were scores of craters, hardened flows of lava, mountain peaks, and even large flat expanses (called "seas" even though there is no water on the moon). Most prominent are the craters, some of which are several miles across. Most of the craters formed more than 3 billion years ago when asteroids and meteoroids crashed into the moon's surface.

Because the moon has no atmosphere, these asteroids and meteoroids didn't burn up as they would on Earth (which does have an atmosphere). Instead, they hit the surface at full speed (from 20,000 to 160,000 mph). Scientists have counted about 30,000 craters on the moon's surface, some as small as 1/25,000 of an inch and others as large as 10 miles across.

Research Questions

1. Why does the moon shine?

2. Is the sun the largest star?

3. What are the phases of the moon?

4. How long ago was the sun born?

5. What is sunshine?

6. Where is the sun at night?

7. What is an eclipse?

 Web Sites

http://www.skypub.com/sights/eclipses/eclipses.shtml
Here students can find information about some recent and upcoming eclipses of the sun and the moon. This site will unfold the differences between a lunar eclipse and a solar eclipse and teach students how to photograph them. (S: 4–6)

http://www.earthview.com/tutorial/tutorial.html
This site provides information describing eclipses on an introductory level. Children can learn about the causes and pattern of an eclipse, plus the effects of a total solar eclipse. (S: K–3, T: K–3)

http://www.hawastsoc.org/solar/eng/moon.htm
An introduction to general information and statistics about the moon is provided at this site. Children can see pictures, watch a video, or view information on the *Apollo* missions and many other explorations. Both students and teachers will find extensive useful information in this Web site. (S: K–3, T: K–3)

http://nssdc.gstc.nasa.gov/planetary/uhar/
This Web site provides detailed descriptions of all of the lunar missions, including Soviet ones. Pictures and extensive discussions of the lunar data are also provided. (S: All, T: All)

http://www.hao.ucar.edu/public/educational/education.html
This Web site provides students with the opportunity to see pictures and graphics from a high altitude observatory of the sun. In addition, there is basic information about the sun. (S: All, T: All)

 Literature Resources

Asimov, Isaac. (1987). *How Did We Find out About Sunshine?* New York: Walker.
This book traces the scientific discoveries that led to our knowledge of the nature and substance of the sun. Students will also learn about nuclear energy and hydrogen fusion.

Asimov, Isaac. (1991). *What Is an Eclipse?* Milwaukee, WI: Gareth Stevens.

This is a perfect book for a project on lunar and solar eclipses. It is filled with loads of information about the changes in the appearance of both the sun and the moon. Each page contains colorful, beautiful illustrations.

Burton, Jane and Taylor, Kim. (1997). *The Nature and Science of Sunlight*. Milwaukee, WI: Gareth Stevens.

This book scientifically describes sunlight in great detail. It is an extremely organized and well-laid out book with many helpful additions to assist students in learning about sunlight. Each beautiful illustration is described in an explicit paragraph.

Gold, Susan Dudley. (1992). *Countdown to the Moon*. New York: Crestwood House.

This book tells the story of three men and their trip to the moon aboard a spaceship named *Apollo 11*. Within this book, children will find colorful pictures of astronauts, spaceships, Kennedy Space Center, and the moon, and many more informative depictions. This book also contains a helpful glossary.

Milburn, Constance. (1988). *Let's Look at Sunshine*. New York: Bookwright Press.

This wonderfully illustrated book explains sunshine and its many uses and purposes. This book also describes how sunshine works with many other types of weather and explains the difference between night and day. Specific words have been boldfaced so that students can look up their meaning in the glossary located at the back of the book.

Simon, Seymour. (1986). *The Sun*. New York: Morrow.

This is a wondrously illustrated(with photographs) book about our nearest star. Full of incredible information and dazzling facts.

———. (1984). *The Moon*. New York: Four Winds.

Another entry in Simon's journey through the solar system, this book will amaze and delight young astronomers.

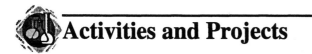

Activities and Projects

1. Encourage students to do the following experiment at home and share with the class their findings and observations.

   A Cosmic Dance—Earth and the Moon: You will need a string, a bright light without a lampshade, and a ball. To learn about the moon's phases, create a model of the sun, moon, and Earth. First, using string, outline a circle on the floor underneath a strong light source. Stand or sit in the middle of the circle. The light represents the sun, you represent the Earth, and the circle represents the moon's path around the Earth. Have a friend hold a ball (the moon) so the light shines on it. While your friend walks around the circle, watch the changing shape of the lighted portion of the ball.

2. Invite each child in class to observe the moon through each of its stages. At the end of their observations, ask them to draw a picture of what they saw on each night and write a brief description of it.

3. Divide students into three small groups. Provide each group with a raisin, an orange, and a beach ball. Invite each group to designate the order of these three items so that they represent the relative sizes of the Earth, sun, and moon. Invite groups to share their deliberations with the class.

4. It takes approximately eight minutes for sunlight to reach the Earth. Challenge students to sit quietly for eight minutes with their eyes closed, pretending that they are rays of sunlight traveling to Earth. After the eight minutes are up, invite the whole class to generate a list of things they saw on their journey.

5. Ask each student to select a letter of the alphabet. Encourage students to work together, brainstorming and/or researching lists of Earth, sun, or moon terms that begin with the selected letters. Combine compiled lists into a class dictionary.

6. Students may wish to create their own sundials. (This will be done outside.) Provide each child with a sheet of paper and a sharpened pencil. Have them place the sheets of paper on the ground and push the pencils straight through the paper into the ground. At the top of each hour, have students mark on the papers where the pencil's shadow falls. Students may wish to check their sundials over the course of several days.

Universe

Introduction

Fifteen billion. That's how many years the universe has been in existence. That's a number almost too large to comprehend, but astronomers have calculated that the universe began about 15 billion years ago. One of the most popular theories about how the universe began is known as the "Big Bang" theory. Scientists believe that 15 billion years ago everything was so close together that the universe was a tiny point (known as a singularity) much smaller than an atom. It is also thought that this singularity was billions and billions of degrees hot.

Suddenly there was a spectacular and incredible explosion (the "Big Bang") and the universe burst into being from its tiny point. Hot material blasted out in all directions. The heat from this explosion was far hotter than the heat from a nuclear explosion or even the heat at the center of the sun. Within seconds of this enormous explosion the universe had expanded to several million miles across. Many scientists (but not all) believe that the universe is still expanding today and will continue to expand throughout its existence. As evidence for this theory they point to the fact that galaxies within the universe are still moving farther apart from one another, as if from the force of an explosion. This idea is confirmed by information gathered by radio telescopes throughout the world.

The "Big Bang" explosion created a young universe that was incredibly hot. As the universe expanded, it began to cool very rapidly. The temperature of the "Big Bang" was estimated to be about 1 billion billion billion degrees Centigrade. One-one hundredth of a second later (less than the time it takes to snap your fingers) the temperature had cooled to *only* $1,000,000,000^0$C.

As materials moved away from the explosion, gases such as helium and hydrogen were created. These are the two most common elements in the universe today. After several million years, these gases collected together into large bodies called galaxies. These first galaxies—known as protogalaxies—were enormous swirling gas clouds that expanded throughout the entire universe. After about 1 billion (1,000,000,000) years, true galaxies with stars and spiral arms began to form from these gas clouds. (Keep in mind that this formation was occurring while the universe was still expanding.) A galaxy is defined as an enormous group of stars, gases, and dust all held together by the force of gravity. Interestingly, astronomers have estimated that the universe is made up of 100 billion separate galaxies, each with 100 billion stars. That means that there are about 10,000 million million million stars in the universe.

Research Questions

1. What is included in the term "universe?"

2. How did the universe come to be?

3. What is a galaxy? Which galaxy do we live in? How many galaxies are there?

4. How many planets revolve around the sun? What are their names?

5. How are stars born?

6. What are black holes and supernovae?

7. How far away is the sun? The moon? The other planets? The next solar system?

 # Web Sites

http://library.advanced.org/18188/english/main/home.htm

This site is entitled From Mars to Pluto. It is filled with information on the planets, people who have affected space exploration, and meteors and comets. There is an interactive quiz for students to test their knowledge. There is also an e-mail address for students to use to submit comments and questions. Finally, there is a section of teacher lesson plans. (S: All, T: All)

http://www.nationalgeographic.com/solarsystem/splash.html

Here students can discover the wonders of the universe using the 3-D Virtual Solar System Guide. As they fly by the sun and planets, children access information about the places they are visiting. (S: All)

http://www.icu2.net/faahomepage/gallery2.htm

This interactive site, The Solar System, allows students to find detailed information on any of the planets, comets, meteorites, or asteroids simply by clicking on the picture of that object. In addition, there are other beautiful space pictures in the kaleidoscope area of the site. This site also provides students with stories about becoming an astronaut, how to build model rockets, and space stations. (S: 4–6)

http://www.dustbunny.com/afk/

Astronomy for Kids is the title of this site for young space explorers. Not only is there interesting information on the planets, including their distances from the sun and the number of moons that each has, but there are also many interactive areas for kids to explore. Children can work on the puzzles that are provided on the site. They may view the sky maps and read the exciting sky facts. Also, kids can send a universe postcard via the Internet. (S: 4–6)

http://library.advanced.org/25763/lmain.htm

Stars: A Mystery of Space is for students of all ages. Here they can watch a movie on the life of a star, visit the planetarium, and vote for their favorite constellation. Children can read stories about star sightings that other young astronomers have submitted, as well as submit their own. There is also a library of the stars that provides information on many different stars and constellations. (S: All)

http://starchild.gsfc.nasa.gov/doc/Starchild/Starchild.html

This site, put out by NASA, is entitled StarChild: A Learning Center for Young Astronomers. The information on this site is divided into two levels: level one is appropriate for the younger elementary school students and level two is designed with older elementary students in mind. Each level contains a variety of universe activities, including math problems and vocabulary word mix-ups. Children can also retrieve the definition of any space word that they don't know from the excellent dictionary. (S: All, T: All)

http://www.pbs.org/deepspace/

Mysteries of Deep Space is a universe resource for both students and teachers. There is a section where kids can ask the experts questions about the universe. In addition, they can test their knowledge of deep space through the trivia game provided on the site. There is also a scrolling interactive time line that tells the entire history of space and the its exploration. For teachers there is a great section filled with classroom activities. (S: 4–6, T: 4–6)

http://kids.msfc.nasa.gov/

This is a highly interactive site called Nasakids. Here students can learn about space and beyond, astronauts, and rockets. They can explore and discover through the interactive puzzles and games on the site. In addition, there is a place where students can view the space art of other children as well as submit their own. Finally, a teacher's corner is an excellent resource for anyone teaching about the universe. (S: K–3, T: K–3)

Literature Resources

Asimov, Isaac. (1989). *How Was the Universe Born?* Milwaukee, WI: Gareth Stevens.

In this book Asimov does a great job of discussing the origins of our universe and the characteristics of the stars in the universe.

———. (1996). *Modern Astronomy*. Milwaukee, WI: Gareth Stevens.

Asimov has created a book for young children longing to discover all about astronomy. They can also learn how they can become astronomers as they "gaze skyward."

Beasant, Pam. (1992). *1000 Facts About Space*. New York: Kingfisher Books.

The easy to read text and cute illustrations of this book help to tell young learners all about galaxies, stars, planets, moons, and modern astronomy.

Branley, Franklyn M. (1981). *The Sky Is Full of Stars*. New York: Crowell.

This book is great for young elementary students because the simple text is easy for them to read and understand. They can use this book to learn about and locate constellations.

Dickinson, Terence. (1987). *Exploring the Night Sky: The Equinox Astronomy Guide for Beginners*. Toronto, Ontario: Camden House.

Questioning minds want to know, and this book has the answers. Through this great resource students can explore a plethora of different topics on the universe, from the moon to things 300,000 light years from Earth.

Fredericks, Anthony D. (2000). *Exploring the Universe: Science Activities for Kids*. Golden, CO: Fulcrum.

This thorough and complete guide to the universe is overflowing with hands-on activities and loads of incredible information. It is a perfect resource for students and teachers alike.

Hopkins, Lee Bennett. (1995). *Blast Off: Poems About Space*. New York: HarperCollins.

The poems in this book are not only fun, they are informative as well. Hopkins does a good job of making facts interesting for young children learning about their universe.

Markle, Sandra. (1992). *Pioneering Space*. New York: Atheneum.
    Markle describes how spacecraft and space stations operate. She also talks about the people who live and work there.

Newton, David E. (1997). *Secrets of Space: Black Hole and Supernovae*. New York: Twenty-First Century Books.
    This book is great for older students who are ready to tackle an in-depth study of the universe. It provides kids with a solid basis of information for understanding what exactly black holes and supernovae are.

Simon, Seymour. (1998). *The Universe*. New York: Morrow.
    Simon's book includes information on almost everything in our universe, including galaxies, solar systems, planets, moons, meteors, comets, and more. He tells the reader about how all these pieces work together.

Snedden, Robert. (1996). *Space*. New York: Chelsea House.
    This book is filled with details about the myths and stories about space and the progress people have made in discovering more about the universe over the years.

Verdet, Jean-Pierre. (1993). *Earth, Sky, and Beyond: A Journey Through Space*. New York: Lodestar Books.
    This exciting story brings the wonders of the sky and space to life, starting right where the sky touches the Earth and journeying out to the edges of the universe, passing many important sites along the way.

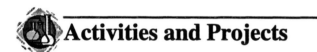# Activities and Projects

1. Invite the students to log on to http://www.dustbunny.com/afk/ and have them explore the information on the various planets provided on the site. Then ask each student to choose one or more of the following statistics and print out this information from the site: distance from the sun, weight, speed, diameter, or any set of facts dealing with the universe that they find interesting. They will need to find this same piece of information for each of the nine planets. Then have them use these statistics to create a visual, such as a graph, diagram, or model, that compares their particular factor among the planets. Display these visuals throughout the classroom and in the hallway.

2. Allow the students to form groups of three or four. Ask each group to log onto http://ww.fourmilab.ch/solar/solar.html and view the diagrams that show the orbit of the planets at that particular moment. Have the students draw or print out this diagram. Then ask them to recreate the scene using a variety of provided art supplies, including foam balls of various sizes, construction paper for rings, and other objects. When the solar system scenes are complete, invite each group of students to travel with their project to a different classroom, where they will explain what they have created.

3. Invite the students to turn the room into outer space. Provide the students with a variety of art supplies such as mural paper, Styrofoam balls, construction paper, paints, posterboard, and so forth. In addition, have resources available to the students in the classroom library, in the school library, and on the Internet, where they can gather ideas for their decorations. They may wish to make planets or moons from the foam balls and hang them from the ceiling. They could cover the walls with space murals and create a

giant sun in a corner of the room. Play some space or space-like music (this could be bought or student created). When the classroom has been completely redesigned, invite other groups of students to come and visit "The Universe."

4. After reading the book *Earth, Sky, and Beyond: A Journey Though Space,* ask the students to discuss what types of things they would see if they were astronauts traveling through space. Create a class list of these sights. Ask each student to pretend she or he is an astronaut and write one or more journal entries about these travels. Encourage students to include not only what they see but also how they feel about the things they are doing and seeing.

5. Introduce the students to *Blast Off: Poems About Space,* by reading a few selections from it. After the readings, ask the students to write their own space or universe poems. Have the book available as well as a variety of other universe and space books where students might find ideas. When the poems are complete, publish them and bind them in a class book. Invite the children to take turns reading a few of the poems in the book to students in other classrooms. In addition, the book should be left in the library for all students to look at.

6. Ask the students to make a list of the different things that they know exist in our universe. They may wish to use the books and Web sites listed above to do this. Afterwards, encourage students to assemble their information into a series of informative booklets. Ask students to determine beforehand if the booklets will be appropriate for primary level students or intermediate level students. After the booklets are complete, invite students to share their information with another class in the school.

Women in Space

Introduction

   Women have made many advances over the years. Prior to 1978, all the astronauts chosen by NASA were male. In 1972, Congress passed an amendment to the Civil Rights Act of 1964 stating that no federal agency could discriminate on the basis of sex, race, religion, or national origin. As a result, women started applying to NASA for jobs. Another major change NASA experienced during that period was in the number of people who would be aboard the space shuttle, from two people to seven. This changed not only the number of positions NASA would need to fill, but also the type of skills needed. In 1983, Sally Ride became the first U.S. woman in space. Now more than 75 women work in different branches of NASA. Many of these women have also been on space missions.

Research Questions

1.   Who was the first woman to go into space? When?

2.   Who was the first African-American woman in space? When?

3.   What is the longest amount of time a woman has been in space?

4.   Where have women visited in space?

5.   How do women go about becoming an astronaut?

6.   Who was the first female commander of a space shuttle?

7.   What woman has logged the most hours in space? How many hours has she logged?

Web Sites

http://www.friends-partners.org/-mwade/articles/womspace.htm
   At this site, are pictures of and links to information on the 36 women who have been in space. The number of hours each has been in flight is also listed. (S: 4–6, T: All)

http://www.galegroup.com/schools/resrcs/womenhst/rides.htm
   This site is dedicated to Sally Ride, the first woman to fly in space. Information is given on her early years, applying and getting into NASA, her *Challenger* experience, and her experiments in space. Further reading on Sally Ride is also provided. (S: 4–6, T: 4–6)

http://ww.jsc.nasa.gov/Bios/htmlbios/payette.html
   This site gives the personal data of Julia Payette, as well as her education, organizations, honors, experiences, and work at NASA. She flew in the STS-96 *Discovery,* a 10-day mission to deliver supplies to the International Space Station. (T: 4–6)

http://quest.arc.nasa.gov/space/frontiers/collins.html

This site focuses on Eileen Collins, the first woman shuttle commander. An interview with her is included, along with information about her earning her pilot's license and learning to fly. (S: 4–6, T: 4–6)

http://quest.arc.nasa.gov/women/intro.html

This site includes profiles of 75 women in NASA. Women are involved in many different branches of NASA, and there are links to more information on many of the women. You can chat with some of the women, and teachers can get teaching tips on how to include the women of NASA in the curriculum. (S: 4–6, T: All)

http://aristotle.ipl.org/inksub/vol1No5/higraph/women.html

This short page provides information on Shannon Lucid and her space records, along with a link to learn more about her. It also gives some information about women in space. (S: 4–6)

Literature Resources

Briggs, Carole S. (1988). *Women in Space: Reaching the Last Frontier*. Minneapolis, MN: Lerner.

This book provides short, vivid biographies of several women who traveled in space. It covers many aspects, beginning with their training at NASA and including their accomplishments on space missions.. This is a must-have book for anyone wanting to learn about women in space.

Burby, Liza N. (1997). *Mae Jemison: The First African American Woman Astronaut*. New York: Rosen.

Pictures and text summarize the life of Mae Jemison from childhood to becoming an astronaut. Easy-to-read text makes this book great for younger students to learn about the first African-American woman astronaut.

Camp, Carol A. (1997). *Sally Ride: First American Woman in Space*. New York: Enslow.

This wonderful book is dedicated to Sally Ride, the first U.S. woman to travel to space. Camp does an excellent job of describing Sally Ride's life in great detail. From growing up to applying for NASA to her *Challenger* mission, this woman has done it all.

Ride, Sally. (1986). *To Space and Back*. New York: Lothrop, Lee & Shephard Books.

This first-hand account by Sally Ride tells of her *Challenger* journey. She writes about different things that happen in space, such as weightlessness. The accompanying pictures are extraordinary.

Stott, Carole. (1997). *Space Exploration*. New York: Knopf.

This is a great reference book that covers a wide variety of topics associated with space. From the astronauts' fashions to living in space, this book will provide a place for children to get the answers to their questions. Teachers may find this book to be a valuable addition to the classroom library.

Activities and Projects

1. Present the Web site http://www.friends-partners.org/-mwade/articles/womspace.htm to the class. Suggest that each student choose a different female astronaut. Students may follow the link to find out more information on their astronauts, such as the amount of time spent in space on different missions. Based on this information, students can create a math story problem. This will be a story that incorporates numbers that the reader will have to determine the proper math function to carry out. (For example, two numbers may have to be added, and the next number may have to be subtracted, etc.). Students are encouraged to trade papers with a partner, who will try to solve the math story problem.

2. Ask the students to read *Women in Space: Reaching the Last Frontier*. Have them imagine they are reporters during the mid-1980s and write a newspaper article about the advancements of women in space travel. This article should be based on the factual information found throughout the book. Post final articles in the school lobby for visitors to see.

3. Ask students to visit the Web site http://www.quest.arc.nasa.gov/women/intro.html. Have each student choose a female astronaut and find out when her birthday is, then use her birthday to determine her astrological sign. They should then create a week's worth of horoscopes for each astronaut. The horoscopes should relate to her career in space. When students are finished, staple the horoscopes together in the form of a small book. Students may then draw a picture of each astronaut's sign. The cover can be created using black construction paper and white chalk.

4. Encourage students to refer to *Women in Space: Reaching the Last Frontier, Mae Jemison: The First African-American Women Astronaut,* and *To Space and Back* to select a female astronaut and draw a picture of her. Students may use crayons, marker, colored pencils, and paint to make their pictures as real as possible. While the pictures dry, ask students to write a short paragraph about their people on 3-by-5-inch note cards. When the pictures are dry, have students attach the note cards. Then invite students to share their women of choice with the class.

Chapter 8

The Human Body

It may be the most incredible machine on the face of the Earth. It is an amazing collection of gears, wires, levers, and pulleys in combination with a host of scientific principles that frequently defies description and constantly amazes even the most die-hard skeptic. What is it? It is the human body—surely one of the most magical and marvelous "packages" in the world. Yes, the body you inhabit is full of wonder, discoveries, and potential investigations that will stimulate and delight everyone who owns one.

In this section your students will be exposed to the marvelous machine they inhabit. They will learn about the different systems of the body that keep us functioning throughout all our daily activities. They will learn how we work, how we think, how we move, and how we operate in a thousand different ways. Indeed, the human body may be one of nature's most incredible laboratories—a laboratory of activities, experiments, and eye-popping discoveries available nowhere else in the scientific world.

Helping youngsters learn about and appreciate their own bodies can be one of the most exciting parts of the study of science. As students peek, prod, and poke into themselves they will gain a deeper appreciation of this marvelous machine as well as learn ways in which the machine can be maintained over an extended period of time. And best of all, that machine is always available for discoveries and explorations at any time of the day or night—a walking laboratory full of possibilities.

Brain and Nervous System

 ## Introduction

The nervous system performs many functions. It controls the action of the muscles and other tissues; the action of the organs; sensations such as smell, taste, touch, pressure, sight, hearing, heat, cold, and pain; and thinking, learning, and memory. The central part of the nervous system is the brain.

The brain is perhaps the most specialized organ in the human body. It is the control center of the body, receiving messages from all parts of the body and sending out orders in return. There are three main parts of the brain: the cerebrum, the cerebellum, and the medulla. The cerebrum is the largest part of the brain. It controls thinking, reasoning, learning, memory, and imagination. It also controls the voluntary movement of the muscles in the body. The smaller cerebellum is located below and behind the cerebrum. This part of the brain coordinates the movements of the muscles so that they operate together smoothly. It's also responsible for the body's sense of balance. The medulla is located at the bottom of the brain and joins the top of the spinal cord. This part of the brain controls the operation of the body's involuntary muscles, including heart action, breathing, digestion, coughing, and sneezing.

 ## Research Questions

1. What are the three parts of the human brain?

2. What part of your brain do you use while reading this question?

3. What is the smallest part of the brain?

4. Are there any nerves in the human brain?

5. How much does an average brain weigh?

 ## Web Sites

http://library.advanced.org/26463/
This site provides a thorough and complete survey of the human brain. Lots of information on all aspects of this marvelous organ. (S: 4–6, T: All)

http://tqjunior.advanced.org/4371/index.htm
This site has tons and tons of information about the brain. Students will be spending hours here. (S: 4–6)

http://www.exploratorium.edu/memory/index.html
The Memory Exhibition offers young scientists an online dissection of a sheep's brain as well as all sorts of memory tests. Great! (S: 4–6).

http://www.imcpl.lib.in.us/nov_nerv.htm
Students get to see a complete illustration of the human brain, with all the important parts labeled. (S: 4–6)

 # Literature Resources

Holm, Sharon. (1998). *101 Questions Your Brain Has Asked About Itself but Couldn't Answer.* Brookfield, CT: Millbrook Press.
The seven chapters in this book provide readers with a thorough and complete examination of the human brain. Lots of information in these pages.

Parker, Steve. (1998). *Brain and Nerves.* Brookfield, CT: Copper Beech.
The author presents a full treatment of how the human brain works, including memory and learning as well as various nerve diseases.

———. (1995). *Brain Surgery for Beginners: And Other Major Operations for Minors.* Brookfield, CT: Millbrook Press.
The author offers a detailed discussion of the central nervous system. He also describes the other body systems, emphasizing the brain's role in controlling each.

Simon, Seymour. (1997). *The Brain: Our Nervous System.* New York: Morrow.
This outstanding book exposes the many wonders of the human brain and nervous system. The information is presented in a stimulating and engaging fashion.

 # Activities and Projects

1. If possible, obtain a calf or sheep brain from your local butcher. Ask students to locate and identify the cerebrum, cerebellum, and medulla. Point out how large the cerebrum is and how its surface is folded in many places. Cut into the gray matter of the cerebrum and note the white matter underneath. Ask students to note how the cerebellum is attached to the rest of the brain and how the medulla connects with the other parts of the brain.

2. Invite students to log on to one or more of the Web sites listed above. Provide small groups of students with large sheets of newsprint and ask each group to illustrate the major parts of the human brain. If possible, obtain X-rays of human heads (from your local hospital or doctor) and invite students to pinpoint selected sections of the brain directly on the X-rays.

3. Obtain a chart of the human nervous system from your local hospital or a medical supply company. Ask students to locate the central nervous system (the brain and spinal cord). Point out the major nerves that spread out from the brain and spinal cord to every part of the body.

4. **Just for fun:** Duplicate the "Brain Puzzlers" below and present them to your students. Inform them that each "sentence" contains a scientific fact—for example: 16 = O. in a P. (16 ounces in a pound) or 29 = D. in F. in a L.Y. (29 days in February in a leap year). Answers are provided with each puzzler.

    A.P. = 14.7 P.P.S.I. at S.L. (air pressure is 14.7 pounds per square inch at sea level).

    32 = D.F. at which W.F. (32 is degrees Fahrenheit at which water freezes).

    P. + E. = W.C. (precipitation and evaporation equals the water cycle).

    9 = P. in the S.S. (nine planets in the solar system).

    24 = H. in a D. (24 hours in a day).

    Y. – S. – S. – A. = W. (year minus summer minus spring minus autumn equals winter).

    B.W. = 100 D.C. (boiling water equals 100 degrees Celsius).

    3L. of the E. = C. + M. + C. (three layers of the Earth are crust, mantle, and core).

    On M. 88D. = 1Y. (on Mercury 88 days equals one year).

    T. = 32 (32 teeth).

5. If possible, obtain an anamod of the human brain for classroom display (an anamod is a three-dimensional model constructed from flat pieces of cardboard). Anamods are available from Delta Education (P.O. Box M, Nashua, NH 03061, 800-258-1302, Catalog No. 57-010-1474; at this writing it is priced at $411.95). After students have had an opportunity to observe the anamod (or a similar illustration), challenge them to create their own three-dimensional model from pieces of stiff cardboard.

Circulatory System

Introduction

The circulatory system is made up of the heart, blood, and blood vessels. The heart pumps the blood, which moves through blood vessels, to every part of the body and back again in about 30 seconds. There are three main functions of the body's circulatory system: It (1) carries digested food to the cells in the body, (2) brings oxygen to the cells for burning the food and producing heat and energy, and (3) takes away the waste materials produced by the cells and carries these materials to organs that remove them from the body.

Research Questions

1. How many miles of blood vessels are there in the human body?

2. What is the role of the heart?

3. What are arteries? What are veins?

4. What are some diseases of the circulatory system?

5. What is a heart attack?

Web Sites

http://tqjunior.advanced.org/5777/cir1.htm

This great site for kids was developed by kids to show how the body gets blood to travel all around it. Highlighted terms can be clicked on to present a definition. This site also provides information about the heart, blood cells, and other parts of the circulatory system. (S: 4–6)

http://tqjunior.advanced.org/5250/Circ.htm

A short but good description of the circulatory system is given at this site, which is just one page of a site dedicated to the systems of the human body. It was written for kids by kids and is easy to understand and use. (S: 4–6)

http://www.mayohealth.org/mayo/9902/htm/heart/heart_1.htm

This is a terrific site for teachers and students to "take apart" the heart and see how it functions and allows blood to travel all around the body. At this site, students can choose to view the heart parts and the whole heart, both internally and externally. (S: 4–6, T: All)

http://www.imcpl.lib.in.us/nov_circ.htm

This site is for teachers who would like to know the scientific terminology of the parts of the circulatory system. Included is a brief overview of how the circulatory system works. (T: All)

http://sln2.fi.edu.biosci/develop/develop.html

This site explains how the heart develops and gains its unique shape while the fetus is still developing. It also discusses how much oxygen the heart needs at the different phases of human growth. (S: 4–6, T: All)

http://sln2.fi.edu/biosci/blood/blood.html

This site is about the role that blood plays in the human circulatory system. The composition of blood is explained and functions of blood in the body are discussed. (S: 4–6, T: All)

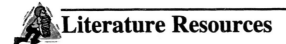# Literature Resources

Bender, Lionel. (1992). *Science Facts: Human Body: The Human Body: Its Mysteries and Marvels*. New York: Crescent Books.

A composite of interesting facts about the human body, this book also discusses the building blocks of the human body. Real-life photographs and diagrams help the reader to understand what the cell looks like.

Cole, Joanna. (1989). *The Magic School Bus Inside the Human Body*. New York: Scholastic.

Ms. Frizzle takes her class on a field trip inside the body of one of her students, Arnold. The class learns how blood is circulated throughout the body as they hitch a ride on red blood cells. Children will enjoy this book because they will be able to see how the circulatory system works.

Gaskin, John. (1985). *The Heart*. New York: Watts.

This book discusses the heart and the job it does pumping blood throughout the body, as well as how to keep it healthy. Younger children will be able to read and understand the text and pictures in this book.

Parker, Steve. (1989). *The Heart and Blood*. New York: Watts.

A great reference for how the heart and blood work together in the circulatory system, this book incorporates photographs, illustrations, and drawings.

Parramon, Merce. (1994). *Invisible World: How Our Blood Circulates*. New York: Chelsea House.

The pictures and photographs in this book are excellent. Each illustration has a description allowing the reader to learn much about the structure and functions of the circulatory system. This book is a must-have for any unit dealing with the circulatory system and can be easily understood by children in grades three and above.

Ward, Brian R. (1982). *The Heart and Blood*. New York: Watts.

This is a great reference book for students on how the circulatory system works. A glossary is provided at the back of the book to further explain the parts of the circulatory system.

Activities and Projects

1. Explain that heart rates are constantly changing, depending on the activities we engage in. Ask your students how they can alter their own heart rate and to write down these methods. Teach your students how to take their radial pulse (on their wrist). After your students have been sitting for at least five minutes, have them take their pulse and record it. Have them then stand and again take their pulses, observing and recording any changes. Ask students to try to change their heart rates, writing down what they hope to accomplish, what they did, and what their results were. Discuss what the students discovered about their heart rates. Ask them if they think that their circulatory system was working harder at any one point, and if so, when and why?

2. Have students keep a "healthy heart log" for one month. During the month, ask students to record the ways that they have helped to keep their hearts healthy. Encourage students to consider diet, exercise, stress levels, and lifestyles Allow time during the month for students to share their observations with their peers. Ask students to make note of any changes in their health habits in their logs and to feel free to ask questions as they arise.

3. Have students work in groups of three or four to create a "circulation system" dictionary. In this dictionary they should include photographs, pictures, notes, article clippings, and anything else that they find relevant to the topic (encourage them to use the Web site and literature resources above). When all the dictionaries are completed, compile them in one big three-ring binder and keep it in a central location in the classroom.

4. If possible, obtain a calf's heart from the local butcher shop. Pare away the fatty material present, and point out to students how muscular the heart walls are. Ask students to identify the ventricles and auricles before you begin to cut the heart open. Make incisions on either side of the lower narrow end of the wall. When you enter the ventricle, cut away more material so that students can see the cavities more clearly.

5. Demonstrate to students how to make a stethoscope using three funnels, a glass Y-tube, and two long plus one short pieces of rubber tubing. Ask students to take turns listening to each other's heartbeats. Then ask them to compare their heartbeats when they are quiet with their heartbeats after they have exercised vigorously for one or two minutes.

Digestive System

Introduction

For food to be used by the body it must enter the bloodstream, where it is carried to all cells in the body. The food we eat is too large and too complicated to be sent directly into the bloodstream; therefore, food has to be broken down, simplified, and changed into a dissolved form that the cells can use. The changing of food into a simpler, dissolved form that can enter and be used by the body is known as digestion. Digestion is carried on by special organs that make up the digestive system. The digestive system is divided into two parts: the alimentary canal and the digestive glands. The alimentary canal is the tube through which the food moves into the body. It includes the mouth, throat, esophagus, stomach, small intestine, large intestine, rectum, and anus. The digestive glands include the salivary glands, liver, pancreas, gastric glands of the stomach, and intestinal glands of the small intestine.

Research Questions

1. How long is the entire alimentary canal?

2. What are some diseases of the digestive system?

3. How should people take care of their digestive systems?

4. What is the role of the small intestine?

5. What does the liver do?

Web Sites

http://www.innerbody.com/image/digeov.html
At this site students can observe a complete and thorough illustration of the human digestive system. This illustration is perfect for downloading for other activities. (S: All)

http://tqjunior.advanced.org/5777/dig1.htm
This is a complete and thorough introduction to the digestive system. Lots to look at and learn at this site. (S: All)

http://www.ama-assn.org/insight/gen_hlth/atlas/newatlas/digest.htm
This is a great site for kids. Filled with an incredible array of information and illustrations, the site offers lots to learn. (S: 4–6).

Literature Resources

Ballard, Carol. (1997). *The Stomach and Digestive System*. Austin, TX: Steck-Vaughn.
    Lots of basic information makes this book a great addition to any classroom library or human body unit.

Holub, Joan. (1999). *I Have a Weird Brother Who Digested a Fly*. Morton's Grove, IL: Albert Whitman.
    This is a silly rhyme about a sister who tricks her brother into swallowing a fly. The fly goes through the boy's digestive system and eventually gets flushed away. A great read-aloud!

Maynard, Jacqui. (1999). *I Know Where My Food Goes*. Cambridge, MA: Candlewick.
    Science is clearly and humorously conveyed in this engaging tale of the eating (and eventual digesting) of some pizza. Another good read-aloud for young students.

Parker, Steve. (1997). *Digestion*. Brookfield, CT: Copper Beech.
    This is a complete and thorough introduction to the digestive process, particularly suited to older readers.

Stille, Darlene. (1998). *The Digestive System*. New York: Children's Press.
    This book describes the functioning of the digestive system simply and explains the process of digestion.

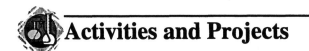

Activities and Projects

1. Into each of three small plastic cups, pour three tablespoons of milk. In the first cup put two tablespoons of water. Cover the cup with a sheet of plastic wrap, using a rubber band to hold the wrap in place. In the second cup, put two tablespoons of a weak acid such as vinegar or lemon juice and cover as above. In the third cup put two tablespoons of an enzyme such as meat tenderizer and cover as above. After one to two hours ask students to observe the changes that have occurred in each cup. The changes that occurred in cups two and three are similar to the digestive process in the stomach.

2. Ask students to create an imaginative newspaper, with "reporters" providing information from throughout the digestive system. Students should divide the newspaper into sections similar to the daily newspaper, such as "Sports" (slalom down the alimentary canal); "Fashion" (designing the perfect stomach); "Architecture" (the structure of the liver); and "Horoscope" ("Selected morsels of food will be dispersed throughout your body and will provide you with strength and vitality.").

3. Ask students to make an oversized, two-dimensional model of the alimentary canal. Have them cut out pictures of food items from old magazines and affix each one to selected spots on the model. Ask students to describe the events that lead to the food's "arrival" at each particular spot in the digestive system.

4. Blow up a balloon and explain to students that the balloon, like the human stomach, expands when filled. Measure out 23 feet of yarn or string for each student. Explain that the small intestine in an adult's body is this length when stretched out.

5. Ask students to imagine themselves as a piece of food traveling down the digestive tract. Lead them through a visual imagery exercise in which they mentally travel from the mouth through the stomach and down into the lower parts of the digestive system. Ask students to write about their "voyages" through the digestive system, describing some of the sights and sounds they experienced.

Diseases

 ## Introduction

By definition, a disease is something that causes an "un-easiness" in the body. This may be the result of an infection, an imbalance, or a hereditary factor. Diseases are typically classified as acute, chronic, malignant, or benign. *Chronic* and *acute* have to do with the duration of a disease, *malignant* and *benign* with its potential for causing death.

An acute disease is usually one that begins quite suddenly and is soon over. Appendicitis is an example of an acute disease. A chronic disease is one that often begins very gradually and then persists over a long period. Stomach ulcers would be an example of a chronic disease.

Benign and malignant describe body tumors. Benign diseases are generally without complications, such as warts on the skin. A malignant disease is one that, if left untreated, typically results in death.

Most diseases have a constellation of signs and symptoms. A *sign* is an objective evaluation of a disease determined by a doctor; a *symptom* is subjective evidence of a disease as reported by a patient. For example, a fever is a sign of a disease, and body aches and pains are a symptom of a disease. Signs and symptoms in varying degrees and intensities are indicative of different diseases and illnesses.

 ## Research Questions

1. Why is it beneficial to learn about diseases?

2. What is a disease? What do all diseases have in common?

3. What do people mean when they say they are fighting a disease?

4. What diseases are most common in childhood?

5. What diseases cause the most concern?

 ## Web Sites

http://www.amnh.org/explore/infection/smp_index.html
The material at this site is informative but also enjoyable. Students can join in with the amazing "Microbe Hunters" or try to locate the "Bacteria in the Cafeteria." Some smart basic rules are provided in the "Prevention Convention." (S: 4–6, T: All)

http://www.brainpop.com/health/seeall.html
This is an excellent site for both students and teachers. It enables the student to learn about health and disease in an enjoyable format. There are approximately 25 categories to choose from on the home page. The teacher's page also provides a list of fascinating links. (S: 3–6, T: All)

http://www.cdc.gov/

The Centers for Disease Control is the premier site for obtaining information about any disease or cluster of diseases. Lots of resources for every classroom teacher. (T: 4–6)

http://www.newsnet5.com/news/cancer/kids.html

At this site, specifically geared for kids, students can learn everything they ever wanted to know about cancer. Full of useful information. (S: 4–6)

http://www.discovery.com/exp/epidemic/epidemic.html

This site has loads of information from the Discovery Channel about killer diseases, including how they are tracked and how they are eliminated. (T: All)

Literature Resources

Almonte, Paul. (1991). *The Immune System*. Minneapolis, MN: Crestwood House.

This book explains how the human immune system works. The text looks at how diseases are attacked by our immune system.

Berger, Melvin. (1995). *Germs Make Me Sick!* New York: HarperCollins.

The fun and simple text in this book explains how bacteria and viruses affect the human body and how the body fights them.

Bergman, Thomas. (1989). *One Day at a Time: Children Living with Leukemia*. Milwaukee, WI: Gareth Stevens.

Photographs depicting children who are battling leukemia accompany the text in this book. These children are followed as they are treated for their illness. A section in the back of the book answers questions from children about leukemia and other cancers.

Bryan, Jenny. (1995). *What's Wrong with Me?* New York: Thomson Learning.

This easy-to-read book discusses some common illnesses, from toothaches to wheezing. Various lists in the back of the book recommend books that could be used with this text.

Caffey, Donna. (1998). *Yikes–Lice!* Morton Grove, IL: Albert Whitman.

This is a creative way to explain a common occurrence in elementary schools. Children can learn how one can get lice. In this text a family discovers lice in the home and fights against it. There is also factual information about how lice live and spread.

Harris, Jacqueline L. (1993). *Hereditary Diseases*. New York: Twenty-First Century Books.

This text discusses how genes function in heredity. Each hereditary disease is explained, with symptoms and possible treatments.

Hyde, Margaret O. & Forsyth, Elizabeth H., M.D. (1997). *The Disease Book, Kids Guide*. New York: Walker.

This is an excellent miniature medical guide for children. The explanations of the various diseases are simple for children to understand. Each disease is accompanied with a description of causes, symptoms, treatments, and effects.

Richardson, Joy. (1986). *What Happens When You Catch a Cold?* Milwaukee, WI: Gareth Stevens.
This text describes how our bodies use their resources to fight off infections such as colds and sore throats.

Showers, Paul. (1980). *No Measles, No Mumps for Me.* New York: Crowell.
A little boy explains how medicine has changed over time and how we can prevent ourselves from getting sick.

Silverstein, Alvin. (1977). *Allergies.* Philadelphia: Lippincott.
The various types of allergies and their symptoms, causes, and treatments are discussed in this text. The research being done to find cures for allergic diseases is also covered.

Weitzman, Elizabeth. (1997). *Let's Talk About Having Chicken Pox.* New York: Power Kids Press.
This book examines the causes of chicken pox, how you feel when you have them, and what can be done to treat them.

Wiener, Lori S., Ph.D., Best, Aprille, and Pizzo, Philip A., M.D. (1964). *Be a Friend: Children Who Live with HIV Speak.* Morton Grove, IL: Albert Whitman.
This is an outstanding text! This book is for children, by children. Children with HIV share their thoughts and insights about having HIV. This is an excellent book to reach out to children about HIV.

 # Activities and Projects

1. Ask students to visit the school nurse to obtain information about illnesses present in your school. Have them display the data they collect in some format that is easy for others to understand, such as graphs, charts, or diagrams.

2. If possible, take the students to visit a nurse in a day care center, pediatrician's office, or nursing home. Ask students to interview the nursing personnel about epidemiology and why it is important. Encourage them to obtain some epidemiological information about illnesses that are present in one of these facilities.

3. Ask students to choose a disease that they want to find out more about. Encourage them to use literature and Internet resources to get necessary information relating to their chosen disease topic. Ask students to create a book with information about their chosen disease. For example, a student may choose chicken pox. The cover of the book may be a face of a child with chicken pox. Then inside the book the student will comment on how you might get chicken pox, what you can and cannot do when you have chicken pox, and other factual information along those lines. Each student's book can be placed in the class library.

4. If possible, obtain petri dishes from the biology department of your local high school. Ask students, working in groups of three or four, to wipe the cotton swabs on various surfaces, then wipe their cotton swabs on the already prepared petri dishes. Place the petri dishes in an appropriate incubation location (check with the biology teacher).

Over a period of several days or several weeks, ask students to observe their petri dishes and note any growth on the medium. Invite the biology teacher to make a short presentation to your class on the organisms that are growing.

5. Ask students to interview their parents about what they do to prevent disease and illness at home. What precautions are taken around the house to prevent the spread of germs and/or diseases? Have students assemble their collected information in an informative chart or graph for display in the classroom.

Excretory System

Introduction

The removal of waste materials from the body is called excretion. The human body produces many kinds of waste materials: carbon dioxide, excess water, used digestive juices, mineral salts and nitrogen compounds, and undigested and unused food.

The body gets rid of waste materials in different ways. The lungs give off carbon dioxide and some water in the form of water vapor. The skin gives off perspiration, which contains water and dissolved mineral salts. The kidneys remove waste materials such as mineral salts and protein compounds from the blood. These wastes, together with excess water, form a liquid known as urine. The undigested and unused food, together with used digestive juices, pass through the large intestine and out of the body as feces.

Research Questions

1. What organs are included in the excretory system?

2. What would happen if we didn't have an excretory system?

3. What are some diseases of the excretory system?

4. How can humans properly maintain the excretory system?

Web Sites

http://members.tripod.com/mumfordg/excretory/index.htm
This is an excellent site on excretion. Very descriptive pictures are presented to aid students in obtaining a clearer understanding of the subject. (S: All)

http://sln.fi.edu/biosci/systems/excretion.html
On this site students will discover how the body is continuously working to remove dangerous waste. (S: 4–6)

http://ww.encyclopedia.com/articles/04314.html
A simple definition of excretion is given in this Web site. Students can also click on highlighted icons to explore additional information. (S: 4–6)

http://library.advanced.org/10348/find/content/excretory.html
On this page students will find loads of information about the excretory system. This site also offers related links that students can visit to obtain graphics of the excretion process. (S: All)

http://members.tripod.com/npc11bio/excretion.htm
This site presents valuable information about the excretory system in a question and answer format. (S: 4–6)

Literature Resources

Gomi, Taro. (1993). *Everyone Poops*. New York: Kane Miller.
This comical, fiction book lets students at a young age know that everyone poops! Despite the title, and the reading level, this book is a great introduction about excretion.

Muncsh, Robert. (1989). *I Have to Go!* Toronto: Firefly Books.
This fiction book deals with going to the bathroom. This is a fun way to introduce a unit on the excretion system.

Parker, Steve. (1995). *What If . . . The Human Body*. Brookfield, CT: Copper Beech.
This is a good book, written for students at a variety of levels. It presents the topics in the form of questions, such as What if the body had no excretory system? The information is very complete.

Silverstein, Alvin, Silverstein, Virginia & Silverstein, Robert. (1994). *The Excretory System*. New York: Twenty-First Century Books.
This is an excellent book devoted to the excretory system. It includes great drawings and relates the subject matter to the students. A must-have for this subject.

Activities and Projects

1. Ask students to cut out an outline of a human body from black construction paper. Then have them cut out the major organs of the excretory system from colored construction paper. They can use Velcro strips to attach the organs to the torso cut out. Ask students to label each organ and provide a brief description of its function and maintenance.

2. Using pantyhose and tennis balls, demonstrate how muscle contractions "propel" lumps of food through the digestive tract. Put the tennis ball in one end of the pantyhose. Grip the starting end with one hand, and with the other grip the pantyhose just below the ball, pushing it until it reaches the end. Discuss with the students the similarities between this demonstration and the removal of body wastes from their own bodies.

3. Ask students to lick their wrists after they have returned from recess or an activity in the gym. Point out that the salty taste is caused by the presence of mineral salts in their perspiration. The salts were left behind after the perspiration evaporated.

4. If possible, obtain the kidney of a calf or sheep from your local butcher shop. Ask students to note the size and shape of the kidney. Point out where a large artery and a large vein enter the kidney. Cut the kidney lengthwise in half with a very sharp knife. Ask students to note the many tubes in the tissue near the surface of the kidney and the large chamber where the urine collects. Point out to students that the urine leaves this chamber and travels through a duct that empties into the bladder.

Growing and Changing

Introduction

Growth is a very complex process that begins at birth and continues until a child is between 16 and 22 years of age. Girls usually reach their full adult height by the age of 16. Boys reach their full height by about age 20. Diet, hormones, and heredity determine growth. Having a balanced and nutritious diet positively affects the amount of growth a child will experience over her or his developmental years. Lack of some nutrients can affect a child's eventual height.

Hormones secreted by the pituitary gland, a small gland at the base of the brain, are also responsible for growth. The hormones are released in small amounts when a child is young. When a child reaches the ages of 9 to 12, the pituitary gland begins to make larger amounts of growth hormones. This is the time when youngsters make the largest growth spurts. Heredity also plays a role in a child's growth. If her or his parents are tall, it is likely that the child will be tall as well. If both parents are short, the child will also have a tendency to be short.

Research Questions

1. At about what age will your body stop growing?

2. Describe at least three physical differences between a six-month-old baby and a newborn.

3. What physical changes will you undergo in the next five years?

4. What determines how fast we grow?

5. How can play be helpful in the growth process?

Web Sites

http://www.kidsource.com/kidsource/pages/Newborns.html

Kid Source On-line presents information on newborns and newborn safety in addition to advice on health, safety, and nutrition for older children. The site also offers a chart on growth and development that is a wonderful source of information on the stages and characteristics of growth and development. (S: 4–6)

http://www.kidshealth.org/tips/OldTips.html

At this site kids can access a daily health tip. Everything is covered, from growth to safety, from vitamins to puberty. A great adjunct to any human body unit. (S: All)

http://www.bu.edu/cohis/kids/kids.htm

This is a very kid-friendly site about health, growth, development, and personal safety. There's lots to explore here! (S: All)

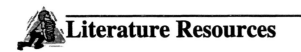

Literature Resources

Bailey, Donna. (1991). *All About Birth and Growth*. Austin, TX.: Steck-Vaughn.

This book discusses how a baby is born and how it grows up. Topics include learning to move, speech, the brain, going to school, adults, growing old, and death.

Cole, Joanna. (1985). *The New Baby at Your House*. New York: Morrow.

This book is written for the older sibling and describes the changes that come about as the result of having a new brother or sister. The photos and text show the reader step by step what is happening to Mom as well as the growing new baby.

Ganeri, Anita. (1995). *Birth and Growth*. Austin, TX: Steck-Vaughn.

This book shows children how humans grow and reproduce. It explains the differences between boys and girls. The book follows the life stages and what happens as we grow into adolescence, adulthood, and late adulthood.

Hurwitz, Johanna. (1987). *Russell Sprouts*. New York: Puffin Books.

This book tells the story of a boy and his transition into the first grade. Topics such as using undesirable language and not growing as fast as peers are covered.

Munsch, Robert. (1986). *Love You Forever*. Willowdale, Ontario: Firefly Books.

In poetic form Robert Munsch weaves a delightful tale of human growth and development. The cycle of life is portrayed along with changes that characterize each stage.

Parker, Steve. (1998). *Reproduction and Growth*. Brookfield, CT: Copper Beech.

This book presents an overview of the human life cycle. The text covers reproduction, heredity, child development, and aging.

Sheffield, Margaret. (1984). *Before You Were Born*. New York: Knopf.

This book tells in a gentle way the story of the first nine months of life, inside a mother's body. Brief text explains each stage in the developing life of the unborn child. Soft, colorful paintings enhances the presentation.

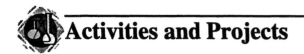

Activities and Projects

1. If possible, take a field trip to a local day care center where students can observe babies, toddlers, and preschoolers at play. Find out the exact age of the various children they'll see, and have the students observe the language, motor play, physical changes, and social interactions of the children at each age. Students should record their observations in a notebook. Following the field trip, discuss what they observed.

2. Have students create a book on human growth and development. Have students use the informational books and the Web sites above to put together a book that classifies changes in growth at various stages of development (infant, toddlers, preschoolers, school-age, and preadolescent). Each stage can be accompanied by a picture of the student at that stage or pictures obtained from old magazines.

3. Invite a pediatrician to speak to the students about growth and development. Have the students prepare questions about human growth and change prior to the visit. Following the visit, have the class create a listing of characteristics of changes that occur at various stages of human growth.

4. When a baby is born, its head is about one-quarter the length of its entire body. As a baby grows, the head becomes smaller in comparison to the rest of the body. Ask students to select several photographs of various family members at different ages. Have them measure the length of each family member's head as well as the length of each person's whole body. What kinds of proportions do the students notice? What is the proportion of the head to the body in infancy, childhood, teenage years, young adult, and adult stages?

5. Invite a family doctor or pediatrician to your classroom to present information on the suggested heights and weights of children at different ages. Make sure students understand that these measurement are only averages and might be different from their own individual height and weight. Ask the doctor to talk about the diet, sleep, and exercise youngsters need to maintain proper growth and development.

Keeping Healthy

Introduction

Here's an interesting question to ask students: Why is it important to stay healthy? Although the answer to that question may be obvious to us as adults, you may discover that your students have some degree of difficulty in responding to that particular question. Too often we ignore our health until we experience a disease, illness, or other medical emergency. It is important for children to know that their individual health is something that should concern them on a regular basis. Also important is the attitude that each person is directly responsible for her or his own health.

The attitudes and practices children develop early in their lives will have a profound effect on their health as adults. It is therefore important that teachers provide information and support in helping students develop healthy lifestyles. Given the increasing cost of medical care in this country, it is vital that children become aware of the practices that may prevent or eliminate later heath problems. Regular visits to a family doctor and dentist, a healthy and nutritious diet, and regular exercise are all critical in helping youngsters grow and develop. They also help form the basis for their continued health throughout their lives.

Research Questions

1. How much exercise should you get each day?

2. What are some common childhood diseases?

3. Why is it important to see a family doctor regularly?

4. What are the food groups on the food pyramid?

5. How can you prevent injury during physical activity?

6. What are some activities that can help you become more physically active?

7. What are some of the things we should avoid to help keep our bodies healthy?

Web Sites

http://www.bennygoodsport.com

On this site, Benny Goodsport and the Goodsport Gang teach children the importance of exercise and good nutrition through a variety of games and activities. The user can learn a number of interesting facts about each member of the gang, as well as about activities that are fun and educational at the same time. (S: K–3, T: K–3)

http://www.fitnesslink.com/redirect.htm
The Fitness Link offers a variety of information on proper ways to exercise and maintain a healthy lifestyle. In the nutrition section the user can discover the best types of food to eat to remain physically fit. Links are also provided to sites that promote good nutrition and offer recipes that are both nutritious and fun. Users can also visit the women's and/or men's locker rooms and enjoy a tour of the virtual gym. (S: 4–6)

 # Literature Resources

Allison, Linda. (1976). *Blood and Guts*. Boston: Little, Brown.
This book tells us what our bodies are made of and exactly how each part functions properly. Not only does this book provide children with an in-depth look at each part of the body, it also provides them with hands-on experiments to discover how various things actually work.

Asimov, Isaac & Dierks, Carrie. (1993). *Why Do We Need Sleep?* Milwaukee, WI: Gareth Stevens.
This book takes a closer look at the importance of sleep. Without the proper amount of sleep each night humans may not be able to function properly the following day. Sleep disorders, such as insomnia, sleepwalking, and nightmares are also touched upon briefly.

Ball, Jacqueline A. (1989). *Hygiene*. Vero Beach, FL: Rourke Corporation.
This book takes a look at feminine hygiene. It provides young women with some tips about how to keep their bodies clean and healthy. *Hygiene* also examines mouth, tooth, eye, ear, hair, foot, and nail care. The book describes body changes, ways to keep germs from spreading, and the proper way to clean and bandage open wounds.

Berger, Melvin. (1985). *Germs Make Me Sick!* New York: Crowell.
This book provides the reader with information about various types of bacteria and viruses. It also offers tips on ways to keep your body healthy and keep germs out of your system. Most important, it suggests when to see a doctor and ways to get better when you are sick.

Cole, Joanna. (1989). *The Magic School Bus Inside the Human Body*. New York: Scholastic.
Ms. Frizzle's class learns about the inside of the human body the best way they can, by entering one! The magic school bus shrinks and is consumed by Arnold, a child in the class. The children travel inside Arnold's body by traveling through the blood stream. They are eventually released from the body when Arnold sneezes. The children can hardly believe what they saw!

Hurwitz, Jan & Hurwitz, Sue. (1993). *Staying Healthy*. New York: Rosen.
This book shows children that healthy habits do not just develop overnight. As young people, they must learn that the choices we make in life will effect our health and fitness well into adulthood, and this book attempts to teach these important details.

Patten, Barbara J. (1996). *The Basic Five Food Groups*. Vero Beach, FL: Rourke Corporation.
This book provides children with the information they need to be sure their bodies get the right nutrients. Through this book children can learn the types of foods found in the five basic food groups as well as how many servings we should eat from each group per day.

Schaefer, Valorie Lee. (1998). *The Care & Keeping of You*. Middleton, WI: Pleasant Company Publications.

This book provides a detailed look a the female body. It helps young girls understand that the changes that are taking place in their bodies during puberty are normal occurrences, and that every girl must go through them at some point in her life. The book provides teenage girls with tips for better hygiene as well as a look at changes that are affecting every part of their bodies.

Taylor, Pam. (1985). *Health 2000*. New York: Facts on File.

Health 2000 provides the reader with a look at how the body works and at healthy living in the twenty-first century. The human body is described as a wonderful machine, and this book takes great care in describing the various systems it is made of. The book also provides the reader with a look at what can be done to keep the body healthy and ways to help create a healthier world.

 # Activities and Projects

1. **Testing for Fat.** Ask your students to think about the last time they ate french fries. Ask for a volunteer to discuss what happened when they wiped their hands on a paper napkin. Explain to your students that foods that have fat in them leave greasy spots on paper. Divide your students into several groups. Ask each group to create a T-square list of foods that have fats in them and foods that do not. Compile a class list of these foods on a large sheet of paper. Have each group complete the following experiment. After the experiment is completed, have your class regroup and discuss what they have learned. If necessary, have your students add foods to or delete foods from the T-square. Display the completed list in your classroom.

Materials for each group:

white paper
paper towel
pencil
cotton swabs

small amounts of the following foods: apple slices, peanut butter, potato chips, cheese, milk, and lemon juice

---

    a. List the foods on the sheet of paper. Place the sheet on a paper towel.

    b. For messy foods, dab the food with a cotton swab. Make a spot by rubbing the swab gently on the paper beside the name of the food. Foods like apple slices and cubes of cheese can be picked up and rubbed directly on the paper.

    c. Continue making spots on the paper with the food items.

    d. Allow the spots to dry. Later check the paper. Put an asterisk next to the foods that have the fat, and share your observations with your classmates.

2. For one week have your students record in their journals everything they eat and drink, including snacks. At the beginning of the following week have students discuss some of the things they consumed during the previous week. Compile a class list of things that were commonly consumed. Keep this list for use at a later date. Discuss what types of things could have been avoided, or substituted, to help maintain a healthier lifestyle. Encourage your students to try to make choices that are healthier when it comes to snacks. Before completing the unit on keeping healthy, ask your students to record everything they eat and drink again for one week. At the end of the second week compile a second class list of types of food and drinks commonly consumed. During which week did your students make healthier decisions? Why? Create a Venn diagram to note the similarities and differences between the two weeks. Display it in the classroom.

3. Invite a D.A.R.E. teacher or officer to come into your classroom to talk to your students about the dangers of drugs and alcohol. Encourage each student to think of one good question to ask the presenter. At the conclusion of the presentation, assist your students in creating a bulletin board to display in your school to help warn other students about the dangerous effects drugs and alcohol have on the body. If possible, also help your students create and illustrate various posters to hang in businesses around your community.

4. After discussing the importance of exercise with your class, divide your students into groups of three or four. Ask each group to brainstorm to compile a list of various exercises a person could do to stay healthy and keep in shape. These exercises could be ones they learned in physical education class, come from their background knowledge, or come from children's literature in the classroom. From each list, encourage the groups to choose the three most creative exercises to present to the class. Once each group has decided on their exercises and are sure they are able to demonstrate them properly, provide each group with an opportunity to do so. Each member of the group should have an active role in the presentation. Ask the rest of the class to write a brief description of each exercise in their health and fitness logs. Once each exercise has been demonstrated, the rest of the class should be able to practice it with the presenting group.

5. At the beginning of the unit ask students to create what they perceive to be a healthy menu for one day. Have each student record her or his "healthy" menu in individual health and fitness logs. Prior to completing the unit, have students create healthy menus using what they have learned about keeping healthy and fit. Have each student create a T-square comparing the similarities and differences between both menus. As a class, discuss whether the original menus were actually healthy. Why or why not?

6. **Demonstration by adult only:** Push a straightened paper clip through a peanut, Brazil nut, or cashew. Apply a lighted match to the nut. The nut will burn, giving off heat energy. Pour some cooking oil into a small saucer and place a piece of soft string in the oil, with one end of the string protruding above the oil and hanging over the side of the saucer. After the string has become saturated with the oil, apply a lighted match to the end of the string. The string will act as a wick, and the oil will burn for some time. Point out to students that when foods are digested in the body, they give off heat energy, just as in the demonstration. The human body needs this energy in order to function. Burning fat is one way our bodies create energy. This energy is necessary to maintain proper health.

Muscular System

Introduction

There are more than 600 muscles in the human body. The purpose of muscles is to cause movement. There are two kinds of muscles: voluntary muscles and involuntary muscles. Voluntary muscles are muscles we control; they move whenever we want them to move. For example, the muscles that move the bones of the skeleton are known as voluntary muscles. Voluntary muscles may be connected to the bones by tendons, they may be connected to other muscles, or they may be connected directly to the bones.

Involuntary muscles are muscles that we cannot control. The action of these muscles is controlled by the nervous system. These muscles move blood through the circulatory system, food through the digestive system, and air in and out of the respiratory system. A special kind of involuntary muscle found nowhere else in the body is the heart muscle.

Muscles work in only one way, by tightening and contracting. When muscles contract, they become shorter and thicker, and in this way exert a pull. Muscles can only exert a pull, never a push.

Research Questions

1. What are muscles?

2. What are the two types of muscles?

3. What is a skeletal muscle?

4. How do muscles work?

5. What do muscles need to work properly?

Web Sites

http://www.innerbody.com/image/musfov.html
From this Web site, students can view the human muscular system as well as cell types, nerve and muscle connections, wrist and forearm rotation, and examples of muscles. The site gives an overall view, as well as separate front and back views, of the muscular system. (S: All)

www.imcpl.lib.in.us/nov_musc.htm
This site shows a diagram of the human muscular system. The Bundles of Energy lists some facts about the muscles in our bodies. (S: 4–6)

http://donke.com/orthodo/menu.htm
  Muscle page for kids! gives students the opportunity to investigate different muscle groups. All of the categories provide a picture of where the muscle is located, its job, and what the technical names mean (e.g., biceps = two-headed). (S: 4–6)

Literature Resources

Avila, Victoria. (1995). *How Our Muscles Work*. New York: Chelsea House.
  This book is geared towards the older elementary student, containing more in-depth information. It discusses the functions of muscles and where they are found in our bodies.

Parker, Steve. (1997). *Look at Your Body: Muscles*. Brookfield, CT: Copper Beech.
  This book provides information about muscles: how they work, that animals have more muscles than humans, that muscles come in different shapes and sizes, and how we control muscles. The author takes a deeper look at the main sections of the body and how we use muscles.

Showers, Paul. (1982). *You Can't Make a Move Without Your Muscles*. New York: Crowell.
  The author utilizes descriptive pictures to show some ways that we use our muscles. The book is filled with general knowledge about the muscles in our bodies and how they work.

Silverstein, Dr. Alvin, Silverstein, Virginia, & Silverstein, Robert. (1994). *The Muscular System*. New York: Twenty-First Century Books.
  This book is geared toward upper elementary students. Broken into three main sections, it covers everything having to do with muscles. Definitely a valuable resource!

Simon, Seymour. (1998). *Muscles: Our Muscular System*. New York: Morrow.
  Simon shows us how and when our muscles work, what they are made of, and the different kinds of muscles there are. He discusses the muscles in the main sections of our bodies—face, arms, legs, and torso—and what our muscles need to stay healthy.

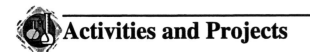
Activities and Projects

1. Ask individual students to stand in front of a mirror. Encourage them to move (contract) various muscles in their bodies (facial, arm, leg, etc.). Ask them to discuss the movement they see. Afterwards, ask students to log on to several of the Web sites listed above and locate those muscles. Encourage students to discuss any relationships between what they saw in their own bodies and what they discovered on a particular site.

2. Ask individual students to lay down on a large sheet of newsprint. Other students can draw an outline of each student's body on the newsprint. Encourage students to cut out their own individual body outlines and post them on a wall of the classroom. Using the Web sites and literature listed above, students should pencil in selected muscles in their own bodies on their personal body outlines. Plan time to discuss the similarities and differences between students (boys versus girls, for example).

3. Before reading any of the literature to the class or having them visit the Web sites, ask the students to make some general predictions about the muscular system. For example: How many muscles are there in the human body? Where is the biggest congregation of muscles? After they record their predictions, have them visit the Web sites and read the books to confirm or disprove their guesses.

4. If possible, invite students to visit a local physical rehabilitation center or chiropractor. Encourage students to talk with the personnel about the muscular system. What are some of the ways in which we can protect our muscles? How should we properly exercise our muscles? What are some diseases or illnesses of the muscular system? Ask students to gather the information in the form of an informative brochure or newsletter.

5. If possible, obtain a chicken's foot from a local butcher. Cut away some of the skin and flesh to expose the strong, white tendons. Pull the tendons one at a time. Some tendons will make the toes bend, whereas others will straighten the toes. Because the tendons are attached to muscles, students will note that the muscles only pull, and never push, regardless of how the toes move.

Reproductive System

Introduction

One of the most important and most fascinating of the natural processes is the reproduction of living organisms. Reproduction produces new individuals of the same kind. Every kind of organism must reproduce, otherwise the species will die or become extinct. Unlike other mammals, however, humans do not have a specific breeding season. They are able to reproduce throughout the year. The reproductive systems of a male and a female produce special cells that must join together to create a new human.

Research Questions

1. How is menstruation in females a part of human reproduction?

2. What are some differences between male and female reproductive organs?

3. What is sexual intercourse?

4. How are babies born?

5. How many eggs does a woman produce at a given time?

6. How long does it take for a baby to grow inside a mother?

7. What is puberty?

Web Sites

http://www.always.com/growing_jr/index.html
All the information kids will ever need to know about puberty and menstruation is located in this Web site. Although this Web site is mainly aimed toward the female viewer, all students can benefit from the information provided. (S: 4–6)

http://www.pregnancycalendar.com/first9months/
This is a multimedia journey through the first nine months of an unborn child's life. Children are able to follow the fetus's progress and development just by a simple click of the mouse. (S: 4–6, T: 4–6)

Literature Resources

Blank, Joani. (1983). *A Kid's First Book About Sex*. San Francisco: Yes Press.

Although this book doesn't discuss how babies are born, it does focus on sexual behavior and reproduction. It answers most questions that a child might have about puberty, sex, and reproduction. Illustrations are provided on each page, with explanations of each.

Cole, Joanna. (1993). *How You Were Born*. New York: Morrow.

Using clear and concise language, the author explains how humans are conceived, develop, and are born. Color photographs are included throughout the text as well as a note to parents as an introduction to the book.

Gravelle, Karen & Gravelle, Jennifer. (1996). *The Period Book*. New York: Walker.

This book is primarily written for adolescent girls. It thoroughly discusses what a period is, why it happens, what it feels like, and what to do when you get it. Everything that girls don't want to ask but need to know about menstruation, changes, and puberty is answered in this little book.

Harris, Robie H. (1994). *It's Perfectly Normal*. Cambridge, MA: Candlewick Press.

The text discusses puberty and the changes that both boys and girls go through, the conception and gestation of babies, and sexually transmitted diseases. This book is an excellent source of information and provides answers to the question asked by so many young children: Where do babies come from?

Johnson, Eric W. (1990). *Love and Sex and Growing Up*. New York: Bantam.

This book is aimed at children between the ages of eight and twelve who are in grades 3–7. Children will find extensive information about puberty, sex, love, becoming an adult, reproduction, and sexually transmitted diseases

Kitzinger, Sheila. (1986). *Being Born*. New York: Grosset & Dunlap.

This book provides factual information about being born, the development and growth of a fetus, and the fertilization and gestation periods of a human life. Photographs accompany the knowledgeable and well-written text.

Mahoney, Ellen Voelckers. (1993). *Now You've Got Your Period*. New York: Rosen.

Although this book is written mainly for adolescent girls, it describes and explains puberty, reproduction, and growth of both males and females. Children will learn about themselves and about the opposite sex and what is or will be going on inside them.

Parramon, Merce. (1994). *The Miracle of Life*. New York: Chelsea House.

This book contains information about how life begins, both male and female reproductive systems, puberty, how the body forms, fertilization, how a fetus grows, and how humans develop. Detailed color illustrations are located throughout the book to help children better understand the text.

Activities and Projects

1. Invite students to research the Web sites and literature above. Ask them to assemble specific information into informative brochures for other students at their grade level. Students can interview other students throughout the school to solicit questions about reproduction. Those questions can serve as the foundation for a brochure directed specifically at students.

2. Ask students to explore several of the Web sites listed above. Have a class discussion about the sites that were most helpful. Which site was geared mostly for kids? Which site answered most of their questions?

3. Invite a biology teacher from the local high school or a college professor from the local college's biology department to visit your class. Ask that individual to present information on the human reproductive system in comparison with the reproductive systems of other animals, specifically mammals. What similarities are there, and what differences?

4. Encourage students to share the Web sites and literature listed above with their parents. If appropriate, you may wish to discuss with students the value of frequent discussions with parents about sexual reproduction and how the Web sites and literature resources listed above can assist in that process.

Respiratory System

Introduction

Respiration is the process in which the human body takes in air and then uses the oxygen from that air. Our body cells need this oxygen to function. Air is taken in (or inhaled) through the mouth and nose. Then it passes into the trachea, the hollow tube from the mouth to the lungs. Inside the lungs, the trachea divides into smaller and smaller tubes that eventually lead to very small air sacs inside the lungs. Oxygen passes through these air sacs into the body. At the same time, carbon dioxide—waste from the body cells—passes from the blood into the sacs. The blood then takes the oxygen to all parts of the body.

Research Questions

1. How do your lungs work?

2. Why do body cells need oxygen?

3. What are some diseases of the lungs?

4. How can we keep our lungs healthy?

5. Under normal conditions, how much air do you inhale? Exhale?

Web Sites

http://tqjunior.advanced.org/5777/respl.htm

At this site, students can view the respiratory system of animals other than humans. They can tour the body to view the path air takes. (S: 4–6)

http://www.yucky.com/body/index.ssf?/systems/respiratory/

A complete and thorough introduction to the human respiratory system: This site has it all! Loads of fascinating data and tons of great graphics makes this a super site. (S: All)

http://www.imcpl.lib.in.us/nov_resp.htm

This site provides a simple, brief explanation of the body's "air bags." A great illustration. (S: 4–6)

http://www.ama-assn.org/insight/gen_hlth/atlas/newatlas/lung.htm

This is a complete introduction to the respiratory system, including the major organs and the ways in which they function together. (T: All)

Literature Resources

Parker, Steve. (1997). *The Lungs and Respiratory System.* Austin, TX: Steck-Vaughn.
   Filled with double-page spreads, this book covers basic aspects of the respiratory system: organs, functions, diseases, and medical treatments.

Roca, Nuria & Serrano, Marta. (1994). *The Respiratory System.* New York: Chelsea House.
   Detailed drawings and pictures are the highlight of this book. There are simple experiments along with basic information on the functions of various parts of the respiratory system.

Sandeman, Anna. (1995). *Breathing.* Millbrook, CT: Copper Beech.
   In this book, diagrams superimposed over color photographs of children and animals enhance descriptions of the respiratory and skeletal systems of the human body.

Silverstein, Alvin & Silverstein, Virginia. (1995). *Respiratory System.* New York: Twenty-First Century Books
   This is a complete and thorough introduction to the respiratory system by two authors who know how to demystify some of the marvels of science.

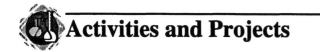

Activities and Projects

1. Ask students to take 3-by-5-inch index cards and tape or tie them to various places inside and outside the classroom (for example, the side of a cabinet, on the ceiling, outside the door to your classroom, on a branch of a nearby tree). On each card, ask students to smear a thin film of petroleum jelly. After several days, ask students to note the amount of pollutants on each card. Which card had the most? Why? Check the cards over a span of three to four weeks.

2. Invite students to write to the National Institutes of Health (Building 31, Room 2B19, Bethesda, MD 20892, 301-496-8855) to request information or literature on some of the diseases of the lungs as well as research being conducted to prevent or reduce the dangers of those diseases. Plan opportunities for students to share that information with other classes.

3. Invite students to investigate several of the Web sites and do an analysis of the information presented. Which site was most informative for students? Which site was most informative for teachers? Which site was most complete or interesting? Students should construct their own rubric for evaluating these sites (or any other sites, for that matter). What makes one "human body" site more informative or interesting than another?

4. Provide students with various art materials (e.g., balloons, straws, pipe cleaners, construction paper, string). Ask them to create three-dimensional models of the human respiratory system. Students may need to consult several Web sites and/or literature resources to ensure that their models are anatomically correct. Provide opportunities for students to display their models for other classes.

5. If possible, obtain a portion of the lung of a calf, sheep, or pig from the local butcher shop. Ask students to note how spongy the lung tissue is. Examine a section of this lung under a microscope and locate a cluster of the air sacs that are found throughout the tissue. Point out that a fleshy wall surrounds each air sac. Depending on the power of the microscope, students may be able to see the capillaries in the walls.

Senses

Introduction

The nervous system makes it possible for the human body to have many sensations. Different sensory nerves located in special sense organs send nerve impulses (messages) to the brain, which recognizes these impulses as sensations. These sensations include touch, pressure, heat, cold, pain, smell, taste, sight, hearing, and balance. All of these sensations come from five sense organs: the skin, nose, tongue, eyes, and ears.

Research Questions

1. What is the difference between external and internal senses?

2. Why do humans need pain? What causes pain?

3. Which sense is the most important?

4. Which sense is the least important?

5. Which sense is most important in animals?

Web Sites

http://tqjunior.advanced.org/3750/

This site is a wonderful source of information for kids. An introduction about the nervous system as a whole leads into detailed sections about each of the senses. Also included in this site are activities, a glossary, cool links, and "sense-sensational" facts in each section. (S: 4–6)

http://faculty.washington.edu/chudler/neurok.html

Neuroscience for Kids offers information about the nervous system in general, the five senses, experiments and activities for each area, and educational resources. Current events links regarding new discoveries in brain research are also available. (S: 4–6, T: All)

http://www.wlu.edu/-Web/bp/brainpk.html

This is definitely a unique site in which students can "poke" a specific area of the brain with the mouse to get a response (sometimes humorous!). The five senses are addressed, and appropriate level discussion questions are also included on this really cool site. (S: 4–6, T: All)

http://sln2.fi.edu/qa97/me9/

This site basically provides teachers with a beginning lesson on the five senses for younger (K–3) students. Activities for individual students to do, as well as classroom and outside activities, are included, and a senses scavenger hunt dealing with charting skills appears at the end. (T: K–3)

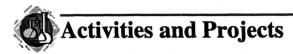

Literature Resources

Byles, Monica. (1993). *Experiment with Senses*. Minneapolis, MN: Lerner.

This book includes simple experiments to illustrate the concepts of the senses, including photographs, diagrams, and drawings.

Cole, Joanna. (1994). *You Can't Smell a Flower with Your Ear: All About Your 5 Senses*. New York: Price Stern Sloan.

Written by the best-selling author of the Magic School Bus Series, this book provides kids in grades 1–3 with activities and experiments they can do to test and trick their senses.

Hickman, Pamela. (1998). *Animal Senses: How Animals See, Hear, Taste, Smell, and Feel*. Toronto: Kids Can Press.

This book provides information and pictures for all levels of learners and shows children how to compare the senses of animals to their own.

Ripoll, Jaime. (1994). *How Our Senses Work*. New York: Chelsea House.

Geared toward older kids (ages nine through twelve), this book describes how the sense organs work and how they provide information for the brain to process.

Tytla, Milan. (1993). *Come to Your Senses (All 11 of Them)*. Winnipeg, Canada: Annick Press.

In this book younger readers (grades 1–3) can explore the senses and how they work. It also covers pressure, hot, pain, muscle and joint, tilt, and balance.

Activities and Projects

1. Bring in various objects from home that stimulate the senses. For example for hearing, a box of paper clips, cymbals (loud), a paper fan (soft); for sight, colors in shades of pastels, fluorescent, and bright; for taste, lemon (sour), strawberry (sweet), and coffee (bitter); for touch, a piece of fur (soft), sandpaper (rough), and a rock (hard); for smell, old milk (bad, rotten), cinnamon (good, sweet), and sulfur (bad). Pass around these objects and ask the children to experience them by touching, tasting, smelling, seeing, or hearing them. Discuss what the children felt when they participated in this activity and if the objects were familiar or new to them. Have they ever experienced these feelings before? If so, when? After discussing the objects, ask each student to write about what stimulates her or his own senses. For example, what tastes good, and what tastes bad, what kind of sounds/music does she or he like or not like, and so forth. Encourage students to illustrate their preferences by drawing or cutting objects out of magazines and creating collages to go along with their paragraphs.

2. A neat way to review the different parts of the eye is to make an edible model of the eye! Hang a diagram of the eye on the board so that all the children can see it, and discuss with the class the different parts of the eye and their function. Explain that they will be making edible models, and ask for volunteers to share what they think each part of the eye could be in terms of a piece of food. For example, use marshmallows for the vitreous humor to hold the shape of the eye (and all the food!), Lifesavers for the iris, a gummy worm for the optic nerve, and Tic-tacs for the pupil.

3. Invite a blind or deaf person to come into the class and speak with the students about their perception of the world. Encourage the speaker to explain what it is like to not be able to see or hear, and what they do to get through everyday situations (e.g., crossing the street, talking to others, reading, etc.). As a follow-up activity, encourage the students to write a story entitled "What My Life Would be Like Without My Sense of _____." Suggest that they include which everyday activities would not be different or impossible for them, and how they would feel as a result of not having that sense.

4. Ask youngsters to talk with their family doctor or a health care worker about some of the ways in which a person should protect her or his eyes and ears. Students may be able to obtain a brochure or informational guide on the care of these sensory organs. Encourage students to write to the American Speech-Language-Hearing Association (10801 Rockville Pike, Rockville, MD 20852) to ask for some descriptive literature.

5. Spread a hairpin until the points are about two inches apart. Blindfold a student and touch the palm of her or his hand with both ends of the hairpin. Repeat the procedure, bringing the points a little closer every time. Eventually the child will say that she or he feels just one point. At this stage both points of the hairpin are touching just one nerve cell. Repeat the experiment on the back of the hand, the forearm, and the back of the neck. Point out the differences in frequency of distribution of the nerve cells in different parts of the body.

Skeletal System

Introduction

Bones are some of the most amazing organs of the human body. Not only do they provide support for the body, but they also protect our other body parts and allow us to move. Connected to those bones by tendons are the muscles, which permit movement and add additional strength and structure to the body.

There are more than 200 bones in the skeleton of the human body. These bones are classified into four main groups: the skull, the spinal column, the ribs, and the limb bones. The skeleton is made of two kinds of material: bone and cartilage. In bone a large amount of hard mineral matter, especially calcium phosphate, has been deposited between the cells, making the bones quite hard. Cartilage has a soft and smooth material, which is tough and flexible, between its cells.

Bones are also important for making scientific discoveries about history. Scientists can learn a great deal of information about prehistoric or ancient peoples by examining bones. By examining bones scientists can determine the age, sex, weight, height, mode of death, and general health of a person who lived thousands of years ago.

Research Questions

1. How many bones does a baby have, and why does it differ from the number of bones in an adult skeletal system?

2. Why do we need our skeletal system?

3. What does the skull protect?

4. What important organs do the ribs protect? How many pairs of ribs do we have?

5. What minerals are found in bones?

Web Sites

http://www.yucky.com/body
   This site is full of interesting facts about the human body. Children can access information by body system or body function. (S: 3–6)

http://www.innerbody.com/htm/body/html
   This site is organized into body systems, and each section is full of interesting facts about human anatomy and physiology. It also includes animations of body functions that kids will enjoy. (S: 4–6, T: All)

http://www.kidshealth.org/kid/body/

Children can use the mouse to roll over the body parts of a child; the organs are identified on the screen. They can also click on "bone" and be directed to an overview, along with nine subcategories, related to the skeletal system. (S: 4–6)

Literature Resources

Arnau, Eduard. (1995). *Invisible World: The Skeletal System*. New York: Chelsea House.

This educational book will give students a wealth of information. It is well organized into concise, specific chapters. It is a great resource about the human skeletal system.

Cole, Joanna. (1989). *The Magic School Bus: Inside the Human Body*. New York: Scholastic,.

This is really a neat book for kids! It is written specifically for kids, and it is filled with a lot of factual information about the human body and how it functions. This would be a great book to read aloud to the class to kick off a unit on the skeletal system or the human body.

Parker, Steve. (1988). *Eyewitness Books: Skeleton*. New York: Knopf.

This is a fun book of interesting facts about the human skeleton and various animal skeletons. Different animal and human bones are compared and contrasted throughout the chapters. In addition, students can learn some really neat things about the history of medicine.

Parker, Steve. (1981). *The Skeleton and Movement*. New York: Watts.

This informational book is nicely organized into short chapters. It contains great pictures and graphics that help to further illustrate various concepts.

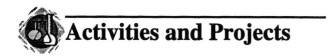

Activities and Projects

1. Have each student generate two to three questions relating to the skeletal system that they would like to have answered. Invite them to access http://www.sciam.com/askexper/medicine/index.html. This is a site where medical science experts are available to answer inquiries.

2. Provide the students with an unlabeled diagram of the human skeletal system. Encourage the children to label the bones by utilizing the following site as a resource: http://sorrel.humboldt.edu/-bioman/index.html

3. **An adult should supervise this activity**. Obtain a whole chicken and boil it for one or two hours in a large pot with some baking soda added. Carefully remove all the meat. With the students, observe the structure of the skeleton. Ask students to draw an illustration of the chicken's skeleton. After the skeleton has cooled, work with the students to remove bone sections from the skeleton. Ask students to note the joints and how they are held together with ligaments (which connect bone to bone).

4. The human skeleton continues to grow until sometime between the ages of 16 and 22. Ask children to record the heights of all their family members. This can be done once each month. Ask students to make predictions about each person's height for the

forthcoming month. Which persons in the family are continuing to grow? Who has stopped growing? Have students create a chart or graph of family members' growth. Friends and other relatives can also be added to the chart.

5. If possible, obtain some X-rays of broken bones from a doctor or nearby hospital. Point out the different types of breaks represented on the X-rays. Discuss with students the need for casts or splints in helping a broken bone to mend. Discuss what might happen if broken bones were not immobilized during the healing process.

6. Soak the leg or thighbone from a chicken in a jar of strong vinegar for four to five days. Remove the bone and wash it in water. Now bend the bone. The vinegar has dissolved and removed the mineral matter from the bone, leaving the soft, flexible animal matter behind. Although the bone still has its original shape and appearance, it will now be soft and flexible enough that it can be easily tied into a knot.

Index

About the Author

Tony is a nationally recognized children's literature expert well known for his energetic, fast-paced, and highly practical presentations for strengthening elementary education. His dynamic and stimulating seminars have captivated thousands of teachers from coast to coast and border to border—all with rave reviews! His background includes extensive experience as a classroom teacher, curriculum coordinator, staff developer, author, professional storyteller, and university specialist in children's literature, language arts, social studies, and science education.

Tony has written more than 35 teacher resource books in a variety of areas, including the hilarious *Tadpole Tales and Other Totally Terrific Treats for Readers Theatre* (Teacher Ideas Press), the highly acclaimed *From Butterflies to Thunderbolts: Discovering Science with Books Kids Love* (Fulcrum), the rip-roaring *Frantic Frogs and Other Frankly Frac-*

Anthony D. Fredericks

tured Folktales for Readers Theatre (Teacher Ideas Press), and the best-selling *Science Adventures with Children's Literature: A Thematic Approach* (Teacher Ideas Press).

Not only is Tony an advocate for the integration of children's literature throughout the elementary curriculum, he is also the author of a dozen children's books, including *Elephants for Kids* (NorthWood), *Exploring the Ocean* (Fulcrum), *Slugs* (Learner), and *Cannibal Animals* (Watts). He is currently a professor of education at York College in York, Pennsylvania, where he teaches methods courses in social studies, science, and language arts. Additionally, he maintains a Web site (http://www.afredericks.com) with hundreds of exciting resources, dynamic activities, and creative projects for the entire elementary curriculum.